STAND for the FAMILY

Alarming evidence and firsthand accounts
from the front lines of the battle

A call to responsible
citizens everywhere

by Sharon Slater
President, Family Watch International

Stand for the Family
By Sharon Slater

Visit us at www.familywatchinternational.org
480.507.2664
fwi@familywatchinternational.org

Library of Congress Cataloging in Publication Data

Slater, Sharon.

Stand for the family : alarming evidence and firsthand accounts from the front lines of the battle : a call to responsible citizens everywhere / Sharon Slater. -- Mesa, AZ : Inglestone Publishing, c2010.

p. ; cm.

ISBN: 978-0-9778814-9-9
Includes bibliographical references.

1. Family policy. 2. Families--Sociological aspects. 3. Marriage. 4. Same-sex marriage. 5. Homosexuality. 6. Abortion. I. Title.

HQ519 .S53 2010
306.8/5--dc22   1007

Editing: Cecily Markland
Cover photo: Helen Robson, www.CapturedMiracles.org
Cover layout and design: Leslie Thompson
Book layout and design: Jana Cox, Legend eXpress Publishing, www.legendexpress.biz

Printed in Canada
Inglestone Publishing, Mesa, Arizona

About the Author

Sharon Slater has dedicated the past ten years of her life to defending marriage, family and life. Whether in a remote village in Africa, addressing 1.5 million people at a pro-marriage rally in Spain, or opposing challenges to family values in the United States, Canada or at the United Nations, Sharon is an internationally recognized leader in the effort to protect and promote the family and family values at the international, national and local level.

In 1999, Sharon co-founded Family Watch International (FWI), a nonprofit organization in consultative status with the United Nations, and she currently serves as its president. Among other activities, Sharon writes a biweekly column for *The Family Watch* a free e-newsletter with readers in over 160 countries around the world.

Sharon's extensive involvement in international adoption issues, including her own efforts to adopt three Mozambican AIDS orphans, also led her to develop FWI's Families For Orphans project. She has also been active in defending marriage and the family in her local community and was selected to represent American Mothers, Inc., as the 2007 Arizona Mother of the Year.

In all of her activities to protect the family, Sharon, along with her husband Greg, has worked as an unpaid volunteer. She has assigned all proceeds from this book to Family Watch International or its affiliates to support efforts to defend the family and family values.

Sharon holds a Bachelors degree in Family Sciences. Before becoming involved in family issues, Sharon was a certified interpreter for the deaf and an instructor of American Sign Language at the university level. She also is fluent in Spanish and Portuguese.

Sharon and her husband Greg are the parents of seven children, four biological and three orphan siblings from Mozambique whose parents died of AIDS. She and her family reside in Gilbert, Arizona.

Table of Contents

Introduction vii

1. Witnessing the Assault at the International Level. 1

2. Deceptive Tactics. 13

3. The Case for the Traditional Family. 29

4. The Sexual Rights Movement. 45

5. Debunking Common Arguments Used to Advance Homosexual Rights . . 61

6. The Assault on Motherhood. 75

7. The Assault on Life 89

8. The Assault on Parental Rights 107

9. The Assault on Our Children's Sexuality 123

10. Who Could be Against the Traditional Family and Why?. 141

11. The Assault on Gender 157

12. Defending Traditional Marriage 173

13. Pornography's Assault on the Family 191

14. The Assault on Religion 211

15. Uncovering Common Anti-Family Strategies 229

16. Immunizing Your Family Against the Assaults. 239

17. Will You Stand for the Family?. 247

Appendices:

    About Family Watch International 251

    The "I Stand For the Family" Petition 253

In appreciation …

Thank you to the many friends, family members and colleagues who helped make this a reality.

While acknowledging the help from all of these people in bringing this book to fruition, as the author I take sole responsibility for what is presented in these pages.

Introduction

Ten years ago, I never pictured myself writing a book like this. Back then, I knew that there were some who didn't hold the same values as I did, but I had no idea there was a massive movement that was literally working to undermine what matters most. Since then, on multiple occasions, I have come face to face with individuals and organizations that are committed to destroying the traditional family.

Initially I was quite shocked, and I asked myself more than once, "Who could be against the family? What could possibly be their motivation?" Though it is still hard for me to fathom, I now know a great deal about their motives and methods. I also recognize just how pervasive and calculated the attacks on the family are.

This book was written to help you understand how these attacks can affect you and your family and what you can do about them. This book will provide you with tools you will need to help you withstand the destructive forces seeking to undermine the traditional family.

My intent in writing this book is not to scare you, but to help you become more aware and, along with that awareness, to provide you with a great deal of hope. There is great reason to hope as there are more good people around the world who believe in the importance of the family than those who do not.

Please understand that while I have deeply held religious convictions about the traditional family, *this is not a religious book*. To present my case, I rely entirely on personal experiences and firsthand accounts, documented research, social science data, logic, commentary, and testimony of experts, as well as the lessons from history and just plain common sense.

It also is important for you to know that this is not a moneymaking venture for me—quite the opposite actually. Many good people have invested a great deal of time and money to help me produce this book. All proceeds from sales of this book will go to Family Watch International, a nonprofit organization that is actively and effectively involved in this fight.[1] I currently serve, on a volunteer basis, as the president of Family Watch.

A Worldwide Movement for the Family

As a mom of seven children, I personally do not relish being involved in this fight. My time is very valuable to my family. But I am doing this because of what is at stake: the very future of my family and yours for generations to come. Our children will inherit the fruits of our labors or the results of our indifference.

Although many battles in defense of the traditional family have been won, many also are beginning to be lost; and the consequences of losing the overall war are catastrophic. The health and wellbeing of our children, our economy, and even our nation, as well as the world we know, depend on our successful defense of the traditional family.

The good news is we can still turn things around. We can reverse dangerous trends. We can win more of the small battles and eventually win the war. I have seen too many miracles to doubt. They happen whenever a small band of dedicated people joins together to protect marriage, family and life. These miracles, some of which I will recount in this book, have occurred at the international, national and local level.

Many who reviewed early drafts of this book reported that they now see the world differently and are better able to identify previously hidden threats to their family, to their community and to the nation as a whole.

In addition, as people are becoming aware of what is happening and are coming to understand the consequences of inaction, we are becoming a strong force, one that is having a great impact.

Tips for Reading This Book

In most of the chapters of this book, I begin with personal experiences, firsthand accounts, and compelling—and sometimes dramatic—experiences of people working to protect the family. These are educational by themselves and will illustrate how close to home these issues are.

---

[1] Family Watch International (FWI) is a 501(c)(3) nonprofit international organization founded in 1999. FWI is not affiliated with any religious group, political party or faction. FWI works at the United Nations (UN), in countries around the world, and in the United States to preserve and protect marriage and the family and to promote family-based solutions to world problems. See Appendix I for a description of FWI's mission, focus areas, objectives and activities.

Following the personal experiences and anecdotes, in each chapter you will find data, logic and legal analysis. While a bit heavier, I would encourage you to at least skim these sections; even a cursory look at the supporting evidence will emphasize the seriousness and the magnitude of the assaults being waged on the family. Coupled with the personal experiences, the accompanying data will help you be better prepared to protect your own family and to help hold the line against these relentless assaults.

Please note that some sections of this book are particularly disturbing. Much care and consideration has gone into determining which material to include and how much to tone it down. I knew that too much sugarcoating would defeat the purpose and skew the true picture of just how heinous the attacks are. At the same time, I understand that some may find certain topics particularly upsetting. For that reason, I have provided warnings in sections where some of the material may be particularly disturbing. These will be clearly identified, so feel free to skip past those sections if you so choose.

Let me reiterate, while a great deal of the information in this book is disturbing, I hope you won't become discouraged. With the help of the media, the opposition often appears to be the majority; however, the truth is that only a small minority is behind these organized attacks on our families. *But if they are left unopposed—by the well-intentioned, "live and let live" majority—this minority will continue to grow and will eventually win.* If they win, we lose. You lose. Your children and grandchildren lose—perhaps for many generations to come.

So, as I mentioned, at the very least, this book will enable you to protect and strengthen your own family. As you read it, I hope you also will feel compelled to join me and other moms and dads, grandmas and grandpas, aunts and uncles, children and grandchildren, community leaders, legislators, religious leaders, and politicians across the world who are working to preserve, protect and promote the family. They are our "Family Watchers," and you will learn more about them throughout the book and especially in the last chapter. If you feel so inclined, I urgently invite you to join us. Success largely depends on you and me and others like us who join the small, but growing, army of common citizens who are currently defending the traditional family. Throughout the book I will show you simple things you can do to help.

It is time to Stand for the Family, time to draw a line in the sand and to shore up our families and our communities, even while stopping the destructive forces that are seeking to take them down. I hope you will heed the call this book extends. I hope you will understand that your voice is important and that one person can make a big difference. I hope with this information in hand, you too will choose to Stand for the Family.

Chapter 1

Witnessing the Assault at the International Level

"Who are you?" the United Nations delegate urgently asked me. My heart was beating fast as she dragged me into the hall during a brief break in an intense UN negotiating session in Geneva, Switzerland.

Who was I? I was a full-time mom. But somehow I had managed to help this UN delegate support her pro-family position during heated negotiations.

That UN conference was one of the pivotal points in my life. At the time, I was a typical stay-at-home mom with all the trimmings—carpooling, soccer games, a busy husband, and four active children, the youngest just entering kindergarten. I had never been actively involved in a cause and didn't even like to get a babysitter for an afternoon, let alone to travel across the world to a United Nations conference.

Yet, at that UN meeting, I came face to face with disturbing events that would change the course of my life. There, I had my first glimpse of the calculated, organized, worldwide assault on the family and witnessed for myself destructive forces that are affecting our nation and the world as a whole.

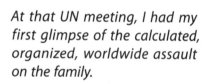

At that UN meeting, I had my first glimpse of the calculated, organized, worldwide assault on the family.

So how did I end up at a UN conference in the first place? In 1999 my husband Greg received an e-mail from his former law professor describing an experience he had in defending the family at the UN. The account had a powerful impact on both my husband and me. We wanted to learn more, so we attended a World Congress of Families[2] in Geneva, Switzerland. A World Congress (not to be confused with a UN conference) brings together government, religious and community leaders; scholars; experts in family issues; and concerned citizens who are working to preserve the family around the world.

---

[2] The World Congress of Families (WCF) is a biennial conference chaired by Dr. Allan Carlson of the Howard Center for Family, Religion and Society. (See www.worldcongress.org.)

Although several speakers at the World Congress described the attacks on the family that occurred at the UN, I still found this hard to believe. I had never been exposed to anyone who was actually trying to undermine the family. I wondered why anyone would be against the traditional family. Little did I know that I would soon have the chance to see for myself just who and what was working against all I hold dear.

My First UN Experience

A few months later, I was invited by a friend to attend my first United Nations conference, also held in Geneva.[3] There, we quickly found ourselves surrounded by people seeking to undermine the family.

Much of the opposition to the family was initiated by the "radical feminists" and other special interest groups in attendance, representing nongovernmental organizations (NGOs)[4] from all over the world.

By radical feminists I do not mean women who are working to further the legitimate rights of women. I mean women who espouse a militant, anti-patriarchal ideology that all men oppress women and who work to legalize abortion and to promote lesbian, transgender and homosexual rights, among other things.

The NGO representatives were working closely with the majority of the UN member states, intent on ensuring that the document to be negotiated would promote their anti-family views. I was appalled by their devious tactics.

I was especially surprised to see my own country, the United States, leading the charge to promote policies harmful to the family. I wondered if anyone on Capitol Hill knew what the U.S. delegates at the UN were doing. I was certain the majority of the people in the United States had no idea.

At the opening session, the chairperson announced that the UN delegates would be negotiating various segments of the conference document simultaneously in different rooms. This immediately put poor nations at a

---

[3] This conference was a regional preparatory meeting, part of the five-year review of the progress made on the UN Beijing Declaration and Platform for Action from the Fourth World Conference on Women, originally held in September 1995. This five-year review also is known as Beijing +5.

[4] There are more than 3,000 NGOs in consultative status with the Economic and Social Council of the United Nations. These UN-accredited NGOs are essentially special interest groups that are authorized to participate in UN conferences and they greatly influence the goals, policies and programs of the UN. Out of the more than 3,000 UN-accredited NGOs, only about 20 work together in a small coalition to try to protect the family; and, of those 20, only a small number regularly participate in UN conferences.

disadvantage as many did not have enough delegates to send to each room. It is the developing nations that usually support pro-family positions at the UN, so it seemed this was a calculated move by the conference planners.

My friend and I recognized a man we had seen at the World Congress of Families, and we introduced ourselves to him. Fortunately, he was a veteran pro-family lobbyist. He asked me to monitor negotiations that were being held in a small room.

NGO representatives and UN delegates alike crowded around a small table trying to listen and to get close enough to grab one of the few copies of the document[5] as it was passed out. Incredibly, some official UN delegates even found it difficult to obtain a copy of the very document their country was supposed to be negotiating.

There were no translators and, since the negotiations were conducted in English, those who had a good command of English had a major advantage. This meant people from the United States, Canada, and fluent English speakers from the European Union dominated the proceedings.

There was standing room only. Since the bag I was carrying was heavy and bulky, I set it down in the corner and moved toward the front so I could hear. Some UN delegates also had to remain standing even though NGO representatives, who are supposed to be observers, had prominent places at the table. One NGO representative proceeded to present her feminist "wish list" of proposed amendments to the document. It seemed that the feminist NGO representatives were running the show, and it was difficult to distinguish between them and the UN government delegates.

I had been instructed by the more experienced pro-family lobbyist to note which delegates made comments favorable to pro-family positions. My page remained blank. It appeared there wasn't a single pro-family delegate in the room.

Instead, I heard outrageous demands. Many of the radical ideas discussed in an earlier women's caucus meeting were being proposed for inclusion in the document. (See examples of the feminist agenda pushed at this conference in Chapter 6, "The Assault on Motherhood.") I was shocked that these controversial ideas were even being considered for

---

[5] Each year the Economic and Social Council of the United Nations holds conferences on social issues. The goal at these UN conferences is to produce an influential resolution or, on occasion, a binding treaty on the topic of the meeting. Every sentence of every paragraph is discussed and negotiated word by word until "consensus" is reached and an outcome document is adopted that member states agree to implement.

inclusion in a UN document and found it hard to believe that not even the U.S. representative was opposing them.

Finally, a woman across the room raised her hand and meekly requested that respect for "religious" diversity be added to the document.

Her suggestion sounded benign, so I was surprised when all the delegates—including the delegate from the United States—strongly opposed it. The other delegates actually laughed at her and condescendingly remarked that it was neither necessary nor appropriate to include respect for religion in the document.

At the time, I didn't know that "respect for religious and cultural values" is one of the most controversial phrases in UN negotiations. This is because the radical feminist agenda runs directly counter to all of the world's major religions, and if countries are required to respect religious values, the feminists cannot force their agenda on the world.

Radical feminists see religion—and particularly denominations they consider "patriarchal"—as the major barrier to women's "empowerment." In other words, this was a very significant addition.

The delegate, trying to defend her proposal, insisted that respect for religion was already included in several other UN documents and the other delegates challenged her to prove it. The delegate's English skills were limited, so she fumbled and stuttered.

I started shaking. I realized that in my bag in the far corner of the room I had the very tool that would help this delegate defend her position. My bag contained a small language guide[6] that identified UN consensus language in favor of the family from previously negotiated UN documents. The section on religion contained the exact citations this delegate needed to support her position.

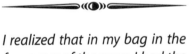

I realized that in my bag in the far corner of the room I had the very tool that would help this delegate defend her position.

Could I possibly squeeze my way over to the corner where my bag was, find the language guide with the citations, and hand it to the delegate before I was thrown out?

[6] Roylance, S. *A Guide for Language Supportive of the Natural Family in the Six Core International Treaties and the Seven Major UN Conference Documents.* (1999). South Jordan, UT: Worldwide Organization of Women & United Families International.

Nervously, while everyone in the room was distracted with the tension of the argument, I made my way through the tightly packed room back to my bag, found the guide, and opened it to the right page. Though I could tell those around me were becoming annoyed, I squeezed back through the crowd, made my way over to the brave delegate, and stood behind her. My heart was pounding. I wasn't sure that UN protocol allowed me to hand her information during negotiations. I waited until attention was diverted from her for a moment, discreetly placed the booklet into her hands, and pointed to the references on religion. Because she was flustered and didn't know who I was or what I was handing her, at first she didn't even look at it. The argument continued.

After what seemed like forever, the delegate suddenly realized that I had handed her just what she needed. She quickly raised her hand, announcing that she had found the citations.

After the delegate read them to the group, the chairman announced, "The Beijing Platform! You must find precedence for your suggestion in the Beijing Platform for Action, as that is the document we are reviewing."

At no point had the chairperson asked anyone else to similarly support their amendments. The delegate's face fell. How could I help her now? I then remembered that the night before, when I had stayed up late studying a copy of the Beijing Platform, I had underlined and starred the references to religion.

Could I squeeze back through the crowd to my bag again? I had already been the recipient of several hostile looks, and I needed to make sure I wasn't too obvious. The room was warm, and someone had just opened a window, so I acted as if I needed to get some air and made my way to the window. Then slowly, I pushed my way around the perimeter of the room until I reached my bag and found the needed references.

In the meantime, someone had handed the delegate a thick booklet containing the Beijing Platform, and she was frantically trying to find a reference to religion. I made my way back over to her, handed her my booklet with the underlined references, and told her it was the Beijing Platform. She looked very stressed and nervous, and I felt exactly the same. Because I was unsure of the UN rules for NGOs, I was worried I might do something out of order and get thrown out.

She raised her hand and exclaimed that she had found the Beijing references and then asked for permission to leave the room to consult. She then pulled me into the hallway, introduced herself as the delegate from the Holy See (that is, the Vatican, which has observer status at the UN), and asked, "Who are you?"

I was a nobody by UN standards. However, I just happened to be in the right place at the right time with the right tool to help a UN delegate support her pro-family position during intense UN negotiations. The whole experience was quite surreal.

> *I just happened to be in the right place at the right time with the right tool to help a UN delegate.*

The delegate explained that it was difficult for her to follow the arguments as she was new to the UN and her English skills were limited. Using the Beijing Platform and my UN language guide, she and I discussed possible rebuttals to the arguments being presented.

It was a life-changing experience to be an eyewitness to what occurred and to see that someone as inexperienced as I could actually play an active role in influencing UN negotiations.

Peer Pressure Impacts Negotiations

After that experience, I joined my friend in another room to witness negotiations calling for a worldwide repeal of all laws against homosexual acts. The tension in the room was almost palpable. Again, the organizers had chosen a small room, and people were standing wall to wall.

Among those standing was the Vatican delegate I had helped earlier. I tried to get inside the room so I could send her a friendly look to give her some moral support, but the room was too crowded. She had been standing through several hours of exhausting negotiations, and she looked totally frazzled. Incredibly, she was being pressured by all the countries represented in the room to agree to the homosexual provision.

She had firmly held her ground to that point, but since these negotiations required consensus[7], the entire room was pressuring her to cave in.

---

[7] Consensus at the UN is generally defined as the absence of a formal objection. If one or more UN member states speaks up and refuses to accept a provision under negotiation, they can usually prevent it from being adopted. However, there is tremendous pressure put on delegates during negotiations to not hold up consensus. Often delegates who are opposed to a provision that the majority of countries are in favor of are pressured into entering a reservation to that provision, stating their country will not be bound by it. They can also issue a statement clarifying their interpretation of provisions in a negotiated document.

The pressure against her intensified until, finally, she left the room to call her superior on her cell phone. She then charged back into the room and interrupted the proceedings. With all eyes on her, she announced that the Vatican was withdrawing its opposition to the homosexual provision.

I was stunned.

The room erupted with cheering and clapping, and there was an air of jubilation as they thanked her. The opposition had won! They did not even continue to negotiate the last few paragraphs of the document because they now had what they really wanted. It seemed that the whole conference had been organized to pass that one phrase.

The Vatican delegate later told us that her superior had decided it was not worth the struggle because these were just preliminary negotiations. She said the homosexual provision would be taken up in later negotiations in New York where they would have more support from other delegations not present at this regional meeting.

I did not fully understand, but I commended the delegate for her efforts and tried not to show my disappointment. She looked relieved that it was over and thanked us for our support. She said it made a big difference to see us there. She said just knowing that she was not alone filled her with peace. She apparently held out as long as she did because of the support she felt from us.

It was unbelievable to me that peer pressure and intimidation could play such a crucial role in UN negotiations that affect the entire world. At that moment, the idea was indelibly impressed upon my mind that if more people had been there to give her moral support, she may not have caved in.

Processing it All

After returning home from that first UN conference, I had even more questions.

Yes, I had seen some pretty disturbing things but, I wondered, did these obscure UN negotiations occurring halfway across the world matter? Could these UN documents have any impact on my family? Did a mom living in Gilbert, Arizona, even need to worry about any of this?

One thing that was clear was that many of the UN participants had made it their life's work to influence UN negotiations. If they thought it was so important, maybe it was. I wondered if there were similar influential people or groups or other policy-making bodies around the world with the same drive to destroy the family. What about in my local community? Or in my children's schools?

Round Two

In my journey to find answers to my questions, a few months later I participated in a continuation of these negotiations at a UN conference held in New York. Again, the pro-family NGOs were vastly outnumbered by the feminists and homosexual activists. Again, I was disturbed to observe Canada, the European Union and the United States (under the Bill Clinton administration) together pushing a sexual rights agenda.

It is important to note that Muslim countries often are fearless in standing up for the family. A delegate from Pakistan, nicknamed "Superman" by one of my colleagues, led the battle on the floor this time. He gave an impassioned plea to Western countries to stop wasting the delegates' time with sexual rights provisions and, instead, to start working on the issues that matter most to women in poverty—i.e., basic health care, clean water, food and shelter. The head of the Nigerian delegation later asked me, "So why is the West so obsessed with sex?" I looked at him, shrugged my shoulders, and replied, "I wish I knew."

Delegates from Sudan, Iraq, Poland, Syria, Nicaragua and other countries all rallied to squelch the efforts that had been mounted. Fortunately, with the help of the pro-family coalition, they defeated some bad provisions. However, the victories did not come easily.

Raining on Their Parade

Each night at the UN, the feminists held an official caucus meeting. As we entered their meeting room, it was clear that these women were angry with the pro-family contingent. Apparently accustomed to controlling a lot of what happens at the UN, they were extremely unhappy about our presence. I was dumbfounded to witness the "weeping, wailing and gnashing of teeth" as woman after woman vented, and some literally shed tears.

The protocol seemed to be to introduce yourself, state the organization you were with, and then proclaim, "... and I am a lesbian." Again, I found this shocking at a UN forum. After such introductions, they would either cry or yell, complaining about the pro-family presence. One young girl, who looked to be about 18 years old, began to cry and said, "I am a lesbian, and I am so angry at these people! So many years of hard work to help women, and it is all being destroyed!"

Another young girl declared, "This used to be the only safe place for us, and now they've ruined it!"

For years, the UN has been the stomping grounds for radical feminists and homosexual activists to effectively and quietly push their agenda upon the world with little or no opposition. We were ruining their party.

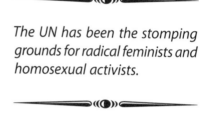

The UN has been the stomping grounds for radical feminists and homosexual activists.

Finally, an older woman announced, "I am a lesbian, and I am so angry that I just want to go home, but if I do, they will win!"

After listening to this for some time, I raised my hand. When I began to speak, some of the women tried to stop me, but the chairwoman, who was head of the Women's Environment and Development Organization (WEDO), firmly reminded them that I had just as much right to be there and to express my opinion as they did.

I said, "I am a woman, and I care about other women just like you do. I know it may not seem like that to you, but it is true. I and others who are here with me just believe in helping women in a different way than you do."

The meeting ended and my colleague Lynn Allred and I went up to the chairwoman, introduced ourselves and thanked her for being fair. She responded that it was an open meeting. Then she looked at us and said something to the effect of, "You girls are young and obviously not acquainted with much of the world, and you are naïve. When you get older and are wiser, you will see the world in a different way. You are in the minority. The world is changing."

Just before this conference, on March 7, 2000, the State of California had overwhelmingly passed Proposition 22 defining marriage as the legal union of a man and a woman.[8] Lynn looked the chairwoman in the eye

---

[8] In May 2008, four California Supreme Court Justices overturned Proposition 22, stating that it was unconstitutional. But, in November 2008, California voters passed Proposition 8, which amended the state constitution and defined marriage as between a man and a woman. In May 2009, the California Supreme Court rejected legal challenges to Proposition 8.

and asked, "If we are in the minority, then why is it that California, one of the most liberal states in one of the most liberal countries in the world, just decided by an overwhelming majority to affirm that marriage should be between a man and a woman?" The chairwoman was speechless. There was nothing she could say.

On a lighter note, at one point a member of a prominent feminist NGO approached us and said there was a disturbing rumor that the pro-family coalition was importing "attractive young women to seduce the delegates." She demanded that we explain ourselves. We frumpy mothers looked at each other and tried not to laugh as one of us replied, "Look around. This is as good as it gets, and if we qualify under your definition of attractive young women, then we'll take that as a compliment!"

Our Message Impacts Negotiations

As the UN conference continued, the negotiations proceeded at an excruciatingly slow pace. Social liberals and conservatives locked horns on issues related to sexual orientation, reproductive rights (abortion), sexual rights, parental rights, and family-supportive language. Both sides were frustrated with how slowly the work was moving. The mood spiraled downward, and the verbal attacks increased. As a way to counteract the accusations and provide a reality check, the pro-family coalition leaders planned a blitz to pass out flyers to all of the conference participants. One of our flyers said, "If the West was not so preoccupied with sex, the document would be done."

Social liberals and conservatives locked horns on issues related to sexual orientation and sexual rights.

There were about 30 people in our ad hoc pro-family group. We spread out and distributed flyers to as many delegates as we could. Somehow, it appeared to the opposition that there were hundreds of us. Within 10 minutes it seemed everyone had a copy. I had stationed myself at the bottom of the escalator and asked those getting off, "Did you see this yet? Come have a look!" Most everyone took one. Some thanked me, and others gave me dirty looks.

One lady looked at me, crumpled the flyer, and threw it at my feet. Several smiled sarcastically and said they had already seen it. Warm reception or not, our flyer definitely had an impact, and the tide started to turn in our favor as more and more UN delegates felt emboldened to speak out on family issues without fear of being accused of "holding up the document." The other side became less strident in their efforts to promote their sexual agenda.

What happened to the actual document under negotiation? All references promoting abortion and broad sexual rights were eliminated. It was a huge victory for the pro-family coalition.[9]

Why Focus on the UN?

Some may think it strange that a book about protecting the family begins with incidents from the United Nations, a seemingly distant organization. However, you will soon see exactly how negotiations at the UN and at other international meetings are undermining families worldwide. Also, once you understand the strategies and attacks on the family at the international level, you will more readily recognize them closer to home where the same tactics are used—sometimes by the same groups or their affiliates.

So, while the first part of this book focuses on what happens at the UN and how that is endangering families worldwide, in subsequent chapters I will show you how similar groups and people are working at the national, state and local levels to undermine the family.

Forces Working to Destroy the Family

Experts agree that, worldwide, the traditional family as an institution is slowly disintegrating. Yet, how exactly is this coming about? What forces are at work to destroy the family? Of course, it is not just one person, group,

---

[9] I have represented various pro-family organizations at UN conferences and at other events discussed in this book. For the most part, however, I have represented either Family Watch International (FWI), the organization for which I have served as president since 1999 or United Families International, for which I served as president from 2001 to 2006. Also, at each UN conference, I and others at Family Watch have worked with the pro-family coalition, which consists of a number of small, but effective, nongovernmental organizations working at the UN to protect life and the family. To avoid repetition and bogging down the narratives of my UN experiences, I typically have not identified which organization I was representing for each experience. All of the successes I discuss in this book were supported by a number of dedicated volunteers and staff from the various organizations with whom I have worked.

law, policy or movement that is the root cause of the breakdown of the family. Rather, there are multiple forces that, when combined, are having a devastating impact.

You most likely could easily identify some of these sources as you have seen them at work in your own community, perhaps even in your own family. Yet, like me, you may not fully comprehend how effective the enemies of the family truly are.

As I expose the aspects of what is behind the various assaults on the family, you will see that there are some well-intentioned individuals and groups who are actually being used as pawns, and there also are well-intentioned people who unknowingly promote policies that harm families. And you will learn how your tax dollars are supporting groups and projects that undermine the family.

The Sexual Rights Movement and the Family

As you read about the various groups and individuals who are working to weaken the family, you may notice that most share a common goal: They seek to create a right to sex outside of marriage without having to take responsibility for the consequences. When sex occurs outside of marriage, it doesn't matter if it is heterosexual, homosexual, premarital or extramarital; the evidence shows that any sexual activity outside of a traditional marriage, sooner or later, is damaging to the individual and to society, and especially to the institution of the family.

Sadly, what many are trying to promote as a "right" to sexual activity comes at a cost that is much greater than most realize. Indeed, as the traditional family disintegrates, children are hurt, economies decline, and nations are weakened. (See Chapter 3 for supporting data.)

Yet, almost daily, we see examples of how pervasive this disintegration is. Shortly before we went to print with this book, a UN official publicly revealed his animosity toward the family. Representing the United Nations Population Fund (UNFPA), he unabashedly declared that the breakdown of the traditional family is a "triumph" for "human rights." He further claimed that high rates of divorce and out-of-wedlock births are not a social crisis, but rather, represent a "triumph" of "human rights" against "patriarchy." UNFPA, receives millions of dollars annually to promote "family planning." Yet it would seem that their true goal is to "plan" the traditional family out of existence.

Chapter 2

Deceptive Tactics

From my first experience at the UN, fast forward eight years to 2008. Then president of Family Watch International,[10] I arrived in New York during the second week of another UN conference[11] on women with a well-seasoned team of veteran UN lobbyists.[12] Upon entering the UN, our team quickly discovered that a resolution being negotiated on HIV/AIDS had a serious problem.

While the resolution appeared to be fairly innocuous, it contained a paragraph that was "taking note" of another very dangerous document. The offensive document, called the International Guidelines on HIV/AIDS and Human Rights[13] and referred to hereafter as "the HIV/AIDS Guidelines," called upon member states to:

- Legalize abortion;
- Legalize same-sex marriage;
- Punish people who criticize same-sex relations;
- Repeal laws against adultery, fornication, oral sex and sodomy;
- Enact laws to protect homosexual behavior; and
- Provide children with explicit sex education.

The resolution being negotiated only made reference to the title of the HIV/AIDS Guidelines. The title

> *Had the UN delegates been aware of the content of the HIV/AIDS Guidelines they were being asked to "take note" of, many would have flatly rejected them.*

---

[10] Family Watch is one of the handful of pro-family NGOs in consultative status at the UN, which means we can participate in UN conferences to try and influence the outcome. Please see "About Family Watch International" at the end of the book for a more detailed description.

[11] This conference was the 52nd Session of the UN Commission on the Status of Women (CSW), held in New York from February 25 to March 1, 2008.

[12] Representing FWI at this conference were myself; Lynn Allred, FWI Director of Communications; and Annie Franklin, FWI Director of International Activities.

[13] The exact wording of the proposed text was "taking note of the Guidelines on HIV/AIDS and Human Rights, as adopted by the Second International Consultation on HIV/AIDS and Human Rights."

sounded reasonable, but none of the provisions were listed. Had the UN delegates been aware of the content of the HIV/AIDS Guidelines they were being asked to "take note" of, many would have flatly rejected them. Unfortunately, the delegates were being purposefully misled and were unknowingly endorsing these radical provisions. This was a classic example of the underhanded processes used to develop anti-family policies at the UN.

The HIV/AIDS Guidelines supposedly were designed to prevent AIDS. Yet the homosexual behavior promoted by these guidelines is known to increase HIV/AIDS infection rates. Clearly, some were using these UN negotiations not to fight AIDS, but to move the radical feminist and sexual rights agendas forward. (Chapter 4 will discuss the sexual rights agenda in detail.)

Unlike UN conventions and treaties,[14] which become binding on UN member states once they sign and ratify them, a UN resolution like the one negotiated at this conference generally is not binding. However, people work hard to insert provisions into resolutions that support their agendas because, once adopted, the provisions in UN resolutions can be considered UN-approved language.

When repeated often enough, phrases and concepts in nonbinding UN documents (such as resolutions, declarations and reports) can become part of "customary international law," which activist judges and legislators then rely on to shape domestic laws as they see fit. So any UN document (whether binding or not) has the potential to eventually influence national, state and even local laws.

Exposing the Deception

It was unfortunate that no one else had recognized the problem with the HIV/AIDS Guidelines before we arrived. It was late in the process. We quickly created a flyer to expose the abortion and homosexual provisions to the UN delegates, and we faxed the flyer to the UN offices of the countries participating in the conference. The flyer asked the delegates to call for the deletion of the paragraph endorsing the HIV/AIDS Guidelines.

---

[14] In the United States, a UN treaty or convention (another word for a legally binding UN document) must be signed by the President and then ratified by a two-thirds vote of the Senate. If this happens, it becomes binding in the United States and has supremacy over other legislation or regulations.

Our Family Watch team personally lobbied as many delegates as possible, both those who were friendly and unfriendly to our cause. My colleague Annie Franklin lobbied French-speaking delegates. I lobbied delegates in Spanish and English. Lynn Allred was one of the few pro-family representatives able to slip into the negotiating room. Lynn monitored the negotiations and kept us apprised of their progress.

A woman entering the negotiation room took our flyer, glanced at it, and laughed. She said we were wasting our time because she worked for UNAIDS (the UN agency dealing with AIDS issues), and they were in full support of everything in the HIV/AIDS Guidelines. It is not uncommon for representatives from UN agencies to pressure delegates in closed-door negotiations to support their positions.

The next day, the delegates from Syria, Sudan and Egypt (all of whom had been provided with our flyers) valiantly tried to get the troublesome language deleted, but failed. They needed more support. At this point, it was essential to find more allies among the UN delegations who would have the courage to speak out against the HIV/AIDS Guidelines. We contacted the African coordinator for Family Watch, who lives in Uganda, and he immediately facilitated a conference call with the Ugandan Minister of Ethics and Integrity. The Minister grasped the seriousness of the threat and quickly called Uganda's UN office in New York to ask them to assist us in removing the reference to the HIV/AIDS Guidelines.

The Ugandan Ambassador immediately came over and, after speaking to the woman chairing the negotiations, assured us that the offending language would be removed.

However, just before the start of the final negotiating session, I caught up with the chairwoman in the hallway and asked if the reference had been removed. She smiled and said, "Maybe next year." Apparently the Ambassador had been deliberately misinformed, and, after all our efforts, the reference to the Guidelines was still in the resolution!

The Ugandan Ambassador had gone out on a limb to help us, especially since we had asked for his help so late in the process and his country was not even a member of the commission negotiating the resolution. He agreed to help us find a way to remove the reference to the Guidelines in a future UN meeting.

Braving Two Storms

A year later, at the 53rd Session of the Commission on the Status of Women, our Family Watch team arrived in New York City along with a massive snowstorm that forced airport closure right after we landed. Undeterred, our team braved the storm to stand in the long line for the usual clumsy UN security registration process. The wind chill factor lowered temperatures to just above zero, but the storm raging outside was nothing compared to the tempest brewing inside the halls of the UN.

For this conference, the UN had adopted the theme of "The equal sharing of responsibilities between women and men, including care giving in the context of HIV/AIDS." The goal was to dictate how men and women should share household responsibilities. The negotiations, as ludicrous as it sounds, included a long discussion on how to ensure that fathers who take family leave do not use it to, for example, "play golf."

Before the conference began, we already had seen proposals that were being circulated behind the scenes to push "sexual and reproductive rights" (read: abortion, promiscuity, homosexuality and transgenderism) as the solution to the AIDS pandemic and abortion as the solution to maternal mortality.

In a UN panel sponsored by Sweden and Norway promoting sexual and reproductive rights, we heard Norway's State Secretary to the Minister of International Development, Mr. Hakon A. Gulbrandsen, state: "The most dangerous day for a woman is the day she gives life." The underlying theme was that giving birth is too dangerous for women; therefore, not only should all mothers have the right to abort their babies, they would be better off to do so.

Ironically, statistics show quite the opposite—i.e., giving birth is safer than having an abortion,[15] and even if there is a problem with the pregnancy, it is never necessary to *kill* the baby to save the mother. In extremely rare cases it may be necessary to *deliver* the baby to save the life of the mother, which could result in the death of the baby, but there is never a need to deliberately *kill* the baby.

---

[15] See the section "The Multiple and Serious Complications of Abortions for Mothers" on page 100.

Family Watch in the Trenches

At 11:30 p.m. on the second-to-last night of the negotiations, I sat near the Vienna Café in the United Nations building, just outside conference room eight, where intense negotiations were taking place. A handful of countries were standing strong against the rest of the world to try to keep "reproductive health services" (UN speak for abortion) out of the final document. Likewise, they also were trying to remove the words "comprehensive sex education" (UN speak for explicit sex education, which promotes homosexual ideology and promiscuous sexual behavior to children as young as 10). Brave delegates also were fighting to preserve a phrase calling for "full respect for religious and cultural values" of each country's people.

During a U.S. briefing earlier that week, U.S. delegate Ellen Chesler announced that one of the United State's main goals at the conference was to ensure the inclusion of "comprehensive sexual and reproductive health and rights" in the document. When a person representing a homosexual group asked what the UN was doing to protect their rights, a U.S. delegate responded that they would start by trying to insert a reference to "various forms of the family" in the document. (This term is quite controversial at the UN because it can connote families based on same-sex relations.)

Ironically, while at a previous UN conference, the U.S. delegation under the Bush administration had helped us defeat a proposal to establish a new UN super office to promote women's rights. Yet, at this conference, under the Obama administration, the United States was promoting the creation of this office to be funded initially with $500,000,000. The effort to establish it was spearheaded by International Planned Parenthood and by prominent abortion advocates. So, we handed out materials outlining how the super office would likely be used to promote abortion. Unfortunately, the UN General Assembly later passed a resolution approving the creation of this office.

Family Watch also launched a new caucus, "The AIDS, Orphans and Africa Caucus," where my foster son Luis, from Mozambique, shared his story of losing both his parents and then his brother to HIV/AIDS. We facilitated a discussion on the importance of family in the life of a child. When Luis explained that, once his parents died, he had to beg for food for his younger siblings and how he had yearned to be adopted, many of the UN delegates from Africa and others present were in tears. We then shared our story of bringing Luis and his siblings into our family.

We discussed how millions of children like Luis might not have lost their parents to AIDS if effective HIV/AIDS programs emphasizing abstinence before marriage and fidelity in marriage had been implemented and followed in Africa. Instead, failed "safe sex" programs (i.e., "anything goes but just use a condom") are promoted by the UN, while HIV/AIDS infection rates continue to increase across Africa.

Back to the negotiations. They were closed (meaning only UN delegates were allowed into the room) and lasted all night, until 5 a.m. At one point early in the morning, a U.S. representative came out of the negotiations to take a breather. I overheard her state to members of our coalition that there was a UN resolution on HIV/AIDS being concurrently negotiated. She said the resolution, which would be adopted the next day, had absolutely "nothing controversial in it." This was the same resolution the Ugandan Ambassador had tried to help us with the previous year.

I showed the U.S. delegate our materials, indicating that the Guidelines endorsed by the resolution called for legalization of same-sex marriage and abortion.

I then reminded her that President Obama, as a candidate, had clearly stated that he was against legalization of same-sex marriage and then asked her what the position of the United States was in regard to this document that called for the legalization of same-sex marriage and abortion.

She smiled and responded, "We support it." I then asked, "Are you telling me that the Obama administration supports a call for the worldwide legalization of same-sex marriage and protections for men having sex with men?" (I already knew this administration supported a call for abortion rights.)

She responded, "We support that document."

The rest of the pro-family coalition continued to focus on the "Agreed Conclusions," the main document being negotiated, while my son Luis and I turned our efforts to lobbying to remove the reference to the radical HIV/AIDS Guidelines in the other document. We were excited when we learned that this was being negotiated by the African countries. I was amazed at how the African UN delegates responded to Luis as we approached them in the hallways and showed them direct quotes from the Guidelines. I let Luis do most of the talking, and, despite his broken English, they listened to him.

We were directed to several key delegates, and fortune was on our side when we met an African man who asked us if he could help us. To our surprise, he was a delegate from Uganda! We explained our concern, and I told him our history in working with his Ambassador. He promised to help. However, we were told that it really was too late as an agreement had already been reached to not re-negotiate the troubling reference to the radical HIV/AIDS Guidelines.

Even though we were told it would be useless, later that morning, our UN coordinator Annie Franklin took Luis to again lobby against the HIV/AIDS Guidelines as the delegates were holding the final meeting before adopting the resolution.

Then to our delight, we learned that somehow our efforts had paid off, and the reference to the HIV/AIDS Guidelines had been deleted. I was ecstatic. Our team had worked hard with a very low probability of success, and yet we had made a difference.

In particular, it was sobering to realize that the reference to the Guidelines had likely been removed due largely to Luis's lobbying efforts. To think that a boy, orphaned by AIDS, and with limited English skills, could have such an effect on a UN document! This reinforced the fact that all it takes is someone who is willing to take a stand for the family, and miracles can happen.

When the negotiations concluded on the main document, we learned most of the language we were seeking to have deleted was removed. This was a great victory for the pro-family coalition.

Author's Note: Now that you are halfway through the second chapter you might be thinking this book is only about the battle to protect the family at the United Nations. While it's true that these first two chapters give you a window into the broad assault on the family at the UN, the upcoming chapters will each focus on a different aspect of the battle against the family and show you how these attacks are being implemented at the international, national, state and local level. Be prepared to read shocking information exposing the sexual rights agenda, which by stealth, is making inroads into our homes, schools and communities.

The next section will show you how the UN can have a direct impact on our lives by greatly influencing our laws and policies and even the education of our children. This is important information that few people are aware of so please share it with others. The more people that understand what is really going on at the UN and how it can affect them, the more voices we will have to stop the ongoing assault on the family.

Why Should *You* Care about What the UN Does?

The United Nations was established to deal with relations between member states, largely in the context of preventing war, resolving conflict, maintaining peace and addressing disasters. However, increasingly, the UN has been intruding into relationships between governments and their people, and even into the level of the family.

——————— »«(●)»« ———————

UN member states have direct authority *over their people and* laws, but the UN greatly *influences that authority.*

——————— »«(●)»« ———————

The individual governments of the 192 UN member states have direct *authority* over their people and laws, but the UN greatly *influences* that authority.

And this makes the UN very powerful indeed. The UN influences governments, and even families, around the world with *money, ideas,* and *words.*

Let's start with money. As the saying goes, "He who holds the purse strings, holds the power." The UN has billions of dollars to implement its agenda. The UN's budget is largely derived from member states (i.e., your tax dollars at work) and it uses that money to implement its agenda in individual countries around the world.

The UN can also make development aid to poor countries contingent upon their implementation of UN social policies. In addition, the UN gives monetary grants to special interest organizations (NGOs) that are aligned with its philosophies. Many of these NGOs then work to challenge national laws that protect the family. UN documents are increasingly filled with language calling upon governments and the UN to work with NGOs or "civil society" to implement their agenda.

And how does the UN use ideas and words to influence governments? If treaties are developed as a result of UN negotiations, they are binding on member states that ratify them and are enforceable under their respective national laws. Fortunately, this is a voluntary process and not all member states always sign or ratify every UN treaty. And if they do, sometimes countries make explicit reservations to provisions that could be used to pressure them to change their laws, for example, on sexual rights or abortion.

In addition to treaties, the UN issues resolutions, declarations and other documents that reflect thoughts and ideas discussed in formal settings at UN conferences. If those thoughts and ideas are repeated often enough and in enough venues, they eventually establish international norms and greatly influence the actions of member states.

Many of the ideas discussed at the UN relating to social policies are quite radical. They are not representative of the views of most people in the world, and almost always run counter to the welfare of the traditional family. Unfortunately, although the people and groups working to influence the UN with their radical anti-family ideology represent a minority view in the world, they can be perceived to be the majority since they are the ones most engaged in the process. Because anti-family groups are always there in large numbers, they have tremendous influence on UN documents and programs.

While many poor policies are promoted by the United Nations, the UN also does a great deal of good in helping countries in crisis due to war, famine, disease and drought. And to clarify, not everyone who works at the UN is anti-family. There are many dedicated delegates from pro-family countries who sometimes just need support to stand up against radical ideologies. Unfortunately, it is difficult to extricate all of the bad from any good that comes out of the UN.

The following are five specific ways the UN and international policies can affect families across the world:

1. International policies often trickle down to the national, state and local level.

Increasingly, U.S. judges are looking outside the Constitution to international laws and policies to make court decisions. For example, in 2002, two homosexual men were charged with committing sodomy, which was against the law in their home state of Texas. They appealed their case all the way to the U.S. Supreme Court in the infamous *Lawrence v. Texas* case.

The decision[16] overturned all anti-sodomy laws in the United States. The majority opinion, written by Justice Anthony Kennedy cited the European Convention on Human Rights, the European Court of Human Rights, the Wolfenden Report from Great Britain, and the rulings of other nations as support for its position that the U.S. Constitution was out of step with international developments concerning homosexual rights. Much of that foreign anti-family jurisprudence was influenced by policies developed at the UN.

The Massachusetts Supreme Court later used some of the U.S. Supreme Court's reasoning in *Lawrence v. Texas* to mandate the legalization of same-sex marriage in that state.

The Massachusetts decision then set off a number of other state battles over same-sex marriage; and, as explained later, it also affected the content of the curricula in that state's own public schools.

2. UN agencies create and fund programs that sexualize children.

A good example of this is a UNICEF-funded Web site[17] that targets 12- to 17-year-old youth and encourages abortion, masturbation, homosexuality and other sexual activities. Here are some direct quotes from their Web site:

- *You're thinking about getting into some loving? You want sex ... Let's get the basic low down on contraceptives ... Play safe, be confident—you don't need anyone's permission to use them and contraceptives give you the freedom to have fun without fear!*

(Notice that there is no mention of condom failure rates, which are especially high among youth.)

- *Remember, girls of any age have a right to: A free, safe abortion. You don't need anybody's permission.*

---

[16] *Lawrence v. Texas*, 539 U.S. 558 (2003).
[17] UNICEF, the United Nations Children's Fund, is the UN agency charged with protecting the world's children. I have intentionally left out the address for this UNICEF-funded Web site as I felt it would be inappropriate for any youth who may pick up this book to be directed there. For more information, contact us at www.familywatchinternational.org

- *Most people fall in love with someone of the same sex at least once in their lives, often during the teenage years.*

One section of the Web site, which I chose not to quote directly, encourages youth to masturbate and gives specific instructions on how to do so. The Web site also reveals some of its major financial supporters:

> *Major funding ... is provided by the Henry J Kaiser Family Foundation and the Bill and Melinda Gates Foundation. Other funders include the South African Government and UNICEF.*

The stated goal on their Web site is to reduce "*the negative consequences of premature and adolescent sex by promoting sexual health and healthy lifestyles for young people,*" yet they are blatantly promoting promiscuous sex among youth.

3. UN policies create international norms that can affect your family.

A nation does not even have to formally agree to be bound by a UN document or declaration for it to impact its people. For example, the city of San Francisco independently adopted the notorious anti-motherhood, anti-family UN CEDAW Treaty, even though the U.S. Senate for nearly 30 years has refused to ratify it because of its radical provisions. (There is, however, an emerging effort in the U.S. Senate to ratify the CEDAW treaty.)

4. UN committees, in concert with NGOs, manipulate member states to change their laws in ways that harm the family.

The UN has established committees to monitor the compliance of UN member states with UN treaties they have signed. These UN compliance committees sometimes interpret treaty language in ways that go far beyond what the original treaty actually says and far beyond what it was understood to mean when it was negotiated by the state parties. They then tell countries they are out of compliance if their laws do not protect such practices as homosexuality or abortion, even though the treaties they are monitoring are silent on those matters.

The UN CEDAW Committee alone has pressured seven countries to legalize prostitution;[18] six countries to decriminalize homosexuality and protect "sexual orientation;"[19] and 66 nations to legalize, remove penalties for, or increase access to abortion.[20]

Even though the recommendations of UN monitoring committees are not legally binding, some nations have changed their laws or how they apply their laws as a result of pressure from these committees.

For example, Peru criminalizes abortion but allows it where a mother's life is in physical danger or to avoid serious and permanent damage to a mother's health. In 2000, the Human Rights Committee (HRC) told Peru that the criminalization of abortion was incompatible with Articles 3, 6 and 7 of the International Covenant on Civil and Political Rights (ICCPR).[21] The HRC said this although the ICCPR does not even mention abortion.

In 2001, medical staff in Peru's Heath Ministry denied an abortion to Karen Huaman, a 17-year-old woman who was carrying a malformed fetus, because Huaman's life and health were not in physical danger. In 2005, the HRC reviewed Huaman's case and ruled, in part, that Peru violated Article 7 of the ICCPR—which prevents torture or cruel, inhuman or degrading treatment or punishment—because Huaman suffered mental depression from her pregnancy experience.[22] The HRC also required Peru to ensure that similar violations did not occur in the future. In 2007, Peru's National Maternal-Perinatal Institute in Lima published responsive guidance.[23]

In Colombia, a similar scenario occurred. In 2006, the same NGO that brought the Peru claim on behalf of Huaman successfully persuaded the Colombian High Court to overturn Colombia's law prohibiting abortion. The Colombian court based its opinion on the recommendations of

---

[18] The countries referred to are the Republic of Korea (2007), Kenya (2007), Netherlands (2007), Fiji (2002), Hungary (2002), Uganda (2002), and Saint Kitts and Nevis (2002).

[19] The countries referred to are Brazil (2007), Honduras (2007), Republic of Korea (2007), Sweden (2001), Kyrgystan (1999), Mexico (1998).

[20] Included are countries in Africa (17), Latin America (20), the Caribbean (4), Asia (13), Europe (4), the Middle East (4), and the Pacific (4). Statistics in this and the prior two footnotes were derived from research done by Thomas Jacobson, UN representative of Focus on the Family, www.focusonthefamily.com.

[21] Human Rights Committee, Seventieth Session, Consideration of Reports Submitted by State Parties Under Article 40 of the Covenant, "Concluding observations: Peru," November 15, 2000 (CCPR/CO/70/PER).

[22] *Karen Noelia Llantoy Huamán v. Peru*, Communication No. 1153/2003, U.N. Doc. CCPR/C/85/D/1153/2003 (2005).

[23] Instituto Nacional Materno Perinatal. Protocolo de Alencion del Aborto Legal. Lima, 2007. Report by Susana Chavez, PROMSEX, 7 February 2007.

the UN CEDAW Committee. Like the ICCPR, CEDAW also does not mention abortion. Several months later, the CEDAW Committee asked Colombia to "indicate whether the Constitutional Court's ruling could have an impact on the possible reform of abortion laws."[24] Indeed, the CEDAW Committee has continued to pressure Colombia to ensure that all women have access to legal abortion services.[25]

Again the original CEDAW treaty, does not mention abortion.

NGOs then sometimes use the bogus rulings of these committees to pressure countries to change their laws. For example, a very powerful NGO, Human Rights Watch (HRW), targeted the small African country of Uganda as part of its campaign to make homosexuality an internationally recognized "human right." HRW claimed that the equality provision of a UN treaty Uganda had signed in 1976, now had to be interpreted as protecting "sexual orientation." None of the state parties to the 1976 treaty would have accepted that interpretation at the time they signed it. Fortunately, Uganda refused to bow to this pressure.

This illustrates an alarming new development now routinely promulgated by some NGOs, some UN agencies, and members of UN treaty monitoring committees which claim that UN documents are evolving documents that are not confined to their original meaning but evolve over time. They insist that provisions in UN documents must now be reinterpreted in light of *their* new and "progressive" understandings of human rights issues.

In other words, they seek to reinterpret UN treaties to mean whatever they want them to mean. They then cite each others' work to support their bogus interpretations and pretend that nations are bound by them. Increasingly, nations are accepting these new interpretations, just as Colombia and Peru did.

I want to reemphasize that no UN treaty includes a right to abortion or unrestrained sexual activity, but the monitoring committees routinely act as if they do.

UN and NGOs in Cahoots

In 1996, a coalition of powerful NGOs, high-level UN officials, and members of UN compliance committees met in Glen Cove, New York, to develop

---

[24] Committee on the Elimination of Discrimination against Women, Pre-session working group, Thirty-seventh session, 15 January-2 February 2007 (August 6, 2007).

[25] See CEDAW/C/COL/CO/6 (02/02/2007).

a plan to advance sexual rights through the UN.[26] They intended to establish a universal right to abortion on demand and other sexual-related rights. [27]

This coalition worked successfully to staff UN agencies and treaty monitoring committees with like-minded individuals who would redefine UN terms and key words in UN documents to promote their agenda. It really was a clever plan, and, as you can see from the previous examples, it has worked brilliantly.

I regularly monitor the e-mail reports from some of the main feminist NGOs working at the UN. They are constantly calling upon their sister groups throughout the world to submit nominees for UN treaty monitoring committees and high-level UN positions to fill positions with their people.

Most people are unaware that these UN committees even exist, let alone how they relentlessly pressure countries to change their laws. Nor are many aware of the UN process used to nominate new members to these committees. Thus, those in the know—i.e., the feminists and, increasingly, the sexual rights activists—have much of the input into and control over the process, thereby exerting great influence on national policies.

A group calling themselves the Sexual Rights Initiative (SRI) offered individuals $500 to create reports on sexual rights abuses regarding "… *reproductive rights, sexual diversity, sexuality education, HIV/AIDS, etc.*" These reports were to target specific countries that were up for review at the next meeting of the UN Human Rights Council. Below are some excerpts from their memo showing how SRI tends to manipulate this UN Council to further sexual rights at the national and regional levels:

---

[26] The plan created in Glen Cove, New York, and a report of how that plan has been successfully implemented by manipulating the UN system to promote abortion has been outlined in *Rights by Stealth, The Role of Human Rights Treaty Bodies in the Campaign for an International Right to Abortion*. Sylva, D., & Yoshihara, S. The International Organizations Research Group. The Catholic Family and Human Rights Institute. Retrieved June 16, 2009, from www.c-fam.org/doclib/20080425_Number_8_Rights_By-Stealth.pdf

[27] UN Population Fund, UN High Commissioner for Human Rights, and UN Division for the Advancement of Women, "Summary of proceedings and recommendations," *Roundtable of Human Rights Treaty Bodies on Human Rights Approaches to Women's Health, with a Focus on Sexual and Reproductive Health Rights, Glen Cove Report* (December 9-11, 1996), p. 6. The CEDAW committee officially "welcomed" findings of the Glen Cove Report. See General Assembly, 53rd Session, "Report of the Committee on the Elimination of Discrimination against Women, 18th and 19th sessions," supplement 38, 1998 (A/53/38/Rev.1), 37-38, http://www.un.org/womenwatch/daw/cedaw/reports/18report.pdf

"The major forum for our work is the United Nations Human Rights Council that offers many more opportunities for State and non-state actors to influence the development and implementation of international law and standards through the United Nations human rights mechanisms. It is an increasingly important venue to develop and advance sexual rights as a critical part of the international human rights framework."

"The Sexual Rights Initiative ... intends to frame sexual rights as both a set of particular rights and as a cross-cutting issue, including the traditional framework of sexual and reproductive rights issues (reproductive rights, HIV/AIDS, sexual orientation and gender identity and so on), but also analyzing sexual rights within a comprehensive human rights framework."

"Hopefully, it will result in stronger and more comprehensive international legal norms that will in turn be implemented at national and regional levels."

If we are to protect the family, there needs to be a massive overhaul of the UN system. By bringing to light and documenting how the UN is being manipulated to promote sexual rights, it is our hope that this book can serve to initiate reform.

If You Had Told Me ...

If you had told me in 1999 that in the coming years I and several other stay-at-home mothers would work closely with United Nations ambassadors and delegates, that we would travel the world in defense of the traditional family, and that we would help government leaders, policymakers and scholars draft language used in UN documents which would be debated during heated negotiations, I would have responded that you were seriously mistaken.

If you had told me that I would be jeered at and mocked while giving a speech on motherhood at a UN forum, or that I would be screamed at by a woman telling me that the family is "the most violent institution in the world," or that another woman would tell me to my face that I was the cause of all the deaths from AIDS in the world because I was trying to convince UN delegates to support a sexual abstinence provision for children, I certainly would not have believed you.

If you had even suggested that I and my colleagues would be invited to the White House by the Bush Administration to advise the U.S. delegation to a major UN conference regarding what their strategy and position on family issues should be, or that we would meet with people like the King of Swaziland and the First Lady of Uganda to discuss sexual abstinence in HIV/AIDS prevention, I would have thought you were delusional.

And finally, if you would have told me that I would one day speak to a crowd of 1.5 million people at a rally in Madrid, Spain, in support of traditional marriage because that fundamental institution was in serious danger of unraveling, I would have seriously questioned your sanity.

Yet, all this and more has happened to my associates and me over the last decade. If a few stay-at-home moms with no previous experience can make such a huge difference, others who simply have a desire to preserve and protect the family can do the same.

The experiences in this book are those of a number of ordinary people who are concerned about the assault on the traditional family. These are eyewitness accounts from mothers, fathers, and some brave youth of the coordinated attacks on the family. These experiences are a testament to the fact that even ordinary citizens with little or no experience can learn, become involved, and make a difference.

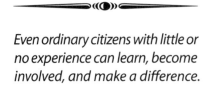

Even ordinary citizens with little or no experience can learn, become involved, and make a difference.

Stand for the Family—What You Can Do

If you are interested in participating in a UN conference to advocate for the family, please fill out an application in the "Family Watch Action Center" section of our Web site at www.familywatchinternational.org. Just click on "United Nations."

"The family is the natural and fundamental group unit of society and is entitled to protection by society and the State." - *The Universal Declaration of Human Rights, resolution 217 A (III), article 16.*

Chapter 3

The Case for the Traditional Family

A Paradigm Shift

Nine months after my husband Greg and I were married, our daughter Julie was born. Fifteen months later, our son Tyler came; and two years later, Michael joined our family. Greg was in law school at the time. All three babies had constant ear infections and acid reflux, and, when they were not taking short, disturbed naps, they usually were crying. None of them slept through the night, and it seemed there was no end in sight.

We all were sleep deprived so most of the time, we were miserable. Greg and I tried various remedies, but none of them worked. I fell into depression for the first time in my life. This was not the life I had planned, and I wondered how I could continue.

Then one night I had a dream in which I was walking by a river in a beautiful canyon, enjoying its serenity and peaceful beauty. All of a sudden, I saw that my little girl Julie had fallen in the river. I immediately jumped in after her. Because I am a strong swimmer, I felt confident that I could save her. I grabbed her and was swimming toward the shore, when I saw that baby Tyler had fallen into the river as well. I panicked, and then remembered that I was a good swimmer. I figured if I gave it my all, I could save them both.

Just as I grabbed Tyler with my other arm, I could see that my newborn Michael had fallen in as well. I realized I could not save them all, and I had to make a choice. For an agonizing moment, I had to consider which one of the three children I would leave behind. Then I woke up.

At that moment, I realized my children were worth more to me than life itself. The thought of losing any one of them was unbearable. These powerful feelings have stayed with me. That day my depression departed—never to return.

There were still dirty diapers, days spent in the doctor's office, dozens of doses of medicine that never seemed to stay down, sleepless and miserable nights, and times of frustration. But never again did I doubt the importance of my work as a mother.

My children are my great joy and well worth a thousand times my investment. Julie, Tyler, Michael and Jessica, as well as our three foster children from Mozambique—Luis, Amelia and Afonso—are the primary reason I felt compelled to write this book.

Let's now take a look at what the majority of Americans think of children, marriage and family.

—————⫘⫘—————

Americans over the age of 18 overwhelmingly support the institution of man/woman marriage.

—————⫘⫘—————

The Majority of People Support Traditional Marriage

A study released by the National Fatherhood Initiative showed that Americans over the age of 18 overwhelmingly support the institution of man/woman marriage. In fact, the study found, of the 1,500 people surveyed:

- 89 percent believe, "All things being equal, it is better for children to be raised in a household that has a married mother and father."
- 86 percent of singles who have never married would like to be married one day.
- 93 percent of the married adults surveyed said they would marry their spouse all over again.

Yet, the actions of many often do not reflect these positive views and aspirations to marry. Increasingly, in the United States and elsewhere, people are delaying marriage or not marrying at all; or if they do marry, almost half of the marriages end in divorce. What many don't realize are the consequences that follow these lifestyle choices.

All Family Structures Are Not Equal, Even If We Want Them To Be

Many people claim that alternative family forms—such as single parents, cohabiting couples, homosexual unions and families broken by divorce—are equal to the natural family as far as their effects on individuals and society. If you think about that concept, it is illogical. When you start with different material, you can't help but end up with different results.

Research demonstrates conclusively that alternative family forms are like the different houses built by the first two pigs in the famous "Three Little Pigs" story. One chose to build his home of straw and the other, of twigs. In an excellent article, titled "The Physics of the Natural Family: Why Families Don't Fall Down,"[28] Paul Mero points out that, although the homes of the first two pigs may have been easy to construct and required little time and commitment, only their brother's home made of bricks (i.e., traditional marriage and values) was able to protect them from danger.

> *Social science research has conclusively proven that a strong family, based on marriage between a man and a woman, is the best environment for protecting, nourishing and developing individuals.*

Marriage Versus Other Family Structures

Social science research has conclusively proven that a strong family, based on marriage between a man and a woman, is the best environment for protecting, nourishing and developing individuals—this family structure provides significantly better outcomes than any other alternative.

There are specific social benefits called "social goods," which flow from man/woman marriage. These social goods are derived from the complementary physical, emotional, and spiritual union of a male and a female.

The institution of man/woman marriage:

- Channels sexual relations in a manner that provides the greatest benefit to individuals and society.
- Helps men live more responsibly and productively.[29]
- Transforms men into husbands/fathers and women into wives/mothers.
- Binds potential parents together to raise the biological children they create.

---

[28] Mero, P. T. (2007, May 11). *The physics of the natural family: Why families don't fall down.* The Sutherland Institute, Retrieved June 6, 2009, from http://www.sutherlandinstitute.org/uploads/physicsoffamily.pdf (excerpted with permission).

[29] Ahituv, A., & Lerman, R. I. (2005, January). *Job turnover, wage rates, and marital stability: How are they related?* Social Science Research Network, IZA Discussion Paper No. 1470. Retrieved April 18, 2008, from http://ssrn.com/abstract=560241

- Legally binds fathers to their biological children. (Mothers are always present at birth, but not so with fathers.)
- Provides the optimal environment in which to raise children.
- Generates the best outcomes in the areas of health, wealth and overall happiness for men, women and children.

Research findings illustrate that the "social goods" derived from man/woman marriage begin to disappear when individuals live outside of the married man/woman family structure. Studies show that any deviation from man/woman marriage generally results in serious negative outcomes for individuals and families. The evidence supporting this is remarkably consistent and compelling.

Research findings illustrate that the "social goods" begin to disappear when individuals live outside of the married man/woman family structure.

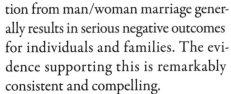

Just because some children find themselves in less-than-ideal family situations, we should not pretend that one family structure is as good as any other. Nor should we pretend that these alternative situations don't have consequences and that there are no differences in likely outcomes for children living outside of a traditional family.

Indeed, researcher Paul R. Amato found that if Americans valued marriage as much today as we did in the 1960s and early 1970s, each year fewer children would fail a grade in school or be suspended from school, and fewer children would need psychotherapy, engage in violence, smoke cigarettes, and consider or attempt suicide.[30] Mr. Amato is only one of the many scholars who have reported such findings after extensive study of family life.

The next section highlights some of the research from well-documented studies showing different outcomes for individuals based on their family structure. These representative studies only scratch the surface of the available research. Many more references are available.

This information can be used with teenagers and young adults to help them understand the likely outcomes from different lifestyle choices they might make.

---

[30] Amato, P. R. (2005). The impact of family formation change on the cognitive, social, and emotional well-being of the next generation. *The Future of Children, 15(2)*, 75-96.

Outcomes According to Family Structure

When compared to single adults, married adults:

- have significantly higher average household income.[31]
- generally have better physical health.[32]
- generally have better emotional health.[33]
- are happier.[34]
- are more likely to be productive and engaged citizens.[35]
- drink and smoke less.[36]
- live longer.[37]
- have lower rates of domestic violence.[38]
- report they find more meaning and purpose in life.[39]
- experience more satisfying sex lives.[40]

When compared to children of non-married parents, children of married parents:

- are less likely to be aborted, abused, or neglected.[41]

---

[31] U.S. Census Bureau. (2002). *Statistical Abstract of the United States: 2001*. Washington, D.C.: U.S. Government Printing Office.

[32] Schoenborn, C. A. (2004). Marital status and health: United States, 1999-2002. Advance Data from Vital and Health Statistics; No 351. Hyattsville, Maryland: National Center for Health Statistics.

[33] Marks, N. F., & Lambert, J. D. (1998). Marital status continuity and change among young and midlife adults. *Journal of Family Issues, 19*(6), 652-686.

[34] Lee, G., Seccombe, K., & Shehan, C. (1991). Marital status and personal happiness: An analysis of trend data. *Journal of Marriage and the Family, 53*(4), 839-844.

[35] Keyes, C. L. (2002). Social civility in the United States. *Sociological Inquiry 72*(3), 393-408; Keyes, C. L. The mental health continuum: From languishing to flourishing in life. *Journal of Health and Social Behavior 43*(2), 207-222.

[36] Schoenborn, supra note 29.

[37] Kaplan, R. M., & Kronick, R. G. (2006). Marital status and longevity in the United States population. *Journal Of Epidemiology and Community Health, 60*(9), 760-765.

[38] Stets, J. E., & Straus, M. A. (1998). The marriage license as hitting license: A comparison of assaults in dating, cohabiting and married couples. *Journal of Family Violence, 4*(2), 161-180.

[39] Wilcox, W. B., Waite, L., & Roberts, A. (2007). *Marriage and Mental Health in Adults and Children*. Research Brief No. 4. Center for Marriage and Families, Institute for American Values. Retrieved June 6, 2009, from http://www.americanvalues.org/pdfs/researchbrief4.pdf

[40] Whitehead, B. D., & Popenoe, D. (2000). The *state of our unions: 2000: The social health of marriage in America*. New Brunswick, NJ: The National Marriage Project.

[41] Sedlak, A. J., & Broadhurst, D. D. (1996). *The third national incidence study of child abuse and neglect (NIS-3)*. U.S. Department of Health and Human Services. Washington, D.C.; Jones, R. K., Darroch, J. E., & Henshaw, S. K. (2002). Patterns in the socioeconomic characteristics of women obtaining abortions in 2000-2001. *Perspectives on Sexual and Reproductive Health, 34*(5), 226-235.

- spend more time with, and receive more affection from, their fathers.[42]
- are less likely to have a premarital birth in high school.[43]
- have higher grade point averages and lower dropout rates.[44]
- do better economically.[45]
- have better physical health and increased life expectancy.[46]
- are less likely to have emotional or behavioral problems.[47]
- engage in fewer risky behaviors (e.g., premarital sex and substance abuse).[48]
- are less likely to divorce as adults.[49]
- experience a lower rate of sexually transmitted diseases (STDs).[50]

When compared to married couples, cohabiting couples:

- have worse physical and mental health.[51]
- earn less and possess fewer assets.[52]

---

[42] Hofferth, S. L., & Anderson, K. G. (2003). Are all dads equal? Biological versus marriage as a basis for paternal investment. *Journal of Marriage and Family, 65*(1), 213-232.

[43] Moore, K. A., et al. (1998). Nonmarital school-age motherhood: family, individual, and school characteristics. *Journal of Adolescent Research, 13*(4), 433-457.

[44] Schneider, B., Atteberry, A., & Owens, A. (2005). *Family matters: Family structure and child outcomes.* Birmingham: Alabama Policy Institute. Retrieved June 6, 2009, from http://www.alabamapolicyinstitute.org/pdf/currentfamilystructure.pdf

[45] Thomson, E., et al. (1994). Family structure and child well-being: Economic resources vs. parental behaviors. *Social Forces, 73*(1), 221-242.

[46] Tucker, J. S., et al. (1997). Parental divorce: Effects on individual behavior and longevity. *Journal of Personality and Social Psychology, 73*(2), 381-391; Mauldon, J. (1990). The effects of marital disruption on children's health. *Demography, 27*(3), 431-446.

[47] Kelleher, K. J., et al. (2000). Increasing identification of psychosocial problems: 1979-1996. *Pediatrics, 105*(6), 1313-1321.

[48] Flewelling, R. L., & Bauman, K. E. (1990). Family structure as a predictor of initial substance use and sexual intercourse in early adolescence. *Journal of Marriage and the Family, 52*(1), 171. Retrieved September 12, 2008, from Research Library database (Document ID: 1718139).

[49] Amato, P. R., & DeBoer, D. D. (2001). The transmission of marital instability across generations: Relationship skills or commitment to marriage? *Journal of Marriage and Family, 63*(4), 1038-1051.

[50] Newbern, E. C., et al. (2004). Family socioeconomic status and self-reported sexually transmitted diseases among black and white American adolescents. *Sexually Transmitted Diseases, 31*(9), 533-541.

[51] Pienta, A. M., et al. (2000). Health consequences of marriage for the retirement years. *Journal of Family Issues, 21*(5), 559-586; Hortwitz, A. V., & Raskin, H. (1998). The relationship of cohabitation and mental health: A study of a young adult cohort. *Journal of Marriage and the Family, 60*(2), 505-514.

[52] Hao, L. (1996). Family structure, private transfers, and the economic well-being of families with children. *Social Forces, 75*(1), 269-292.

- are much more likely to separate.[53]
- experience more conflict and violence.[54]
- receive less social support from friends and family.[55]

When compared to married women, cohabiting women:

- have more depression and three times the alcohol problems.[56]
- are three times as likely to experience physical aggression.[57]
- experience at least three times the amount of violence.[58]
- are more likely to suffer sexual abuse.[59]

When compared to children in married households, children in cohabiting households:

- will receive a smaller share of their parents' income for education.[60]
- are more likely to cheat in, or be suspended from, school.[61]
- are more likely to engage in delinquent behavior.[62]
- face dramatically higher rates of physical and sexual abuse.[63]
- show poorer emotional development.[64]

---

[53] Binstock, G., & Thornton, A. (2003). Separations, reconciliations, and living apart in cohabiting and marital unions. *Journal of Marriage and Family, 65*(2), 432-443.

[54] Brown, S. L., & Booth, A. (1996). Cohabitation versus marriage: A comparison of relationship quality. *Journal of Marriage & the Family, 58*(3), 668-678.

[55] Popenoe, D., & Whitehead, B. D. (2002). Should we live together? What young adults need to know about cohabitation before marriage: A comprehensive review of recent research. New Brunswick: National Marriage Project.

[56] Horowitz, A. V., & White, H. R. (1998). The relationship of cohabitation and mental health: A study of a young adult cohort. *Journal of Marriage and the Family, 60*(2), 505-514.

[57] Salari, S. M., & Baldwin, B. M. (2002). Verbal, physical and injurious aggression among intimate couples over time. *Journal of Family Issues, 23*(4), 523-550.

[58] Ibid.

[59] Waite, L. J., & Gallagher, M. (2000). The case for marriage: Why married people are happier, healthier, and better off financially. New York: Doubleday, 41.

[60] DeLeire, T., & Kalil, A. (2005). How do cohabitating couples with children spend their money? *Journal of Marriage and Family, 67*(2), 286-295.

[61] Wilcox, W. B. et al. supra note 36.

[62] Ibid.

[63] Thomson, E., et al., supra note 42; Schnitzer, P. G., & Ewigman, B. G. (2005). Child deaths resulting from inflicted injuries: Household risk factors and perpetrator characteristics. *Pediatrics, 116*(5), 687-693.

[64] Sarantakos, S. (1996). Children in three contexts: family, education and social development. *Children Australia, 21*(3); Meltzer, H., et al. (2000). *Mental Health of Children and Adolescents in Great Britain*. London: Office for National Statistics, The Stationery Office; Hao, L. (1997). *Family Structure, Parental Input, and Child Development*. (1997, March). Paper presented at the Population Association of America Conference, Washington, D.C.

When compared to married adults, separated or divorced adults:

- are more than twice as likely to commit suicide.[65]

- experience noticeably higher rates of violence by spouses, ex-spouses and/or boyfriends.[66]

- suffer greater economic hardships (especially women).[67]

- experience greater depression, substance abuse, and poor health.[68]

When compared to children of married couples, children whose parents divorced:

- are less likely to attend and graduate from college.[69]

- are more likely to experience economic hardship and deep poverty.[70]

- are more likely to experience depression or anxiety in their 20s or 30s.[71]

- have twice the risk of experiencing serious psychological problems.[72]

- are more likely to get involved in early sexual activity.[73]

- are more likely to use drugs and alcohol.[74]

---

[65] Kposowa, A. J. (2000). Marital status and suicide in the National Longitudinal Mortality Study. Journal of Epidemiology and Community Health, 54(4), 254-261; Wilcox, W. B., et al., supra note 36.

[66] Rennison, C. M., & Welchans, S. (2000). Intimate partner violence. (NCJ 178247). Rockville, MD: U.S. Department of Justice, Bureau of Justice Statistics.

[67] Finie, R. (1993). Women, men and the economic consequences of divorce: Evidence from Canadian longitudinal data. *Canadian Review of Sociology and Anthropology*, 30; Bianchi, S. (1999). The gender gap in the economic well-being of nonresident fathers and custodial mothers. *Demography*, 36(2), 195-203; Waite, L. J., & Ghallagher, M., supra note 56, 180.

[68] Liu, H., & Umberson, D. J. (2008). The times they are a changin': Marital status and health differentials from 1972 to 2003. *Journal of Health and Social Behavior*, 49(3), 239-253; Schoenborn, C. A. (2004). Marital Status and Health: United States, 1999-2002. Advance Data from Vital and Health Statistics. (No. 351). Hyattsville, MD: National Center for Health Statistics; Coombs, R. H. (1991). Marital status and personal well-being: A literature review. *Family Relations*, 40(1), 97-102.

[69] Johnsson, J. O., & Gahler, M. (1997). Family dissolution, family reconstitution, and children's educational careers: Recent evidence from Sweden. *Demography*, 34(2), 277-293.

[70] Thomas, A., & Sawhill, I. (2002). For richer or for poorer: Marriage as an antipoverty strategy. *Journal of Policy Analysis and Management*, 21(4), 587-599; Ross, C. E., & Mirowsky, J. (1999). Parental divorce, life-course disruption, and adult depression. *Journal of Marriage and the Family*, 61(4), 1034-1045.

[71] Ross, C. E., & Mirowsky, J. (1999). Parental divorce, life-course disruption, and adult depression. *Journal of Marriage and the Family*, 61(4), 1034-1045; Cherlin, A. J., et al. (1998). Effects of parental divorce on mental health throughout the life course. *American Sociological Review*, 63(2), 239-249.

[72] Wilcox, W. B., et al., supra note 36.

[73] Flewelling, R. L., & Bauman, K. E. (1990). Family structure as a predictor of initial substance use and sexual intercourse in early adolescence. *Journal of Marriage and the Family*, 52(1), 171.

[74] Short, J. L. (1998). Predictors of substance use and mental health of children of divorce: A prospective analysis. *Journal of Divorce & Remarriage*, 29(112), 147-166; Wallerstein, J. S., Lewis, J. M., & Blakeslee, S. (2000). *The unexpected legacy of divorce: The 25-year landmark study*. New York: Hyperion; Flewelling, R. L., & Bauman, K. E. (1990). Family structure as a predictor of initial substance use and sexual intercourse in early adolescence. *Journal of Marriage and the Family*, 52(1), 171-181.

- are more likely to cohabitate or divorce.[75]

When compared to heterosexual men, men who engage in homosexual behavior:

- experience a significantly higher rate of domestic violence with their partners.[76]
- are up to seven times more likely to attempt suicide.[77]
- have a lower life expectancy by 20 to 30 years.[78]
- have an incidence of HIV/AIDS that is up to 430 times higher.[79]
- have three times the number of drug and alcohol dependencies.[80]
- are significantly more promiscuous, with very few maintaining fidelity.[81]
- are more than twice as likely to have an STD.[82]
- are significantly more likely to engage in pedophilia.[83]
- are much more likely to have mental and emotional disorders/illnesses.[84]

---

[75] Amato & DeBoer, supra note 46.

[76] Owen, S., & Burke, T. W. (2004). An exploration of the prevalence of domestic violence in same-sex relationships. *Psychological Reports, 95*(1), 129-132.

[77] Saunders, J. M., & Valente, S. M. (1987). Suicide risk among gay men and lesbians: A review. *Death Studies, 11*(1), 1-23.

[78] Cameron, P., Cameron, K., & Playfair, W. (1998). Does homosexual activity shorten life? *Psychological Reports, 83*, 847-866.

[79] Odets, W. (1994). Report to the American Association of Physicians for Human Rights, as cited in Goldman, E. L. (1994). Psychological Factors Generate HIV Resurgence in Young Gay Men. *Clinical Psychiatry News.* October, 5.

[80] Craig, R. J. (1987). MMPI-derived prevalence estimates of homosexuality among drug dependent patients. *The International Journal of Addictions, 22*(11), 1139-1145; Fifield, L., Latham, J. D., & Phillips, C. (1977). *Alcoholism in the gay community: The price of alienation, isolation, and oppression.* Los Angeles: The Gay Community Service Center; Fenwick, R. D., & Pillard, R. C. (1978). *Advocate guide to gay health.* New York: E. P. Dutton.

[81] Rothblum, E., & Solomon, S. (2003). *Civil unions in the state of Vermont: A report on the first year.* Burlington: University of Vermont Department of Psychology; McWhirter, D. P., & Mattison, A. M. (1984). *The male couple: How relationships develop.* Englewood Cliffs: Prentice-Hall.

[82] Laumann, E. O., Gagnon, J. H., Michael, R. T., & Michaels, S. (1994). *The social organization of sexuality: Sexual practices in the United States.* Chicago: University of Chicago Press.

[83] Freund, K., & Watson, R. J. (1992). The proportions of heterosexual and homosexual pedophiles among sex offenders against children: An exploratory study. *Journal of Sex and Marital Therapy, 18*(1), 34-43; Erickson, W. D., Walbek, N. H., & Sely, R. K. (1988). Behavior patterns of child molesters. *Archives of Sexual Behavior, 17*(1), 77-86.

[84] Sandfort, T. G., et al. (2001). Same-sex sexual behavior and psychiatric disorders: Findings from the Netherlands mental health survey and incidence (NEMESIS), *Archives of General Psychiatry, 58*(1), 85-91; New study confirms higher level of psychiatric disorders among men and women engaging in same-sex behavior. (2008, February). Retrieved June 8, 2009, from National Association for Research & Therapy of Homosexuality Web Site: http://www.narth.com/docs/studyconfirms.html

- are at higher risk of deliberate self-harm.[85]

When compared to heterosexual youth, youth who engage in homosexual behavior:

- are at increased risk of suffering major depression and generalized anxiety disorder.[86]
- are associated with more school and runaway problems.[87]
- are more likely to attempt suicide.[88]
- experience a much higher rate of alcoholism.[89]
- are more likely to engage in substance abuse.[90]
- are more likely to engage in high-risk sexual behavior.[91]

When compared to heterosexual women, lesbian women:

- are significantly more likely to be victims of domestic violence.[92]
- experience a much higher rate of sexual coercion by their partner.[93]
- are more likely to use drugs and alcohol.[94]

---

[85] King, M., Semlyen, J., Tai, S. S., et al. (2008). A systematic review of mental disorder, suicide, and deliberate self harm in lesbian, gay and bisexual people. *BMC Psychiatry, 18*(8), 70-87.

[86] Fergusson, D. M., Horwood, L. J., & Beautrais, A. L. (1999). Is sexual orientation related to mental health problems and suicidality in young people? *Archives of General Psychiatry, 56*(10), 876-80.

[87] Savin-Williams, R. C. (1994). Verbal and physical abuse as stressors in the lives of lesbian, gay male, and bisexual youths: Associations with school problems, running away, substance abuse, prostitution, and suicide. *Journal of Consulting and Clinical Psychology, 62*(2), 261-269.

[88] Silenzio, V. M., et al. (2007). Sexual orientation and risk factors for suicidal ideation and suicide attempts among adolescents and young adults. *American Journal of Public Health, 97*(11), 2017-2019.

[89] Orenstein, A. (2001). Substance use among gay and lesbian adolescents. *Journal of Homosexuality, 41*(2), 1-15.

[90] Blake, S. M., et al. (2001). Preventing sexual risk behaviors among gay, lesbian, and bisexual adolescents: The benefits of gay-sensitive HIV instruction in schools. *American Journal of Public Health, 91*(6), 940-946; Russell, S. T., Driscoll, A. K., & Truong, N. (2002). Adolescent same-sex romantic attractions and relationships: Implications for substance use and abuse. *American Journal of Public Health, 92*(2), 198-202.

[91] Ibid.

[92] Brand, P. A., & Kidd, A. H. (1986). Frequency of physical aggression in heterosexual and female homosexual dyads. *Psychological Reports, 59*(3), 1307-1313.

[93] Waterman, C. K., Dawson, L. J., & Bologna, M. (1989). Sexual coercion in gay male and lesbian relationships: Predictors and implications and support services. *The Journal of Sex Research, 26*(1), 118-124.

[94] Lewis, C. E., Saghir, M. T., & Robins, E. (1982, July). Drinking patterns in homosexual and heterosexual women. *Journal of Clinical Psychiatry, 43*(7), 277-279.

- have a significantly higher risk of developing general anxiety disorder.[95]
- are twice as likely to attempt suicide.[96]
- are at higher risk for breast cancer.[97]
- are at higher risk of deliberate self-harm.[98]

Statistics for Children of Same-Sex Couples

After examining available studies in this area, researcher Dr. Trayce Hansen found that, compared to other children, those raised by homosexual parents are 4 to 10 times more likely to engage in homosexual behavior.

Dr. Hansen cites the conclusions of the researchers Judith Stacey and Timothy Biblarz, who, after reviewing 21 different studies, concluded that children parented by homosexuals are different in terms of sexual behavior and preference.[99]

Compared to other children, those raised by homosexual parents are 4 to 10 times more likely to engage in homosexual behavior.

Some studies have claimed to find no differences in children parented by homosexuals. However, independent evaluations have concluded that these studies do not meet minimum scientific standards. Some of the problems associated with these studies include:

- Very small size samples.
- Reliance on "self-reporting" by the same-sex parents themselves who may have a vested interest in representing their children to be as normal as possible.

---

[95] Cochran, S. D., Mays, V. M., & Sullivan, J. G. (2003). Prevalence of mental disorders, psychological distress, and mental health services use among lesbian, gay, and bisexual adults in the United States. *Journal of Consulting and Clinical Psychology*, 71(1), 53-61.

[96] Saghir, M. T., et al. (1970). Homosexuality. IV. Psychiatric disorders and disability in the female homosexuals. *American Journal of Psychiatry*, 127(2), 147-154; King, M., Semlyen, J., et al. (2008). A systematic review of mental disorder, suicide, and deliberate self harm in lesbian, gay and bisexual people. *BMC Psychiatry*, 18(8), 70-87.

[97] Brandenburg, D. L., Matthews, A. K., Johnson, T. P., & Hughes, T. L. (2007). Breast cancer risk and screening: a comparison of lesbian and heterosexual women. *Women & Health*, 45(4),109-30.

[98] King, M., Semlyen, J., Tai, S. S., et al. (2008). A systematic review of mental disorder, suicide, and deliberate self harm in lesbian, gay and bisexual people. *BMC Psychiatry*, 18(8), 70-87.

[99] Hansen, T. A review and analysis of studies which assessed sexual preference of children raised by homosexuals. Retrieved June 8, 2009, from http://www.drtraycehansen.com/Pages/writings_sexpref.html

- Self-selection of some of the subjects through homosexual advocacy magazines.
- Failure of the researchers to control for children who were raised during their formative years by heterosexual parents who later broke up and entered into same-sex unions.[100]

This flawed research has been used to promote the legalization of same-sex marriage and the adoption of children by same-sex couples.

The Multi-Billion Dollar Cost of Family Breakdown

Any deviation from the traditional married family structure generally leads to such things as poverty, crime, violence, substance abuse, disease and other problems that world governments must spend millions of dollars trying to fix. From a purely economic perspective, there are enormous tangible costs to society that emanate from family breakdown. A landmark U.S. study released in 2008 revealed that the breakdown of the family costs U.S. taxpayers a staggering $112 billion every year![101] To arrive at this figure, a group of distinguished scholars and economists considered only the following costs:[102]

- Costs to taxpayers from divorce and out-of-wedlock childbearing;
- Costs for government programs to single parents, such as child welfare, housing assistance and food stamps;
- Losses in tax revenue from taxpayers who are thrown into poverty after family breakdown; and

---

[100] In an exhaustive scientific review of the same-sex parenting studies, Dr. George Rekers—who is a Professor of Neuropsychiatry and Behavioral Science, Research Director for Child and Adolescent Psychiatry, and Chairman of Faculty in Psychology at the University of South Carolina School of Medicine—characterized those studies as follows: "... the few studies available are biased with regard to subject selection in that they generally report on a small group of research subjects which are not randomly selected and which do not constitute a scientifically representative sample of homosexual parents and their children. Furthermore, although the research designs of the available studies are replete with numerous other methodological deficiencies, many of the authors make illegitimate generalizations or unwarranted conclusions from their flawed research studies." Rekers, G. & Kilgus, M. (2001). Studies of homosexual parenting: A critical review. *Regent University Law Review*, 14(2), 343-382. Family Watch International's Family Policy Brief, titled Same-sex Parenting and Junk Science, which can be found on the FWI Web site (www.familywatchinternational.org), summarizes the expert critiques of the studies to date on same-sex parenting.

[101] Scafidi, B., The taxpayer costs of divorce and unwed childbearing: First-ever estimates for the nation and all fifty states, Institute for American Values (2008): 5.

[102] See http://www.americanvalues.org/html/coff_mediaadvisory.htm

- Increased taxpayer expenditures for criminal justice and education programs serving children and adults from broken families.

Over the last decade, the cumulative costs of national, state and local expenditures in the United States alone due to family breakdown was more than $1 trillion.

Economics professor Dr. Ben Scafidi explained: "This new report shows that public concern about the decline of marriage need not be based only on 'moral' concerns, but that reducing high taxpayer costs of family fragmentation is a legitimate concern of government, policymakers and legislators."[103]

The study also demonstrates the cost effectiveness of programs that are intended to prevent family fragmentation. David Blankenhorn, president of the Institute for American Values, stated that "Even a small improvement in the health of marriage in America would result in enormous savings to taxpayers. ... For example, a 1 percent reduction in rates of family fragmentation would save taxpayers $1.1 billion."

These new statistics provide a compelling economic argument for preserving laws and policies that protect traditional marriage and the family. By safeguarding the vital institutions of marriage and family, governments could save millions, if not billions, of dollars annually.

Happily Ever After

Statistics supportive of the traditional family can come from unlikely sources. A 2007 Associated Press/MTV poll showed that when youth between the ages of 13 and 24 were asked, "What one thing in life makes you most happy?" the number one answer was "spending time with their families."[104]

Of course, traditional marriages are not without their challenges. However, marriage experts Linda J. Waite and Maggie Gallagher reported that a high percentage of unhappily married couples who stay together resolve their problems and come to enjoy their marriage:

---

[103] Scafidi, B. (2008, April 15). Marriage breakdown costs taxpayers at least $112 billion a year: First-time research reveals staggering annual taxpayer costs for divorce and unwed childbearing, [Press Release]. New York: Institute for American Values. Retrieved June 8, 2009 from http://www.americanvalues.org/coff/pressrelease.pdfWatersmith, C. (2000, March 1).

[104] Associated Press—MTV Poll, Youth Happiness Study. (2007) Retrieved June 8, 2009 from MTV Web site: http://www.mtv.com/thinkmtv/about/pdfs/APMTV_happinesspoll.pdf

Eighty-six percent of unhappily married people who stick it out find that, five years later, their marriages are happier. ... Most say they've become very happy indeed.[105]

Waite and Gallagher further noted:

The very worst marriages showed the most dramatic turnarounds: 77 percent of the stably married people who rated their marriages as very unhappy ... said that the same marriage was either "very happy" or "quite happy" five years later.[106]

These statistics should give hope to individuals who are currently struggling in their marriage.

The Emperor is Stark Naked!

In Hans Christian Andersen's story, "The Emperor's New Clothes," some tailors come into town and convince a king that the fabric they are weaving can only be seen by intelligent people—or those fit for their office. The king, not wanting to be considered stupid, claims to be able to see the nonexistent material and commissions the "tailors" to make him some new "clothes."

As the king marches down the street to show off his new clothes, no one wants to admit they cannot see them, lest they be considered ignorant. So everyone "oohs" and "aahs" and remarks how magnificent the king looks. Suddenly, however, a child in the crowd points at the king and exclaims the obvious—that the king is actually parading through the town stark naked!

Social science research overwhelmingly shows that lifestyle choices can negatively impact a myriad of outcomes for men, women and children.

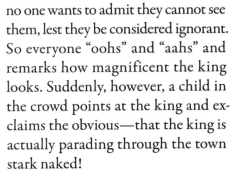

Those who assert that premarital sex, cohabitation, adultery, pornography and homosexuality are private matters with no negative impact to society and individuals are like the tailors in this story. To further their purposes, they claim that anyone

---

[105] Waite & Ghallagher, supra note 56.
[106] Ibid.

who doesn't agree with them—and anyone who fails to not only accept, but also endorse, their lifestyles—is either "intolerant," "bigoted," "old fashioned," or even "stupid."

Not wanting to be thought of as politically incorrect, too many people are afraid to challenge these new "tailors" of our society, despite the fact that social science research overwhelmingly shows that lifestyle choices can negatively impact a myriad of outcomes for men, women and children.

Societies are slowly but surely being swindled by imposter "tailors" who are trying to steal from future generations. In the following chapters, we will take their "fabric" apart, thread by thread.

Stand for the Family—What You Can Do

1. The research on family structure presented in this chapter also can be accessed through our Web site in the Family Policy Resource Center. The information has been organized into a policy brief entitled "Statistics According to Family Structure." This free policy brief can be used as a powerful tool to help people understand why family structure matters to everyone, but especially to children. It can also be used to encourage legislators to protect the institution of marriage. Please share this information with as many people as you can.

2. You may also want to share with legislators the information on the financial cost to society from the breakdown of the family. The full report, "The Taxpayer Costs of Divorce and Unwed Childbearing: First-Ever Estimates for the Nation and for All Fifty States," can be accessed at www.americanvalues.org.

3. Sign up for our free e-newsletter, *The Family Watch,* at www.familywatchinternational.org to receive updates on cutting-edge family issues.

For More Information: Our free Family Policy Brief on "Same-Sex Parenting and Junk Science" can also be found in the Family Policy Resource Center on our Web site.

Chapter 4

The Sexual Rights Movement

In many ways, every aspect of the assault on the family comes down to one underlying movement, the movement to destroy all societal restraints on sexual behavior. As mentioned before, once sex occurs outside of the confines of marriage, the family unit is weakened, and the negative consequences to individual family members can be substantial.

Since the most organized, best funded, and most aggressive component of the sexual rights movement is the campaign for homosexual "rights," this chapter will examine in depth the issues surrounding the movement for homosexual and transgender rights.

Unfairly, many who oppose the creation of homosexual and transgender "rights" are labeled as "hateful" and "homophobic," when quite the opposite is true. Opposing sexual rights can actually be a compassionate position based on a desire to help people avoid lifestyles that are generally fraught with disease and heartache. My heart goes out to anyone who struggles with same-sex attraction or gender identity issues.

To set the record straight, I am adamantly opposed to violence or verbal abuse directed toward anyone—homosexual or heterosexual. However, I am concerned about laws, policies and school programs that promote homosexuality as these can affect the well-being of children and youth. When homosexuality is promoted, children can more easily be persuaded to adopt a homosexual lifestyle and thus experience many of the well-documented negative outcomes associated with this lifestyle.

Interview with a Homosexual

During a long flight several years ago, I had the unique opportunity to have a candid conversation with a homosexual man about his lifestyle and his views on same-sex marriage, homosexual adoption, and other homosexual issues. I think we both learned a lot.

For many years, I had studied the research regarding the origins of same-sex attraction and the issues surrounding homosexuality, so I was somewhat practiced in addressing the standard arguments that are used to justify and promote the homosexual lifestyle. This man was interested in openly discussing his experiences with me and helping me understand homosexuality from his perspective. I have reconstructed our conversation and changed his name to Mike to protect his privacy.

Mike began by telling me that he was certain he had been born gay and had never known anything else. Mike had been teased throughout high school because he was different. Upon graduating, Mike believed he was gay and started living a homosexual lifestyle.

Sharon: Why do you believe that you were born homosexual?

Mike: I've always felt attracted to men. To think about being with a woman is repulsive. My brother is gay too.

Sharon: I have a friend who is a recovered homosexual and is now happily married with children. In fact, he's a therapist who successfully treats homosexuals. If homosexuality is genetic, how is it possible that people have changed their sexual orientation from homosexual to heterosexual?

Mike: He's a fraud. How do you know he has really changed? I don't believe it. He is repressing his feelings, and they will eventually come back.

Sharon: My friend tells me that being recovered doesn't mean you are exempt from temptations. It's what you do with those thoughts and feelings that matters. He says homosexuality is like an addiction. A recovered alcoholic may still crave a drink, a recovered smoker may still be tempted to smoke, and a recovered sex addict (whether heterosexual or homosexual) may face temptation throughout his entire life. For many, recovery doesn't mean perfection. It means one has successfully established a heterosexual relationship that is satisfying and meaningful and no longer acts on homosexual feelings or desires that may persist for a long time. You must be aware of all the social science data indicating that generally the homosexual lifestyle is risky and unhealthy. Do you think it's a good idea to promote this lifestyle by granting marriage rights to same-sex couples?

Mike: Most of the negative statistics would disappear if homosexuals were accepted and could marry. The suicide and drug rates are reactions to being persecuted and unaccepted. If that changed, the negative outcomes would change. Gay marriage could be the cure. By granting gays the right to marry, we can help homosexuals be monogamous and have healthier lifestyles. Right now, there's no reason for us *not* to be promiscuous. We aren't allowed to marry. When you teach abstinence until marriage, that doesn't apply to us. We can't wait until we can get married because we aren't allowed to get married. That should change.

Sharon: If that were true, then why don't these negative outcomes decrease where countries are more accepting of homosexuality and where same-sex marriage is legalized? What about the AIDS rates in the homosexual community? Isn't it risky for homosexuals to have sex with each other since a large percentage of this population already is infected with HIV?

Mike: I've been HIV positive for several years. With advancements in medicine, living with AIDS isn't as bad as before. I refuse to be a "gift giver." Before having sex, I always inform my partner of my HIV-positive status, and I only have sex with a condom. [A "gift giver" is an HIV-positive man who deliberately transmits the HIV/AIDS virus to a sexual partner. Sadly, some homosexual men actually seek to have sex with HIV-positive men.]

Sharon: So do you personally know "gift givers" in the gay community that have unprotected sex in order to infect their partner intentionally? Do you know gay people called "bug chasers" who want to become HIV positive? [A "bug chaser" is a homosexual man who deliberately attempts to contract the HIV/AIDS virus by having unprotected sex with a man or group of men who are known to have the virus.]

Mike: Yes I do. Some gays experience "condom fatigue." They're tired of worrying about infection. It can be liberating to be infected and to have sex with someone else who is positive as well—not having to worry anymore about getting infected.

Sharon: You believe that homosexuals should be allowed to marry, but surely you recognize that many gay men are promiscuous and don't have stable relationships. Do you really think it's a good idea to bring children into such unstable relationships?

Mike: My brother has had the same partner for almost 20 years, and they're very happy together. There are many children in the world who need parents that will love them, and gay couples can provide that. Do you think a child is better off in an orphanage than with a loving gay couple?

Sharon: Children need both a mother and a father for optimal development, and homosexual couples can never provide that. In addition, research shows that homosexual relationships are generally unstable. Several studies I've looked at are difficult to believe. Some of them indicate that the average homosexual man has between 500 to 1,000 sex partners during his life. Is that possible according to your experience? Would you be willing to tell me how many sexual partners you think you've had in your lifetime?

Mike: (Silence) I don't know. I've been to a lot of gay bars over the years, and I've been sexually active for over 20 years. I have no idea.

Sharon: Would you say it's a lot?

Mike: I really don't know.

Sharon: Why do you think you've had so many partners? Do you want to have a committed relationship?

Mike: Yes I do. I've met many men, but it just never seems to work out. I usually just have one-night encounters. It's like I keep searching for something, and I can't find it. Men are men. I think it's harder for men to be satisfied even in heterosexual relationships. Men are generally promiscuous.

Sharon: So have you ever *not* told someone you were HIV positive before having sex?

Mike: Well, it's not easy to face the rejection. When I meet a guy at a bar, it's not the first thing I tell him, but I always do.

Sharon: In the literature I've read, it says that in many cases homosexuals have not had a good relationship with their father. Do you mind me asking what your relationship was like with your father?

Mike: My father and I have a great relationship.

Sharon: What was it like when you were growing up?

Mike: Well, my mother was very protective of me. I was the third of three, and she spoiled me. I didn't have a bedroom, so I slept in the bed with my mom for a long time.

Sharon: Let's get back to your father. What was he like? Controlling, abusive or absent like the literature would indicate?

Mike: My father worked during the night and would sleep during the day, and he had a temper. He would hang his pants on the back of the door by the belt, and when we heard the jingle of the belt, we knew we were in big trouble. My father was very condescending.

Sharon: Do you agree that, statistically, a man having sex with another man, at least in the United States, is at a much greater risk of contracting

AIDS? A study released recently by the CDC[107] says AIDS infections among men who have sex with men in the United States are on the rise, which is a serious concern.

Mike: I heard AIDS was on the decline worldwide, and with new medical developments, many gays don't think it is such a life-altering thing to be infected. Something that's really bothering me is the push by the Bush administration for "abstinence only" sex education, which I believe is really dangerous and is putting sexually active teens at risk. Do you think schools should teach about condoms or "abstinence only?"

Sharon: I think children should be taught that abstinence should be the norm and is what is expected of them, and they also should be clearly taught about the negative repercussions (beyond AIDS) of sex before marriage or outside of traditional marriage. But I do think that some kind of provision should be made to inform those who choose to become sexually active about the risks of unprotected sex. Would you agree that homosexuals have a riskier lifestyle?

Mike: I know a lot of homosexuals who are just fine.

Sharon: All the studies we can find show that, statistically, married men and women and the children in these families fare better in everything that can be measured, including reported levels of happiness, education, wealth, health, crime rates, drug use and other high-risk behaviors. Married men and women even report experiencing greater satisfaction in their sexual relationships than single people. Don't you think it's a good idea to promote such a model so that people can find the greatest happiness and be protected from a myriad of problems? The further we get away from this model, the gloomier the statistical outcomes.

Mike: Did you have sex before marriage?

Sharon: No.

Mike: You mean you never had intercourse before marriage?

Sharon: No. I never did. I waited until I was married.

Mike: What about your husband? Did he have sex before marrying you?

Sharon: No, he didn't.

Mike: (Pause) That's very unusual.

Sharon: My children have said they plan to save sex until marriage.

---

[107] CDC is the acronym for the Centers for Disease Control and Prevention. The CDC is one of the major operating components of the U.S. Department of Health and Human Services. The organization's Web site can be accessed at www.cdc.gov.

Mike: Well, I actually think that abstinence is the best thing for children as well.

Sharon: I've had to fight the curriculum in my daughter's school that promotes homosexual behavior, and premarital and extramarital heterosexual sex for that matter. I don't believe that schools should teach anything that has the potential to sexually arouse children—whether it is heterosexual or homosexual. It's not right, and it's not what the schools are for.

Mike: I can't believe that schools would promote homosexuality. Why would they do that?

Sharon: I know many schools that have and do. You see the pendulum has swung too far. We don't want kids making fun of homosexuals or assaulting them, but the solution isn't to promote homosexuality. The solution is to teach children to be kind and not to single out and pick on others for any reason. [I wanted to say to him, but didn't, "You are HIV positive because of your sexual activity. I don't think it's right or desirable for schools to promote the behavior that has caused you to contract this deadly disease. This isn't an issue of hate; it's an issue of safety for you and for children and teens who are going to be making decisions regarding their sexuality."]

Mike: Here's the problem. We're competing with each other. You want to protect yours, and we want to protect ours. Our teens are sexually active, and so if programs don't teach them about condoms, they're going to be at greater risk. Your kids are not necessarily sexually active, so you want to protect them from sex. We are in competition with each other.

Sharon: I never thought of it that way. We're both trying to protect our own. [And yet, note that Mike also said being infected with AIDS is not such a bad thing.]

Mike: That's right. What do you think about hate crimes? Do you believe in hate crimes?

Sharon: Absolutely not. A crime is a crime, and I don't think it should be punished more if it's a crime against a homosexual as opposed to an overweight or elderly person or a person that may be picked on for another reason. All crimes of violence should be punished equally.

Mike: I really like the way you explain these issues. I can tell that you don't hate me or homosexuals. When I told you I was gay, and then that

I was HIV positive, you didn't act squeamish or back off. I really enjoyed our conversation. We can learn a lot from each other.

Sharon: Thank you! I don't hate homosexuals, although I'm sure some think so because of my position on homosexuality and other related issues. But my positions are compassionate. They stem from caring about the outcomes for homosexual people and for teens considering that lifestyle. My positions aren't derived from hate. We can disagree on the issues and still be friends. I think many people in my camp are misjudged as bigots. That's another reason I worry about hate crimes legislation. How can you judge people's thoughts and feelings? Right now, legislation addressing housing and employment discrimination is being dealt with around the country. I'm against passing this kind of legislation as typically drafted, and I'll tell you why. It gives homosexuals an unfair advantage.

Suppose you were an employer, and you had legitimate reasons for firing an employee who happened to be homosexual. Most employees don't think they deserve to be fired, regardless of their performance. So, the employee you fired immediately throws this new legislation in your face and tries to sue you. How are you going to prove you weren't discriminating because he is homosexual? Why should people get special rights based on their sexual orientation? Did you know that some people (fortunately a very small minority) consider pedophilia a natural and normal sexual orientation? Should we be giving pedophiles special rights too?

Mike: That statement is somewhat offensive to me.

Sharon: Well, it is a reality—that there are many types of sexual behaviors or "orientations." Society has to decide which are healthy and should be protected and promoted and which ones aren't. I happen to believe that only one of them is healthy, and you probably think that at least two are. I think we'll continue to disagree on that point.

After we landed, Mike said, "Maybe it was meant to be that we sat next to each other." He asked to exchange e-mail addresses in the event that either of us had further questions.

Homosexuals vs. Homosexual Activists

Before we go any further, it is critical that we differentiate between *homosexual activists* who are trying to force their lifestyle on others and *homosexuals*, like Mike, who are *not* trying to force their lifestyle on anyone. *Homosexuals* are people who experience same-sex attraction and who may or may not act on that attraction. Not all homosexuals, including some of those who choose to engage in homosexual sex, support the *homosexual agenda*.

Some homosexuals who act on their same-sex attraction openly and honestly admit that their lifestyle is not healthy, but they choose it anyway. Others have sought therapy and have successfully reoriented to hetero-sexuality, and some are even working to protect traditional marriage and the family. You may have friends, acquaintances or family members who experience same-gender attraction, who you care about and who are not trying to force their sexuality on society.

In contrast, *homosexual activists* are people who are pushing an agenda to change our society by changing our laws and values. They are literally seeking to destroy the traditional family. Homosexual activists promote the *homosexual agenda*, which is a calculated, well-planned, well-organized and well-financed effort to mainstream homosexuality into our society by redefining marriage and family and indoctrinating our children about the homosexual lifestyle. We can genuinely care about homosexuals and value them as individuals and still oppose the "homosexual agenda" which is not only harmful to society, but which is also harmful to homosexuals.

> *We can genuinely care about homosexuals and value them as individuals and still oppose the "homosexual agenda."*

The following quotes from activists reveal some of the aspects of the homosexual agenda:

> [Legalizing "same-sex marriage"] *is also a chance to wholly transform the definition of family in American culture. It is the final tool with which to dismantle all sodomy statutes, get education about homosexuality and AIDS into public schools, and, in short, usher in a sea of change in how society views and treats us.*[108]

> *Being queer* [This is not a term I prefer to use, but the author of this quote is using it to describe himself.] *is more than setting up*

---

[108] Signorile, M. (1996, May). I do, I do, I do, I do, I do. OUT Magazine, 30.

house, sleeping with a person of the same gender, and seeking state approval for doing so. Being queer means pushing the parameters of sex, sexuality, and family, and in the process transforming the very fabric of society.[109]

The homosexual activists I am concerned about are the ones who are not content simply to "live and let live." They are the ones who are deliberately and aggressively attempting to destroy all of society's sexual norms and the social institutions—such as marriage and the family—which uphold them.

I believe that Mike's views expressed in his interview with me are representative of many homosexuals who are not actively working to push a homosexual agenda on society. However, excerpts from the following article will show you that there are others in the homosexual community who clearly are seeking to push a harmful sexual agenda.

(Before you read on, I want you to know that I debated for a long time whether I should include excerpts from the following article since it is so disturbing. However, I felt it was important to include at least part of it to help you understand the mindset of the aggressive homosexual activists. In the end, I compromised and left some of the most disturbing parts out.)

Warning: The material that follows is quite disturbing. If you prefer not to read it, please skip to the next section.

The following excerpts are from activist Michael Swift's 1987 article, "Gay Revolutionary," that was actually read into the United States *Congressional Record.*[110]

We shall sodomize your sons. ... We shall seduce them in your schools, in your dormitories, in your gymnasiums, in your locker rooms, in

---

[109] Ettelbrick, P. [former legal director of the Lambda Legal Defense and Education Fund, Executive Director of the International Gay and Lesbian Human Rights Commission]. (1993). Since when is marriage a path to liberation? In Rubenstein, W. (Ed.) *Lesbians, gay men and the law.* New York: The New Press. (pp. 401-405)

[110] Swift, M. (1987, February 15-21). Gay revolutionary. *Gay Community News.* (Washington, D.C.) Written for a homosexual publication, this article by homosexual activist Swift was reprinted in its entirety in the U.S. Congressional Record, 15-21 February, 1987, E3081. Note: While it doesn't seem to change the intent in my mind, homosexual activists say that a "vital first line" that sets this piece up as satire and proves it was never meant as anything more than a joke is always omitted by the religious right (and was omitted in the Congressional Record). While that line may provide some explanation, it seems to only emphasize the underlying desires of the homosexual activists. The line states: "This essay is an outré, madness, a tragic, cruel fantasy, an eruption of inner rage, on how the oppressed desperately dream of being the oppressor."

your sports arenas, in your seminaries, in your youth groups, in your movie theater bathrooms, in your army bunkhouses, in your truck stops, in your all male clubs, in your houses of Congress, wherever men are with men together. Your sons shall become our minions and do our bidding. They will be recast in our image. They will come to crave and adore us.

... We will unmask the powerful homosexuals who masquerade as heterosexuals. You will be shocked and frightened when you find that your presidents and their sons, your industrialists, your senators, your mayors, your generals, your athletes, your film stars, your television personalities, your civic leaders, your priests are not the safe, familiar, bourgeois, heterosexual figures you assumed them to be.

The family unit, which only dampens imagination and curbs free will, must be eliminated.

We shall write poems of the love between men ... stage plays in which man openly caresses man... and make films about the love between heroic men. ... Our writers and artists will make love between men fashionable.

The following are just some of the many examples that could be cited that show how the homosexual activists are succeeding in their efforts:

- A popular song with a catchy tune, "I Kissed a Girl" (sung by a girl), extols lesbian experimentation.
- *Brokeback Mountain*, a controversial film about a cowboy falling in love with another cowboy, did very well at the box office.
- Movies, television shows, reality-based programs, soap operas, songs, musicals, and even children's shows now regularly feature homosexual themes or cast members.

Swift also threatens churches:

All laws banning homosexual activity will be revoked. Instead, legislation shall be passed which engenders love between men ... All churches that condemn us will be closed ... Those who oppose us will be exiled.

Finally, Swift warned:

> *There will be no compromises. We are not middle-class weaklings.*
> *Highly intelligent, we are the natural aristocrats of the human race,*
> *and steely-minded aristocrats never settle for less. Those who oppose*
> *us will be exiled. ... Tremble, hetero swine, when we appear before*
> *you without our masks.*[111]

I'm sure that back in 1987, Swift's dream seemed like a crazy diatribe from a far-out fanatic. However, much of what he fantasized about has already come to pass. People in various countries have been fired or sued for simply stating their personal views on homosexuality or against same-sex marriage.

The Homosexual Activists' Game Plan

In their bestselling book titled *After the Ball: How America will Conquer Its Fear and Hatred of Gays in the '90s*, homosexual activists outlined their strategy to mainstream and legitimize homosexuality in the United States:

1. Do not "draw attention to the gay sex habits that provoke public revulsion."

2. Begin by portraying homosexuals as "victims in need of protection so that straights will be inclined by reflex to adopt the role of protector."

3. Present homosexuals in the media as "wholesome and admirable by straight standards" so that they are "indistinguishable from the straights we'd like to reach."

4. Desensitize people to homosexual issues by inundating the media with gay, lesbian, bisexual and transgender messages.

5. Convert people to the belief that "gayness" is good by influencing "the average American's emotions, mind, and will, through a planned psychological attack, in the form of propaganda fed to the nation via the media."[112]

---

[111] Ibid.

[112] Kirk, M., & Madsen, H. (1989). *After the Ball: How America Will Conquer its Hatred and Fear of Homosexuals in the '90's*. New York: Doubleday.

We can see that in the two decades since these homosexual activists developed their plan, much of it has already succeeded.

A Key Strategy of the Homosexual Agenda

Opinion polls consistently show that those who believe homosexuality is genetically programmed, and therefore immutable, tend to support laws and policies that promote and protect homosexual behavior and that legalize same-sex marriage. Those who believe homosexuality is a programmed trait are also more likely to support measures criminalizing religious speech against homosexuality and to censor research showing the negative statistics associated with homosexuality. Therefore, a key objective of those seeking to mainstream homosexuality in society is to perpetuate the myth that homosexuality is genetic and immutable.

Those who believe homosexuality is genetically programmed, tend to support the legalization of same-sex marriage.

Gay Brains?

In the 1990s, it was widely reported that researcher Simon LeVay found a difference between homosexual and heterosexual brains, thereby supposedly proving that homosexuality is genetic. However, Dr. LeVay himself stated:

> It's important to stress what I didn't find. I did not prove that homosexuality is genetic, or find a genetic cause for being gay. I didn't show that gay men are born that way, the most common mistake people make in interpreting my work. Nor did I locate a gay center in the brain. ... My work doesn't address whether [sexual orientation is] established before birth.[113]

Despite LeVay's public disclaimers, his study has been widely misused to promote the idea that homosexuality is innate. This has been the case even though the opposite conclusion could have been drawn

---

[113] Nimmons, D. (1994, March). Sex and the brain. *Discover, 15*(3), 64. LeVay maintains a Web site in which he discusses the strengths and weaknesses of related research. See http://www.simonlevay.com.

from his study—i.e., homosexual behavior causes brains to develop differently, rather than homosexuality being caused by different brain structures.

Gay Genes?

Then there was the "gay gene" myth. In 1993, another researcher, Dr. Dean Hamer, announced he had purportedly found a "gay gene" which causes homosexuality.[114] But his own study showed that a significant percentage of the homosexuals taking part had *not* inherited this so called "gay gene."

Scientific reviewers also identified flaws in Hamer's method of determining who was homosexual and who was not. In addition, Hamer was charged with research improprieties by the National Institutes of Health for deliberately excluding pairs of brothers whose genetic makeup contradicted his hoped for experimental outcome. Hamer eventually admitted that his study did not support a genetic cause for homosexuality and that female homosexuality was "culturally transmitted, not inherited."[115] However, much of the public and the media still erroneously believe there is a "gay gene," and many homosexual activists continue to site Hamer's discredited study.

There have also been studies which purport to show that when compared to heterosexual men, homosexual men are more often left handed, or they tend to have counter clockwise hair whorls, or their finger lengths are different, or they have different fingerprint ridges. Even if all of these studies were credible, they still don't prove that homosexuality is genetic because most people with these unique characteristics are *not* homosexual. At most, we can say that genetic factors *might* possibly result in an increased *predisposition* to homosexuality. However, a predisposition is not the same as being genetically determined or inevitable. If homosexuality were genetically predetermined, people could not change. The very fact that many people have changed from a homosexual orientation to a heterosexual orientation proves that homosexuality is not genetically determined.

---

[114] Hamer, D. H., Hu, S., Magnuson, V. L., Hu, N., & Pattatucci, A. M. (1993). A linkage between DNA markers on the X chromosome and male sexual orientation. *Science, 261*(5119), 321-327.
[115] Hamer, D., & Copeland, P. (1998). *Living with our genes: Why they matter more than you think.* New York: Bantam Doubleday.

Environmental Factors that Influence Homosexuality

For reasons we do not fully understand, some people appear to be more *susceptible* to developing same-sex attraction just like some people are more susceptible to alcohol, tobacco, drug addictions or other sexual addictions.

Some homosexuals report experiencing feelings of unwanted same-sex attraction at a very early age. They point out that they did not choose to have these feelings; these feelings came to them unsought. This has led some to erroneously conclude that, since this attraction was unwanted, and since they remember being "different" from an early age, it must be genetically determined.

As I told Mike when I met him on the plane, someone I know struggled with same-sex attraction and developed a serious same-sex sexual addiction that lasted for many years. After recovering, he became a licensed therapist and has successfully treated many homosexuals. He maintains that homosexuality is not what someone *is*, rather it is what they *feel* or *do*. Homosexuality describes feelings, behaviors, preferences and inclinations—not personhood or identity.

Our experiences can have a great impact on the development of our sexual orientation. To some extent, people can be trained to react to sexual stimuli just like Pavlov's dogs learned to salivate at the sound of a bell. For example, if an avowed heterosexual were repeatedly exposed to homosexual pornographic images, it is possible that he might eventually be aroused by them.

There are a number of environmental factors that have been shown to influence the development of a homosexual orientation. For example, research shows that a high percentage of children abused by a person of the same sex end up acting out homosexual tendencies when they are older.[116] If homosexuality is genetic and not learned, how can this be explained? Did the perpetrator just happen to choose children who were genetically homosexual? This is not likely.

Some people are sexually attracted to children or animals or have other sexual fetishes. Are their sexual attractions also genetically determined? If

---

[116] Lisak, D. (1994). The psychological impact of sexual abuse: Content analysis of interviews with male survivors. *Journal of Traumatic Stress, 7*(4), 525-548; Gilgun, J. & Reiser, E. (1990). The development of sexual identity among men sexually abused as children. *Families in Society, 71*(19), 515-521.

not, then why would same-sex attraction be genetically determined and not other sexual attractions?

A large percentage of male homosexuals share common experiences in childhood. And while it is not clear what all the causes of same-sex attraction might be, research has identified a variety of common factors that may contribute to the development of a homosexual orientation such as:

- Physical and/or sexual abuse as a child;
- Hostile, detached or absent father;
- Overprotective or controlling mother;
- A feeling that they were not accepted by peers of their own gender.

Regardless of how someone has developed a same-sex attraction, he or she can decide not to act on this attraction in the same way one can decide not to act on an attraction to someone else's spouse, or toward a family member or a child. To say that we cannot help but succumb to all of our sexual desires is to believe that we are no better than animals. Some argue that animals exhibit homosexual behavior, so it is natural and therefore normal for humans to do so as well. However, animals also eat their young. Civilized people do not pattern their behavior after animals.

For More Information: For updates about how the sexual rights movement is being promoted at the international, national and local level, sign up for our newsletter on our Web site at www.familywatchinternational.org.

Chapter 5

Debunking Common Arguments Used to Advance Homosexual Rights

As I was writing this chapter, my daughter Julie sent an e-mail out to her friends asking them to join her Facebook group and to sign the "I Stand for the Family" petition that Family Watch has been circulating. (See the petition at the back of the book.) Julie was pleased to see her group quickly grow from 20 to more than 5,000. However, she also received some negative e-mails from those opposed to her stance on marriage.

To illustrate common arguments used to advance homosexual rights, as well as to provide you with some ideas regarding how to respond to these arguments, I have reproduced some of these communications below.

E-mail from a young lady to my daughter Julie:

I only joined this group so I can write this on the wall. I think what you're doing is horrible. How can you advocate something that limits someone's rights because of someone they love? The fact that traditional families are starting to decline does not directly affect anyone except for those involved. I understand that religion is a strong part of some people's lives but what you must understand is that it is not the same for everyone. If you expect respect for your religious lifestyle please respect people who do not follow your religion.

Gay rights are as important as any other HUMAN rights and there is NO reason that you should advocate against them, regardless of if [sic] those rights do not lead to a "traditional family." I respect that you have your opinions but I ask you to think about the things you are advocating. Your religion is your religion, respect people that are not the same as you and they will do the same for you. Thank you.

I understand that people are always going to have different opinions but realize that yours is one that discriminates against another human being for something that has nothing to do with you. I can't imagine following a religion and listening to a God that would tell me to do that. What you're doing is wrong, and you should be ashamed of yourself, I know I am for you."

Julie's response (which I helped her write):

Dear Jamie, [Her real name has been changed to protect her privacy.]

From your e-mails I can tell you are an open-minded, social justice, human rights advocate kind of a person. I admire that in you. However, you have made several assumptions that are absolutely wrong and somewhat naïve, although I am sure well intentioned. I do not doubt your sincerity.

Here are some of the problems with your allegations:

1. First you ask, "How can you advocate something that limits someone's rights because of someone they love?"

If everyone had a right to marry whomever they love, then you would have to accept polygamy, adult/child marriage, incestuous marriages and other kinds of bizarre relationships that some people promote. Governments sanction marriage not to sanction love, but to secure both a mother and father to their potential offspring so that the next generation will have the most optimal chance of becoming positive contributors to society. No one is trying to stop homosexuals from loving each other; we are simply trying to keep marriage what it always has been for the sake of children.

2. Second you state, "The fact that traditional families are starting to decline does not directly affect anyone except for those involved."

This is a very naïve statement. The social and human costs to society due to the breakdown of the family are monumental. Men, women and children in an intact nuclear family fare better on all measurable indicators; they are wealthier, healthier and happier on everything that can be measured. The further the deviation from that model, the worse the outcomes for the individuals, especially for women and children. Children who live without both biological parents are at a high risk for sexual and physical abuse, crime, delinquency, drug abuse, suicide, etc. Most of our tax dollars are spent trying to deal with the consequences of the breakdown of the family.

3. Third, you think my position is a religious statement when you say, "I understand that religion is a strong part of some people's lives but what you must understand is that it is not the same for everyone. If you expect respect for your religious lifestyle please respect people who do not follow your religion."

You wrongly assume anyone who wants to protect marriage is promoting their religion. The social science data overwhelmingly show that men, women, and children all fare better in a nuclear family, and there are way less costs to society when more people follow that model. Society has a vested interest in promoting that model which has nothing to do with religion. There are people from many different faiths, as well as no specific faith who want to protect marriage because that is what is best for society.

4. You also stress that "Gay rights are as important as any other HUMAN rights and there is NO reason that you should advocate against them, regardless of if [sic] those rights do not lead to a "traditional family."

Your statement is problematic for a variety of reasons:

1. You assume I am against rights for gay people which I am not. I think their human rights should be protected the same as any citizen.

2. You assume that gays should have the right to marry other gays. Gays have the same right as everyone else and that is to marry someone of the opposite sex. Most societies do not consider sodomy, or same-sex marriage to be a right, mainly because of the negative consequences to society and to gays generally when involved in that lifestyle.

3. Finally, just because I have a different opinion than you on this matter does not mean I cannot respect you. Just because I believe the homosexual lifestyle and same-sex marriage are not good for individuals or society does not mean I cannot respect gay people as persons and as friends. I have friends that smoke, yet I think smoking is unhealthy for them and society, and if I could vote to outlaw smoking, I would for the good of everyone. Same with drugs, same with gay marriage. So please be fair and don't call my political efforts to defend marriage "horrible" and tell me I should be "ashamed" of myself just because you do not agree with me. We can agree to disagree with each other on this highly controversial issue yet still respect each other—that is the American way.

Compassion Compels Us to Present the Facts

Someone once said, "An enemy flattereth, but a friend speaketh the truth." We can help people we care about by letting them know the truth about homosexuality and then continuing to love and respect them as individuals, regardless of the choices they make.

"An enemy flattereth, but a friend speaketh the truth."

Many homosexuals experiencing unwanted same-sex attraction feel trapped in this lifestyle, because they have been told they were "born that way" and that it is impossible to change. Since this is not true, the compassionate response is not to condone, embrace, encourage or validate a harmful behavior. Rather, it is to let people know there is a way out and, if they are receptive, to point them to therapeutic help.

Research on the Homosexual Lifestyle

People may be less likely to engage in homosexual behavior or support public policies protecting this lifestyle when they understand the potential negative consequences to themselves, their families and society. In addition to the research on the negative outcomes for those who choose a homosexual lifestyle contained in Chapter 3, consider the following from a report published by the National Association for Research and Therapy of Homosexuality (NARTH):[117]

---

[117] National Association for Research and Therapy of Homosexuality. A comprehensive response to the American Psychological Association's objections to the treatment of homosexuality. Retrieved June 13, 2009, from http://www.narth.com/docs/PhelanReportSummaryFact.pdf

Research has proven that homosexuals (mainly the male representatives) have much greater prevalence of pathology than the general population. This has been proven true in several areas, including the following:

- Suicidal risk-taking in unprotected sex[118]
- Violence[119]
- Antisocial behavior[120]
- Substance abuse[121]
- Suicidality[122]
- Promiscuity[123]
- Paraphilias[124]
- Being paid for sex[125]
- Sexual addiction[126]
- Personality disorders[127]
- Psychopathology[128]

---

[118] van Kesteren, N. M., Hospers, H. J., & Kok, G. (2007). Sexual risk behavior among HIV-positive men who have sex with men: A literature review. *Patient Education and Counseling, 65*(1), 5-20.

[119] Owen, S., & Burke, T. W. (2004). An exploration of the prevalence of domestic violence in same-sex relationships. *Psychological Reports, 95*(11), 129-132.

[120] Fergusson, D. M., Horwood, L. J., & Beautrais, A. L. (1999). Is sexual orientation related to mental health problems and suicidality in young people? *Archives of General Psychiatry, 56*(10), 876-880.

[121] Sandfort, T. G., de Graaf, R., Bijl, R. V., & Schnabel, P. (2001). Same-sex sexual behavior and psychiatric disorders. *Archives of General Psychiatry, 58*(1), 85-91.

[122] de Graaf, R., Sandfort, T. G., & Ten Have, M. (2006). Suicidality and sexual orientation: Differences between men and women in a general population-based sample from the Netherlands. *Archives of Sexual Behavior, 35*(3), 253-262.

[123] Laumann, E.O., Gagnon, J. H., Michael, R. T., & Michaels, S. (1994). *The social organization of sexuality*. Chicago: University of Chicago Press.

[124] Crosby, R., & Mettey, A. (2004). A descriptive analysis of HIV risk behavior among men having sex with men attending a large sex resort. *Journal of Acquired Immune Deficiency Syndrome, 37*(4), 1496-1499.

[125] Schrimshaw, E., et al. (2006). Test-retest reliability of self-reported sexual behavior, sexual orientation and psychosexual milestones among gay, lesbian and bisexual youths: High rates of sexual behavior in the general population: Correlates and predictors. *Archives of Sexual Behavior, 35*(2), 225-234.

[126] Dodge, B., Reece, M., Cole, S. L., & Sandfort, T. G. (2004). Sexual compulsivity among heterosexual college students. *Journal of Sex Research, 41*(4), 343-350.

[127] Zubenko, G. S., George, A. W., Soloff, P. H., & Schulz, P. (1987). Sexual practices among patients with borderline personality disorder. *American Journal of Psychiatry, 144*(6), 748-752.

[128] Sandfort, T. G., de Graaf, R., Bijl, R. V., & Schnabel, P. (2001). Same-sex sexual behavior and psychiatric disorders. *Archives of General Psychiatry, 58*(1), 85-91.

With regard to women who choose the lesbian lifestyle, NARTH reported:

> Lesbians have much greater problems than their heterosexual counterparts, particularly in health issues.[129] Findings from a national survey of approximately 1,925 lesbians, the largest to date, revealed that over 50 percent had considered suicide and 18 percent had attempted suicide; 37 percent had been physically abused; 32 percent had been raped/sexually attacked; and 19 percent had been in incestuous relationships. Almost one-third used tobacco daily and about 30 percent drank alcohol more than once a week."[130]

Consider these disturbing statistics regarding homosexual men:

- A study of homosexual and bisexual men published in the *Journal of Sex Research* found that the average number of sexual partners was 755.2. Some had had thousands of partners.[131]

- In a study of 2,583 homosexuals also published in the *Journal of Sex Research*, an evaluation of the older homosexual men found that "the modal range for number of male sexual partners ever was 101-500." Between 10.2 percent and 15.7 percent had more than 1,000 sexual partners.[132]

- Even though homosexuals represent a very small percentage of the population[133] (estimated at between 1 and 3 percent), about a third of child sexual abuse cases involve homosexuals.[134]

---

[129] Johnson, S. R. & Palermo, J. L. (1984). Gynecologic care for the lesbian. *Clinical Obstetrics and Gynecology, 27*(3):724-731.

[130] Bradford, J., Ryan, C., & Rothblum, E. D. (1994). National lesbian health care survey: Implications for mental health care. *Journal of Consulting and Clinical Psychology, 62*(2), 228-242.

[131] Meyer-Bahlburg, H. F. L., Exner, T. M., Lorenz, G., Gruen, R. S., Gorman, J. M., Ehrhardt, A. A. (1991). Sexual risk behavior, sexual functioning, and HIV disease progression in gay men. *Journal of Sex Research, 28*(1), 3-27. This was the average number of partners for HIV-positive men. The average number of sexual partners for HIV-negative men was 921.9. The highest number of sexual partners recorded for an individual in this study was 23,000.

[132] Van de Ven, P., Rodden, P., Crawford, J., Kippax, S. (1997). A comparative demographic and sexual profile of older homosexually active men. *Journal of Sex Research, 34*(4), 349-360.

[133] Gilman, S. E., Cochran, S. D., Mays, V. M., Hughes, M., Ostrow, D., & Kessler, R. C. (2001). Risk of psychiatric disorders among individuals reporting same-sex sexual partners in the National Comorbidity Survey. *American Journal of Public Health, 91*(6), 933-939.

[134] Blanchard, R., et al. (2000). Fraternal birth order and sexual orientation in pedophiles. *Archives of Sexual Behavior, 29*(5), 463-478.

- A study in Canada showed that life expectancy of young adult homosexual and bisexual men is 8 to 20 years less than for all men. The researchers estimated that if the trend were to continue, nearly half of homosexual and bisexual men who were 20 years old at the time of the study likely would not live to the age of 65 years.[135]

Many homosexual activists claim the negative statistics that correlate with their lifestyle are caused by societal rejection of homosexuals and that if same-sex marriage is legalized and homosexuality mainstreamed throughout society that these negative statistics will disappear. However, in countries where same-sex marriage is legalized and the homosexual lifestyle is more widely accepted, there is no evidence that any of these negative statistics have decreased. This indicates that these negative outcomes are likely caused by the lifestyle itself, rather than societal disapproval of homosexuality.

Homosexuality Can be Successfully Treated

The fact that same-sex attraction can successfully be treated also is evidence that it is not a genetically determined immutable characteristic, such as skin color and race. Each year, thousands of homosexuals in the United States alone successfully reorient from same-sex attraction to opposite-sex attraction.

Dr. Nicholas Cummings, past president of the American Psychological Association personally saw more than 2,000 patients with same-sex attraction. His staff saw another 16,000 patients. They did not attempt to reorient individuals with same-sex attraction to opposite-sex attraction unless patients strongly indicated this as their desired therapeutic goal. Of those with that goal, 67 percent had positive outcomes, with 20 percent of them reorienting to opposite-sex attraction.[136]

Several experts, with assistance from NARTH, surveyed 882 dissatisfied homosexuals. After receiving therapy or engaging in self help, 20 percent to 30 percent of the participants said they shifted from a homosexual

---

[135] Hogg, R. S., et al. (1997). Modelling the impact of HIV disease on mortality in gay and bisexual men. *International Journal of Epidemiology, 26*(3), 657-661.
[136] Cummings, N. (2007, December). Former APA President Dr. Nicholas Cummings describes his work with SSA clients. Retrieved June 16, 2009, from The National Association for Research and Therapy of Homosexuality: http://www.narth.com/docs/cummings.html

orientation to an exclusively or almost exclusively heterosexual orientation.[137] Other studies have produced similar findings.[138]

Compared to the percentages of individuals who recover from any addictive behavior including alcoholism, substance abuse or any kind of sexual addiction, these are very encouraging numbers.

Politics Caused the APA to Remove Homosexuality from its List of Disorders

Although the American Psychiatric Association (APA) removed homosexuality from its list of mental disorders, this clearly was a political decision that was *not* based in science. Dr. Robert Spitzer, a Professor of Psychiatry at Columbia University, originally led the effort in the early 1970s to remove homosexuality from the APA list because at the time he personally believed it was a fixed orientation. Subsequently, he received numerous phone calls from former homosexuals and became aware of other evidence which verified that many individuals had changed their sexual orientation.

Spitzer decided to investigate by conducting his own study and published his findings that many who had received treatment for unwanted same-sex attraction successfully developed exclusive opposite-sex attraction or achieved a level of "good heterosexual functioning."[139]

After publishing his study, Spitzer was immediately attacked by some of his colleagues and by homosexual advocacy groups for stating that homosexuals can change. None of these attacks were based on scientific grounds, as Spitzer's findings were solid. The attacks were politically motivated.

If you point out examples of people who make the change from a homosexual orientation to a heterosexual orientation, activists claim that they must really have been "bisexual" all along, and, therefore, they didn't

---

[137] Nicolosi, J., Byrd, A. D., & Potts, R. W. (2000). Retrospective self-reports of changes in homosexual orientation: A consumer survey of conversion therapy clients. *Psychological Reports, 86*(3 Pt 2), 1071-1088.

[138] Clippinger, J. A. (1974). Homosexuality can be cured. *Corrective and Social Psychiatry and Journal of Behavioral Technology, Methods, and Therapy, 20*(2), 15-28; James, E. C. (1978). Treatment of homosexuality: A reanalysis and synthesis of outcome studies. (Unpublished doctoral dissertation, Brigham Young University); Jones, S. L. & Yarhouse, M. A. (2000). *Homosexuality: The use of scientific research in the church's moral debate.* Downers Grove: InterVarsity Press; Byrd, A. D. & Nicolosi, J. (2002). A meta-analytic review of treatment of homosexuality. *Psychological Reports, 90*(3 Pt 2), 1139-1152.

[139] Spitzer, R. (2003). Can some gay men and lesbians change their sexual orientation? *Archives of Sexual Behavior, 32*(5), 403-417.

really change. Yet, research clearly shows that people can and do change their orientation both ways; and, in proving that homosexuals can change, the foundation of the homosexual agenda crumbles.

There is a growing number of former homosexuals who are beginning to speak out against the discrimination they receive from the gay community. This discrimination becomes especially harsh when former homosexuals talk about the negative experiences that emanated from their former lifestyle. They are ostracized, called liars and frauds, and told they didn't really change. These former homosexuals are beginning to organize and demand that their rights to change not be trampled on.

Perpetuating the myth that homosexuals are "born that way" is so critical to homosexual activists achieving their political agenda that there is a movement within the American Psychological Association (APA) to make it unethical to treat unwanted same-sex attraction. They would deny help to those who want it in order to achieve their social engineering agenda. However, this movement seems to be losing ground. A 1998 publication by the APA claimed that genetic factors played "a significant role in a person's sexuality." However, an updated brochure published in 2009 states:

> There is no consensus among scientists about the exact reasons that an individual develops a heterosexual, bisexual, gay or lesbian orientation. Although much research has examined the possible genetic, hormonal, developmental, social and cultural influences on sexual orientation, *no findings have emerged that permit scientists to conclude that sexual orientation is determined by any particular factor or factors.* (Emphasis added.)

Unfortunately, as statistics show, many homosexuals who were sexually abused as children are more likely as adults to abuse other children. This creates a cycle of abuse and recruit-ment of young boys in each succeeding generation. Instead of perpetu-ating this cycle by giving credence to the myth that homosexuality is

> *Many homosexuals who were sexually abused as children are more likely as adults to abuse other children. This creates a cycle of abuse and recruitment of young boys in each succeeding generation.*

genetic and promoting it with laws, policies and programs, we should offer treatment and support to those who struggle with unwanted same-sex attraction.

Recruiting Children to Homosexuality

Almost two decades ago, David Thorstad, a member of the North American Man/Boy Love Association (NAMBLA) stated in the *Journal of Homosexuality*, "The ultimate goal of the gay liberation movement is the achievement of sexual freedom for all—not just equal rights for lesbians and gay men, but also freedom of sexual expression for young people and children."

Homosexual activists argue that since homosexuality is wholly genetic (which we know it is not), schools have the same obligation to teach about sodomy as they do about heterosexual sex. It is amazing that many school districts have adopted this philosophy and are implementing curricula that mainstream homosexuality. Worldwide, and often under the guise of HIV/AIDS prevention, sex education programs are increasingly encouraging early sexual experimentation so that "questioning youth" can discover their "sexual orientation" or "gender identity."

Unlike traditional heterosexual sex education programs, homosexual-oriented curricula generally include explicit instruction in sexual techniques. They teach children about all the possible sex acts they can engage in. Proponents argue that because some students will be engaging in homosexual acts (i.e., "they can't help themselves—it's genetic"), the schools need to teach all students how to do it safely. The strategy is similar to cigarette manufacturing companies promoting filtered or "low nicotine" cigarettes in ads that appeal to teenagers as a way to "safely smoke."

The more common homosexuality appears, the easier it is for children to think it is normal and even desirable to experiment with it, and thus the more likely they will be to subsequently adopt a homosexual identity. A 10-year-old girl recently came home from school and announced to her mother that she was probably gay. When her shocked mother asked why she thought so, she said that she wasn't attracted to boys. She would much rather be with her girlfriends. Her mother explained that it is normal for young girls to prefer other girls as friends and that attraction to boys was a part of life that would develop later.

This young girl's confusion would likely never have developed without the avalanche of sexually confusing messages sent out through the media, the schools, and other cooperating venues.

"Questioning" youth who react to sexual stimuli involving a person of the same gender might begin to believe that since they felt stimulated, they might be homosexual and begin to experiment with homosexuality. Recently my friend's teenage son came to her very upset and told her he thought he might be "gay." He reported a boy who was known to be "gay" had told him he could tell he was gay and he shouldn't deny it. His mother asked him if he had ever been sexually attracted to other boys and he had not. However, the fact that others thought he was gay caused him to think it was probably true.

It is dangerous to encourage youth to question whether they are gay or not, especially since it might lead to experimentation. Sexual experimentation is like drug experimentation in that it can become an addiction. It is critical that parents find out what is being taught regarding human sexuality in their schools and work to remove curricula that encourages youth to question their sexual orientation. Sadly, we have come to a day that we have to discuss these sensitive topics with our children or risk them succumbing to the sexual indoctrination being thrust on them by society.

Homosexuality and Pedophilia

The terms "homosexual" and "pedophile" are rarely used when a man abuses a boy. Many news reports in the mainstream media (which generally advance the homosexual agenda) regarding the sexual abuse by Catholic priests avoided using the words "homosexual" or "pedophilia," even though the male priests were preying on young boys. If a man has sex with a boy, this is a homosexual act by a pedophile. The media rarely portrays the sexual abuse of boys by men as a homosexual issue.

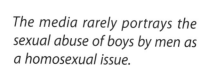

The media rarely portrays the sexual abuse of boys by men as a homosexual issue.

Stand for the Family—What You Can Do

Sometimes all it takes to stop a harmful movement in a community is for someone to have the courage to stand up and speak his or her mind, like the little boy in the story "The Emperor's New Clothes" who was not afraid to point out that the King was naked. Hopefully, the information in this chapter that exposes the sexual rights agenda has helped you see that agenda more clearly so that you can work with us to stop it before it destroys our families.

Here are some things you can do:

- Do not harass, demean or degrade people who struggle with same-sex attraction. Understand that this is a condition they probably have not chosen consciously, and treat them with respect. If they are receptive to it, refer them to places where they can get help.
- Take the time to teach your children that homosexuality is not innate and that it can be changed. You may find some of the research in this chapter helpful toward that end.
- Make sure the curriculum being taught in your local schools does not teach the myth that homosexuality is genetic, immutable and cannot be changed.
- Make sure your schools are not promoting homosexual behavior or promiscuity.
- Support laws and policies that allow people to be treated for unwanted same-sex attraction and that protect man/woman marriage.
- Oppose policies or programs that promote homosexual behavior or that give homosexuals special rights or protections based on their sexual behavior. Once a law is passed protecting "sexual orientation" or homosexuality in any way, that law will be used to try to force others to accept homosexual behavior and will likely be used as a basis to eventually try to legalize same-sex marriage.

For example, states that have granted civil unions for homosexuals have had those civil union laws used against them in the courts to try to legalize same-sex marriage by claiming same-sex couples are not being treated the same as heterosexuals. Remember that all people's rights should be protected whether they be homosexual or heterosexual; however, sexual behavior is exactly that, a behavior, and should not be used as the basis to claim special rights.

For More Information: To access research and scholarly articles on the causes and treatment of male and female homosexual attraction, please go to the Web site of the National Association for Research & Therapy of Homosexuality (NARTH) at www.narth.org. On their Web site, you can also access NARTH's report, "What Research Shows," summarizing the last 125 years of research regarding the medical, psychological and relational pathology in the homosexual population and the efficacy of reorientation therapy. Their executive summary of this report is free.

Our Family Policy Brief, *What You Need to Know About Homosexuality*, can be found in the Family Policy Resource Center of the Family Watch Web site.

Chapter 6

The Assault on Motherhood

When I was pregnant with my fourth child, at 32 weeks along, something was not quite right. During a routine office visit, the nurse took my blood pressure. She took it again, and then again. She left the room abruptly and returned promptly with the doctor. He took my blood pressure on one arm and then the other. The doctor explained that my blood pressure was really high, and he wanted me to go on bed rest over the weekend and come back the following Monday.

He said high blood pressure in pregnant women was the "silent killer," and said, although I may not feel any symptoms, my blood pressure needed to be monitored carefully. I was puzzled. My blood pressure had always been abnormally low.

On Sunday, I stayed home from church, but it seemed unnecessary to do so. I felt absolutely fine. Later that day, a friend of mine who knew I was worried about this "silent killer" stopped by with her husband, who was a doctor. He had brought a blood pressure cuff, and when he took my blood pressure, he looked very worried. He said I should get to the hospital as soon as I could. I still felt fine.

When I arrived at the hospital, they again took my blood pressure, told me I should plan to stay overnight, and checked me in. They kept asking me if I had a headache, but I felt fine.

I woke up at about 4 a.m. in my hospital bed with a splitting headache. I called the nurse to ask for Tylenol. She took my blood pressure, then quickly grabbed my bed and struggled to pull it through the door and into the hall. When she finally succeeded, she leaned against the wall, holding her heart. I think she was having a panic attack.

The next thing I knew, I was seeing double, and my bed was being pushed into a room where doctors and nurses were running around in a panic. I was totally disoriented, but I heard someone say, "We are going to have to take the baby." My leg started convulsing, and a nurse came over and tried to hold it down. They gave me an IV of magnesium sulfate, and I began to calm down. My vision cleared, and my muscles relaxed. They told me they could wait another 45 minutes until my husband arrived, but they also said their concern was for my life, and the only way to protect me was to take the baby as soon as possible.

When my husband arrived, they performed a C-section and whisked my 4-pound 2-ounce, little girl off to the ICU. I barely had a chance to glance at her. They took me to the recovery room and instructed me to try to relax and not to worry about the baby.

Still, my blood pressure would not go down, and my headache persisted. The doctor decided it would be too risky to move me and turned off the lights, leaving me alone in a dark room with an IV of magnesium sulfate dripping into my arm. They asked my husband to leave, as they did not want me to have any stimulation that could possibly bring on a seizure.

The nurse periodically came to check on me, and each time I asked her about the baby. She kept telling me my baby was fine but had to stay in the ICU because she was unable to regulate her own body temperature. The nurse kept promising me I would see the baby soon.

I longed to see my baby. It seemed the nurse was making up excuses. I'm not sure how long this lasted—at least through a double shift for this particular nurse. I worried that our premature baby had died and that they did not want to tell me for fear the news would set off a full seizure. I was distraught, and each time the nurse came in, I repeated my pleas to see the baby.

Finally, a new nurse came on duty. She smiled at me, and I started crying. She asked me what was wrong. I told her I was worried that my baby hadn't made it, and they were keeping it from me. She exclaimed, "You haven't seen your baby? We are going to see that baby right now!" She wheeled my bed straight up to the ICU and took me to my daughter's incubator.

As I reached in the incubator and held my beautiful baby girl, a rush of warmth filled my body and tears of joy came to my eyes. My headache immediately went away, my blood pressure soon dropped, and they were able to transfer me to the maternity ward.

The connection with my baby was so powerful that just holding her healed me. "Baby" Jessica is now 14 years old and is one of the great joys of my life.

Why do I tell you this story? Because I am trying to communicate something I know perfectly but cannot prove—that there is a powerful bond that can develop between a mother and her baby, even while the child is growing in the womb. This bond is deeply beneficial to the child and the mother. When the bond is broken, mother and child suffer. I believe that is one of many reasons why motherhood is so important.

Why is Motherhood under Attack?

A tactic used in the attempt to weaken the institution of the family is to convince married couples to remain childless, to postpone having children, or to drastically limit the number of children they have through abortion.

So how is this tactic being implemented? The well-plotted strategy has been: First, convince women that motherhood is meaningless, degrading and confining, and that childcare is an unfair burden placed on women. Convince them that fulfillment can only be found in competing with men and advancing equally in the workforce. Teach them that postponing or sacrificing professional pursuits for the benefit of their children and family is too much to ask. Better yet, repeal all laws and policies that recognize any differences between men and women. Eliminate special protections or incentives that encourage motherhood, childbearing, or the raising of one's own child and remove "harmful" symbols that stereotype women, like Mother's Day.

Sound familiar? Meet the Radical Feminist Agenda.

Please don't misunderstand me. I support women's rights. I believe that women should vote, own property, advance in careers, receive equal pay for equal work, and be allowed to hold government offices just as men can. I have a college degree, and I ran a successful business with an educational toy and book company, reaching one of the highest levels of management and sales and becoming a member of the company's President's Club. Along with others, I also have found a measure of success in my work at the local, national and international level to preserve and protect the family. However, I strongly believe that the greatest role a woman in our society can play is to be a good mother. Mothers literally hold the future of any society in their hands. No other accomplishment can compare to a job done well as a mother. Dedicated motherhood is not just good for the children. It's good—very good—for the mother, the family and society as a whole.

Yet largely due to the assault by the radical feminists, motherhood increasingly is being devalued. This must be reversed.

The Radical Feminists' Views on Motherhood

As I related earlier, my first experience with the anti-family agenda was at a UN conference in Geneva, Switzerland, in 2000. Before the official negotiations began, my colleague and I attended the women's caucus meetings where the feminist NGOs were formulating their proposals to the document under negotiation. Although the feminists were promoting many good things, many of their demands were so absurd, I was certain they would be ignored. But I was wrong.

They were seeking to:

- Eliminate all "obstacles" to women's empowerment, including children (through planned pregnancy programs and population control), unwanted pregnancies (i.e., through government-mandated, government-funded abortion on demand), patriarchal religions (because they supposedly subordinate women), and capitalism (according to their statistics, women suffer the most economically in free-market economies).

- Ensure that all governments and businesses achieve "parity" by enforcing quotas of 50/50 men-to-women ratios in all important decision-making and upper level employment and government positions, especially in military decision-making positions.

- Ensure that all women enter the labor force where they can realize their full economic value to society, and mandate that governments provide free, full-time daycare for all children.

- Ensure that these proposed women's rights are considered human rights and that all violations of such rights are prosecuted in the International Criminal Court with power to supersede national laws.

When I saw that this was not just a wish list and that many of these ideas were being considered by the delegates for inclusion in the document, I became concerned.

Aren't Mothers Best for Their Children?

A conversation I had with two women conference participants from the Netherlands was quite eye-opening for me. They were advocating for government to encourage mothers to put their children in government-sponsored daycare so they could enter the workforce. They told me they truly believe women who stay home with their children are oppressed by men and are leeches to society.

According to radical feminists, a woman's contribution to society is measured by the amount of money she earns. They pore over statistics comparing the percentages of employed women to employed men. The more women in the labor force, the easier it is for the feminists to show the importance of a woman's contribution to society. Hence, stay-at-home moms are viewed as traitors to the feminist cause.

These particular women were surprised by my questions about the welfare of children in daycare. They truly believed children would be better off in government-sponsored daycare with trained professionals. I told them I was a full-time, stay-at-home mom at that time, but when I previously worked with a toy company, I had visited many daycare centers in the United States. Most of the daycare workers were untrained foreigners who could not get any other jobs. I told them that the children I saw were not well cared for, and many appeared to be distraught. I explained that, as a mother, I love my children more than anyone else, and I would be more likely to be attentive to their emotional and developmental needs. I had seen too many miserable children in daycare who were starving for adult attention and affection.

The women were very surprised. They had never met someone who believed in taking care of her own children. I was an anomaly to them.

Several colleagues and I were able to find only two delegates willing to help us with the daycare provision—one from Hungary, the other from Poland. We worked with them to draft an amendment recognizing the right of mothers to care for their own children.

As we expected, our proposed amendment was met with great opposition. The delegate from the Netherlands said, "I could never support this." And the Canadian delegate said, "We have a real problem with this." The chairman suggested that Hungary and Canada get together to negotiate something acceptable to both countries.

The delegates from the two countries negotiated compromise language that didn't allow either side to get what they wanted. At that point, I realized why UN documents are so convoluted, contradictory and confusing.

But mostly, I wondered what business the UN had in mandating universal social policies such as daycare.

The UN's Assault on Motherhood

No UN treaty is more dangerous to the family than the UN Convention on All Forms of Discrimination against Women, known as CEDAW.[140] CEDAW intrudes on virtually every area of family life—attacking motherhood, life, religion, family roles and parental rights. Here are a few examples that pertain to womanhood and motherhood:

- CEDAW's preamble calls for "a change in the traditional role of men as well as the role of women in society and in the family ..."
- Article 5 of the treaty requires ratifying countries "to modify the social and cultural patterns of conduct of men and women with a view to achieving the elimination ... of practices which are based on ... stereotyped roles for men and women." (Motherhood is one of the "stereotyped roles" for women that the monitoring body of the CEDAW treaty has sought to eliminate.)
- Article 2 of the CEDAW treaty requires the ratifying countries to "embody the principle of equality of men and women in their national constitutions or other appropriate legislation." (While this may sound attractive, it is a sneaky way to force countries to adopt constitutional amendments similar to the Equal Rights Amendment.)

Fortunately, more than 25 years ago, Americans rejected a proposed Equal Rights Amendment (ERA) to the U.S. Constitution. Had the ERA been adopted, the United States would legally have become a gender-neutral society. Among the many negative consequences, the ERA likely would have eliminated occupational benefits and protections for

---

[140] The CEDAW text can be found at http://www.un.org/womenwatch/daw/cedaw/

pregnant women, widow and survivor benefits under Social Security, segregation of women and men in prisons, segregation of boys and girls in public school locker rooms, restrictions on women being drafted into the military and serving equally on the front line, and much more. Full "equality," despite essential differences between the two genders, would have been backed by the force of law.

The ERA flies in the face of science, history, and just plain common sense. Men and women are different physically, emotionally and psychologically—regardless of what any law might try to say. Yet CEDAW seeks to create the same "rights" that the ERA would have created had it been ratified by the U.S. Congress. President Jimmy Carter signed CEDAW in 1980, but, so far, conservatives have been able to block Senate ratification, which is required before a treaty can go into effect in the United States.

That could change in the near future, if it hasn't already. At the time of this writing, there has been renewed talk among some U.S. Congressmen about trying to ratify CEDAW. In fact, in March 2009, the U.S. delegation to the UN gave a briefing in New York, stating that they believed they would soon have enough votes in the U.S. Senate to ratify CEDAW.

This should concern us all.

If CEDAW is ratified by the Senate, it becomes U.S. law. In fact, Article VI, paragraph 2 of the United States Constitution states:

> ... all Treaties made, or which shall be made, under the Authority of the United States, shall be the supreme Law of the Land; and the Judges in every State shall be bound thereby, any Thing in the Constitution [of any State] or Laws of any State to the Contrary notwithstanding.

CEDAW has been aptly described as "the ERA on steroids." I shudder to think what activist judges in the United States could do with our laws if CEDAW is ratified.

A UN committee has been charged with monitoring countries that have ratified CEDAW to ensure their compliance with the treaty. The activities of this committee reveal the pressures we would face in the

United States if this treaty were to become U.S. law. Consider that this committee has:

- Recommended the "decriminalization of prostitution" in China.[141]
- Demanded that Mexico "address the matter of whether it intends to legalize prostitution" and urged it to provide "access to rapid and easy abortion."[142]
- Told the Czech Republic that it was concerned about that country's "over-protective measures for pregnancy and motherhood."[143]
- Told Belarus it was "concerned by the continuing prevalence of sex-role stereotypes and by the reintroduction of such symbols as a Mothers' Day and a Mothers' Award, which it sees as encouraging women's traditional roles."[144]
- Criticized Slovenia because "less than 30 percent of children under three years of age ... were in formal daycare."[145]

If you would like to receive updates about action items or related events occurring in the United States, you can sign up to receive our free e-newsletter, *The Family Watch*, and we can keep you apprised of any developments in the Senate with regard to CEDAW and help you make your voice heard in opposition to ratification by the United States. If CEDAW has been ratified by the time you read this, we need to work toward getting our president to "unsign" the CEDAW treaty.

Here's the problem though: Even if we stop the United States from ratifying the CEDAW treaty, it can still impact our communities if we are not vigilant. In an alarming recent development, radical feminists and other activists have been quietly working to get U.S. cities to independently adopt CEDAW. An e-mail sent out by the Women's Institute for Leadership and Development for Human Rights stated:

> *San Francisco passed an Ordinance that adopted CEDAW as city law and the Mayor allocated $200,000 to the implementation of the Ordinance. ... The effort to adopt CEDAW as local law is now*

[141] Concluding observations of CEDAW: China. 05/02/99. A/54/38, paras. 251-336.
[142] Concluding observations of CEDAW: Mexico. 14/05/98. A/53/38, paras. 354-427.
[143] Concluding observations of CEDAW: Czech Republic. 14/05/98. A/53/38, paras. 167-207.
[144] Concluding observations of CEDAW: Belarus. 04/02/2000. A/55/38, paras. 334-378.
[145] Concluding observations of CEDAW: Slovenia. 31/01/97. A/52/38/Rev.1, paras. 81-122.

being replicated in cities across the United States including Seattle, Eugene, New York and Los Angeles. The campaign was supported by over 200 local, state, national and international NGOs and elected officials including Senators Feinstein (CA) and Boxer (CA).

So don't think that what happens at the UN cannot affect you!

What Do American Moms Think About Working?

A 2007 Pew Research poll focused on the changing attitudes of U.S. women over a 20-year period about working outside the home.

The most interesting finding was that the attractiveness of full-time employment for mothers with children under 18 years had declined. In 1997, 32 percent of women characterized full-time employment as the "ideal" situation. In 2007, only 21 percent thought so.

In that time period, the number of full-time working women who cited part-time work as their ideal rose to 60 percent, compared to 48 percent in 1997. The number who said not working at all would be their ideal was virtually unchanged, 20 percent in 1997 compared to 19 percent in 2007.

While the survey did not specifically probe why there was this change in attitude, some of the other findings suggest at least a partial explanation. Women in the survey were asked to score themselves on a scale of 1 to 10 on how they felt they were doing as mothers, with 10 being the highest. Only 28 percent of full-time working mothers gave themselves a 9 or 10, compared to 41 percent of mothers working part-time and 43 percent of nonworking mothers.

When asked, "What situation is best for children?" 52 percent of full-time working mothers said part-time work was best, and 30 percent said that not working at all was best. Of nonworking mothers, 44 percent said not working was best, and 41 percent said working part-time would be best. How does one explain these statistics?

After more than a generation of being misled by the "Superwoman" propaganda of the feminists, more women now are aware (and in some cases painfully so) of the reality that their responsibilities as mothers take—and deserve—"quantity time." Yet many mothers are finding it very difficult to have even "quality time" with their children when they are under the stress of a full-time job. Many women have come to realize that trying to "have it all" can, and does, shortchange them and their children.

Children Need "Quantity," Not Just "Quality," Time

Jay Belsky is a researcher who, early in his career, held the position that putting children in daycare had no negative effect on them. Belsky's politically correct view was widely publicized, cited and praised by the feminists.

That all changed when he published new data showing that children in full-time daycare do worse than children with stay-at-home moms. He was ostracized and boycotted by many because his new position, while based on sound data, was not politically correct.

Specifically, in citing the *Study of Early Child Care* by the National Institute of Child Health and Human Development (NICHD), which collected data on more than 1,000 children from 10 different American communities, Belsky stated: "This study showed clearly that high levels of nonmaternal care—regardless of its observed quality—predicted the emergence of 'insecure attachments' between children and their mothers and the development of various kinds of 'problem behavior.'"

Some of the "problem behavior" identified in the study included: neediness (e.g., demands a lot of attention, demands must be met immediately, easily jealous), assertiveness (e.g., bragging/boasting, argues a lot), disobedience/defiance (e.g., talks out of turn, disobedient at school, defiant—talks back, disrupts school discipline), and aggression (e.g., gets into many fights; exhibits cruelty, bullying, or meanness; physically attacks others; destroys own things).

> *"... nonmaternal care of the kind available in most communities poses some developmental risks for young children and perhaps the larger society as well."*
> –J. Belsky

Should it really surprise us that research indicates children show more "neediness" and act out more aggressively when they have been left in daycare all day?

The results prompted Belsky to conclude:

> Early, extensive and continuous nonmaternal care of the kind available in most communities poses some developmental risks for young children and perhaps the larger society as well. Nor would it seem any longer tenable to argue that disconcerting evidence highlighting risks associated with high dosages of child care are simply a function of low-quality care. ... [Q]uantity counts when it comes to understanding the effects of early child care on socio-emotional development.[146]

Unfortunately, many mothers are unaware of or ignore such data.

Other studies show that children in full-time daycare are more prone to respiratory and ear infections, most likely because of constant exposure to many other children who may be sick.[147]

The mother who entrusts her child to the care of others when it is not necessary for her to work may reap consequences she never intended.

Mothers—Come Home to Your Children!

I certainly do not mean to be critical of single or married mothers who, of necessity, have to work to make ends meet. My grandmother was a widow who did the best she could to raise my dad and his brother. Many mothers have no choice but to work to provide for their children. These women merit our help and support. However, we don't do anyone any favors by pretending that having a working mother is good for children just because this situation cannot be avoided by some.

Many mothers seek employment to pay for extravagant vacations, fancy cars, big screen TVs, and other luxuries that aren't absolutely necessary. Some families might be surprised to realize that, although the mother is working full time, her employment is actually costing the family. After families weigh the tax implications of two salaries, childcare, the extra family trips to restaurants, work lunches and other work-related expenses, in addition to hiring out cleaning, driving,

[146] Belsky, J. (2002). Quantity counts: amount of child care and children's socioemotional development. *Journal of Developmental & Behavioral Pediatrics, 23*(3), 167-170.

[147] Nafstad, P., Hagen, J., Oie, L., Magnus, P., & Jaakkola, J. (1999). Day care centers and respiratory health. *Pediatrics, 103*, 753-758; Zutavern, A. et al. (2007). Day care in relation to respiratory-tract and gastrointestinal infections in a German birth cohort study. *Acta Paediatrica, 96*(10), 1494-1499.

tutoring and other things, sometimes there is virtually nothing left of mom's salary.

From my experiences visiting orphanages in various African countries, I have discovered that too many are filled with children who are not really orphans. In poor countries, a number of parents drop off their children in orphanages because they actually believe their child will be better off there. At least in the orphanage, they reason, their child will receive regular meals and, most likely, an education. Instead of a better situation, these children are met with crowded conditions, lack of loving care and, in some cases, abuse.

I wish I could somehow find all of those parents and tell them how important they are to their children. I wish I could show them the negative statistics for children growing up in orphanages without the love of their mothers and fathers. Family affiliation, and especially a mother's love, can be more important to a child's future than an education or even clothes or regular meals. Colleen Down drives this point home in her book, *It Takes a Mother to Raise a Village*, by recounting a lesson Mother Teresa learned:

> Mother Teresa, a great advocate for mothers, tells the story of a boy whom the sisters found on the streets of Calcutta. He was living with his mother in a box. The sisters took the boy back to the orphanage, bathed him, fed him, and gave him a clean bed to sleep in. The next day he disappeared. They found him back in the box with his mother. Once again they took him back to the orphanage and once again he ran away. Mother Teresa said she learned a very important lesson that day. A mother, even a mother in a cardboard box, was more important than the physical comforts that the sisters could provide.[148]

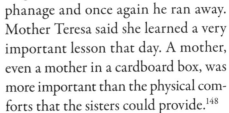

Family affiliation, and especially a mother's love, can be more important to a child's future than an education or even clothes or regular meals.

While visiting orphanages in Africa, I witnessed firsthand the differences between children who had experienced the love of their mother and those who had not. Regardless of why the children were in the orphanage, the impact of being institutionalized was

---

[148] Down, C. (2001). *It takes a mother to raise a village*. Draper: Lightwave Publications.

painfully evident. The clothing and toys we brought largely were ignored at first because what the children really wanted most of all was to be held. Each of us who made those trips wished we had ten arms and five laps so we could hold more of them at once. Then there were the children with the blank stares. They didn't seek love because they didn't know what it was. These are the children I can't get out of my mind.

According to the latest statistics, UNICEF estimates there are more than 150 million orphans throughout the world growing up without the love of a mother—and this number is rapidly increasing. It is mind-boggling to think of the individual and societal ramifications of more than 150 million motherless children.

It is important to re-emphasize—and I don't want anyone to miss this point—that *any mother who is unable to care for her children due to circumstances beyond her control deserves our support and help.* It is a tough road to travel alone. Some mothers are forced to take on the dual burden of motherhood and being the breadwinner. They do the best they can.

Still, let us not extol, promote or give tax incentives to mothers who *choose* to work outside of their home when they don't have to. We must not reward or subsidize that which hurts children and society. Mothers certainly have the right to make that choice, but government and responsible citizens should promote mother care, as that is what is best for children.

Any mother who is unable to care for her children due to circumstances beyond her control deserves our support and help.

Mothers, please do not be deceived into thinking that someone could care for your children better than you or that the extra money is worth it. Don't buy into the idea that self-fulfillment can only come from outside the home or from climbing the corporate ladder. Don't sacrifice your little ones to get ahead in your career. You are more critical, especially in your children's formative years, than all of the other influences combined.

Let us not extol, promote or give tax incentives to mothers who choose to work outside of their home when they don't have to.

The poet William Ross said, "The hand that rocks the cradle is the hand that rules the world." Mothers, keep rocking. Your mark will be felt for generations. Let's work to enthrone motherhood at the center of our national priorities and esteem mothering as the greatest contribution a woman can make in society. May the great men and women of the future be proud to say, as Abraham Lincoln did, "All that I am, or ever hope to be, I owe to my angel mother."

For More Information: Our Family Policy Briefs on the ERA and the CEDAW Treaty can be found in the Family Policy Center section of our Web site at www.familywatchinternational.org. These briefs can be used with policymakers to encourage them to oppose U.S. ratification of CEDAW and to oppose passing the ERA, which is being revived again.

If, by the time you read this, CEDAW has been ratified by the United States, we can inform you of our efforts to have the president "unsign" the CEDAW treaty. *The Family Watch* e-newsletter will keep you apprised of any developments in these areas.

Families for Orphans is a project of Family Watch International, which promotes family-based care for orphans. To learn more about how you can help some of the 150 million orphans in the world, who are growing up without a mother or a father, please go to our Web site at www.familiesfororphans.org.

Chapter 7

The Assault on Life

During a negotiating session at a UN conference on children,[149] our pro-family coalition noticed that a UN delegate from Africa seemed confused by the uproar that the term "reproductive health services" was creating. We tried to convince her that "reproductive health services" can be a code phrase for abortion, but she had a hard time believing us.

We showed her that the World Health Organization's definition of "reproductive health"[150] includes "induced abortion" under the guise of "fertility regulation."

She finally understood and became angry. She exclaimed, "I'm the reproductive health specialist on my delegation. Why was I not informed that 'reproductive health services' can mean abortion?"

She then insisted that we give her one of our "Motherhood" buttons, and she promptly put it on, making a definite political statement that she was in the pro-life camp. She said she was going to make sure everyone on her delegation knew that "reproductive health services" could include abortion, and then she was going to demand that this phrase be clearly defined. With that, she stormed off to the negotiating room, "Motherhood" button and all.

That experience left me to wonder how many other UN delegates did not understand what was really going on during UN negotiations.

Later in the session, a delegate from Canada, in what was either a slip of the tongue or a rare moment of candor at the UN, stated that "reproductive health services" did indeed include abortion. After his statement, there was absolute silence. He had spoken the unspeakable. He must have been reprimanded for his blunder because we didn't see him at the microphone again.

For years, delegates from liberal countries have tried to promote abortion in UN documents by using deceptive and elastic language, but, while at the

---

[149] This was a UN negotiation meeting for the Special Session of the UN General Assembly on Children, convened in 2002 to review the progress made in the area of children's rights since the UN World Summit on Children held in 1990. It was the first UN conference that included children as official members of UN delegations.

[150] To see the World Health Organization's online "Reproductive Health Library," which includes "induced abortion" under "fertility regulation," go to http://www.who.int/rhl/fertility/en/

same time denying that this is what they were doing. Shortly after becoming Secretary of State, Hillary Clinton stated publicly that the Obama administration considered abortion to be a component of "reproductive health." Clinton confirmed what we have been claiming for years but which pro-abortion governments have been denying all along in order to pass reproductive health policies. Wherever they can, pro-abortion activists will interpret "reproductive health" provisions to encompass abortion, even if those who created the provisions never intended them to include abortion.

Uncovering UNICEF's Deception on Abortion

We realized that the battle to educate the UN delegates on how the term "reproductive health services" language was being used deceptively was not over. A delegate from Costa Rica, speaking on behalf of a new voting bloc of Latin American countries called the Rio Group, insisted that since abortion is illegal in many countries, the term "reproductive health services" could not be interpreted to include abortion. Her true agenda became evident, however, when she refused to accept the addition of language clarifying that it did not include abortion.

Fortunately, Leonor Valdes, a former member of the UN Mexican delegation, had joined our team at this conference. She had recently been fired from the Mexican delegation, most likely because she had helped us on the abortion issue at a previous conference. She had with her a copy of a sex-education manual that had been funded by UNICEF and distributed throughout Mexico.

With this manual, we had the very tool we needed to stop the abortion language. This is because UNICEF also was insisting that "reproductive health services" did not include abortion, yet Leonor's UNICEF-published manual listed abortion under "reproductive health."

The UNICEF manual states: "Reproductive health includes the following components: counseling on sexuality, pregnancy, methods of contraception, abortion, fertility, infections and diseases ... abortion services in adequate conditions in countries where abortion is legal."[151]

---

[151]Elementos teoricos para el trabajo con madres embarazadas adolescentes [Theoretic Elements for Working with Mothers and Pregnant Teens] (Mexico: DFI/UNICEF, 1999), p. 66 [translation from Spanish]. Original text: "La salud reroductiva incluye los siguientes componentes: Asesoramiento sobre la sexualidad, el embarazo, los metodos anticonceptives, el aborto, la infertilida, las infecciones y las enfermedades..."

To first get the delegates' attention, we handed them excerpts from the manual, which also tells teens they can find sexual pleasure in various situations, including with animals, with a non-consenting person, or with a person of the same sex.

The manual states: "Situations in which you can obtain sexual pleasure:

- Masturbation
- Sexual relations with a partner—whether heterosexual, homosexual or bisexual.
- A sexual response that is directed toward inanimate objects, animals, minors, non-consenting persons."[152]

The manual goes on to say:

> Here we must insist there is no ideal or perfect relationship between two or several people except the one that gives us the most satisfaction and that which is adapted to our way of being and the lifestyle we choose. This is why we encounter many differences among women.

- Some women like to have relationships with men. And others with another woman.
- Some women like to have gentle relationships with much tenderness and affection while others like rougher, harder stimulation in order to enjoy sexual pleasure.[153]

Delegates were aghast upon reading the excerpts and found it hard to believe that UNICEF had published such a manual. We definitely had their attention. Then we showed them another excerpt that listed abortion as a component of "reproductive health," thereby exposing UNICEF's deception. As you can imagine, distributing these excerpts created quite a stir. In fact, it was front-page news in *The Washington Times* for three days in a row.

I then called my Costa Rican colleague, Rebeca Strachan and asked her to let her new government (a new president had been recently elected) know that their UN representative was promoting an abortion provision. Ms. Strachan faxed our report of the delegate's actions to the Costa Rican

---

[152] Taller de salud sexual y reproductiva para madres y embarazadas adolescentes: Propuesta Metodologica [Workshop on Sexual and Reproductive Health for Mothers and Pregnant Teens] (Mexico: DIF/UNICEF, 1999), p. 89 [translation from Spanish].
[153] Ibid. p. 94 [translation from Spanish].

government, along with a copy of the translated excerpts of the UNICEF manual. Ms. Strachan reported to us that the Costa Rican officials agreed to instruct the delegate to stop promoting abortion.

Our efforts in passing out the excerpts from the UNICEF manual and contacting the Costa Rican government, along with the lobbying efforts of the pro-family coalition, were rewarded when the word "services" in connection with "reproductive health" was completely removed from the document!

To our delight, during the UN General Assembly session following the adoption of the official document, the Costa Rican representative completely reversed her prior position and, instead, spoke in alignment with us against the abortion language. She announced that Costa Rica understood that nothing in the negotiated text could be interpreted to mean abortion and that Costa Rica's constitution recognizes the right to life beginning at conception.

A UN Security Guard's Change of Heart

At another time, while we were waiting outside of closed UN negotiations, we befriended one particular security guard. Before entering the negotiating room, the UN delegates had informed us that things were heating up on the issue of abortion; so while we waited I asked the security guard if he knew what was going on in the room, and he said he did not. I told him that representatives from almost every country in the world were gathered in the room and were deciding one of the most controversial issues of our time—whether nations should legalize abortion. He then shared this story:

> My wife and I had decided not to have children until we were more set in life. However, she got pregnant, so we decided to have an abortion. The day of the abortion, I took her to the hospital and checked her into a room upstairs. I was outside by my car having a smoke, when all of the sudden I had a powerful feeling overcome me. I suddenly realized that upstairs they were about to kill my child. I ran in the door, up the stairs, and into the room, just in time to stop the abortion.

Then he smiled a big smile, pulled out his wallet, showed me a picture of his two-year-old son, and proudly said, "See that boy? He's my son!"

Where Have All the Children Gone?

Harvard graduate and professor Harold Brown warned:

> Since 1973, we have killed between 1.3 and 1.5 million unborn
> future Americans yearly. The price in blood has now exceeded 40
> million, ten times more than have been killed in all of our wars.
> ... Whatever you think about abortion, about all of the potential
> hard cases, can it be right for a nation to kill one-quarter, sometimes
> one-third, of every new generation? Can we ask God to bless us
> while we exterminate ourselves?[154]

Sadly, we have reached a point in our society where one of the most dangerous places for a child is in the mother's womb. The widespread rejection of children has caused seismic changes in our society and to the family structure. Fewer children means shrinking kinship groups.

Sadly, we have reached a point in our society where one of the most dangerous places for a child is in the mother's womb.

Aside from a few exceptions, fertility rates worldwide are in steep decline. Many women are choosing not to bear children. Having only one child is becoming the norm for those who choose to become mothers. Two or more children is the exception in much of the developed world.

When an "Only Child" Marries Another "Only Child"

Where the "only child" is the norm in some countries, we can see the effect on family structure. When an only child marries another only child and they have only one child, this only child will have no siblings, aunts, uncles, or cousins. What a dramatic change to the extended family kinship support structures that have characterized human societies since the dawn of time!

When an only child marries another only child and they have only one child, this only child will have no siblings, aunts, uncles, or cousins.

Since the home as the manufacturing and economic center of life has largely become obsolete, in many

---

[154] Brown, H. (2003, February). Hard truths: Facing facts. *The Religion and Society Report, 20*(2).

countries children are now viewed as an economic burden rather than an asset, and the news of pregnancy is, in many cases, met with condolences instead of congratulations. Because of the interruption to the mother's career, along with the cost of feeding, clothing and educating a child, increasingly children are seen as a curse rather than a blessing. The feminist agenda views children as obstacles, and, therefore, feminists have declared war. Children are the enemy and the womb is the battleground.

Population Explosion or Implosion?

In 1968, in his best-selling book, *The Population Bomb,* author Paul Ehrlich predicted that in the 1970s and 1980s, hundreds of millions of people would starve to death because the earth was overpopulated. The UN bought into this false overpopulation theory. Many UN officials mistakenly believe that limiting populations is the answer to most of the world's problems, including poverty, disease, discrimination against women, and so on.

However, in *Earth Report 2000*, Robert Bailey summarized what has really happened:

- As the world's population quintupled, the world's economies grew 40 fold. (In other words, due to technology, we are doing much more with far less.)
- There is literally too much food in the world and plenty of land.
- Starvation is a political disaster, not a natural one (i.e., the real problem is the allocation and distribution of food, not its physical availability).
- You could move the entire world population inside medium-sized homes, and they'd all fit inside Texas, yielding a population density similar to that of Paris.

The UN has established programs across the world to try to limit the number of children being born. This misguided approach has succeeded, and fertility rates in many countries have decreased sharply. In a speech at the World Congress of Families IV in Warsaw, Poland, Dr. Phillip Longman stated:

> All told, some 59 countries, comprising roughly 44 percent of the world's total population, are currently not producing enough children to avoid population decline, and the phenomenon continues to spread. By 2045, according to the latest UN projections, the world's fertility rate as a whole will have fallen below replacement levels.[155]

The world is not facing a population *explosion*. Rather, the world is facing a population *implosion*. Many countries are not producing enough children to replace their aging populations. Some countries such as France, Russia, Australia and Italy are actually paying women to have more children, and other countries are considering implementing such programs. One region in Russia went so far as to declare a national holiday entitled "Day of Conception." Everyone gets the day off to go home and do his patriotic duty.

This population *implosion* is having a devastating effect on these economies. No babies ultimately means no workforce. Who will support the elderly who are now living longer? Senior citizens have been promised generous social welfare and retirement programs that no longer exist. Even the deafest politicians are beginning to hear the time bomb ticking.

In the United States, the Social Security/Medicaid system will soon be facing a crisis. Contrary to the belief of most Americans, the money the government deducts from your paycheck is not set aside awaiting your retirement. It is spent by the government almost as soon as it is received.

The government is gambling that there will be enough workers from who to collect taxes in order to pay your Social Security benefits when you retire. However, there won't be enough workers because not enough babies are being born to support this system.

---

[155] Longman, P. (2007). Falling human fertility and the future of the human family. Remarks delivered at the World Congress of Families IV. Retrieved June 13, 2009, from http://www.worldcongress.org/wcf4.spkrs/wcf4.longman.htm

According to a U.S. Social Security and Medicare Report:[156]

- "The financial outlook for the Medicare program continues to raise serious concerns."
- Medicare expenditures "are expected to increase in future years at a faster pace than either workers' earnings or the economy overall."
- Fund assets are projected to be exhausted in 2019.

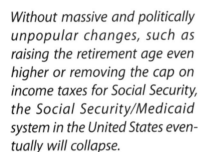

Without massive and politically unpopular changes, such as raising the retirement age even higher or removing the cap on income taxes for Social Security, the Social Security/Medicaid system in the United States eventually will collapse.

Without massive and politically unpopular changes, such as raising the retirement age even higher or removing the cap on income taxes for Social Security, the Social Security/Medicaid system in the United States eventually will collapse.

This should concern all Americans. Similar problems are looming over a number of other countries where the replacement fertility rate is significantly lower than the minimum 2.1 required to maintain a stable population.

UN Still Promoting Population Control

A couple of years ago, I read a booklet distributed at a UN conference which compared a family that chose to have one or two children with a family that chose to have more. It depicted the larger family as irresponsible and unable to care for its children properly and, of course, the smaller family as successful and happy.

The UN consistently fails to understand that *people* are the most valuable economic asset in both developed and developing countries. It is largely the improper allocation of resources and government corruption that perpetuates poverty in developing countries.

Surprisingly, even though UN officials know that the fertility rates of many nations are declining to dangerous levels (because the UN collects

[156] The Boards of Trustees of the Federal Hospital Insurance and Federal Supplementary Medical Insurance Trust Funds. (2008). *The 2008 annual report of the boards of trustees of the federal hospital insurance and federal supplementary medical insurance trust funds.* Baltimore: Centers for Medicare and Medicaid Services. Retrieved June 13, 2009, from U.S. Department of Health and Human Services Web site: http://www.cms.hhs.gov/ReportsTrustFunds/downloads/tr2008.pdf

the data),[157] it still promotes population control worldwide under the guise of "family planning" and "safe sex."

Promoting population control activities in light of the serious negative consequences of falling birth rates is not just illogical—it may constitute societal suicide.

> *Promoting population control activities in light of the serious negative consequences of falling birth rates is not just illogical—it may constitute societal suicide.*

There Are Always At Least Two Victims of Abortion

Abortion, one of the most common surgical procedures in the United States and probably in the world, is a very effective population control method. It is estimated that in the United States alone, a baby is aborted every 23 seconds—between 3,000 and 4,000 abortions every day!

In the United States and throughout the world, the great majority of abortions are not performed because of rape, incest, or to save the life of the mother. Most abortions are done for social reasons. Many women who "choose" abortion, however, are unaware of the serious physical, psychological and spiritual consequences that may plague them for the rest of their lives.

> *In the United States and throughout the world, the great majority of abortions are not performed because of rape, incest, or to save the life of the mother. Most abortions are done for social reasons.*

We should not only be concerned with the millions of babies who have been and will be killed by abortion. We also should be deeply concerned about the millions of abortive mothers who have and will suffer from the serious consequences of abortion.

The following poignant testimonies were provided by Operation Outcry, a project of the Justice Foundation:

---

[157] In the UN publication *World Population Prospects: The 2006 Revision Highlights*, the UN's Population Division recognized that: "Slow population growth brought about by reductions in fertility leads to population ageing, that is, it produces populations where the proportion of older persons increases while that of younger person's decreases. In the more developed regions, 20 percent of population is already aged 60 years or over, and that proportion is projected to reach 33 percent in 2050. In developed countries as a whole, the number of older persons has already surpassed the number of children (persons under age 15), and by 2050 there will be more than twice as many older persons in developed countries than children."

When my doctor told me I could never have children as a result of my abortion, I was devastated. That day I knew I had taken the life of the only child I would ever carry. –Jackie Ballard, Tennessee

There are no words to express the deep dark hole I found myself in [after my abortion], *no phrase to describe the depth of my despair. –Kay Painter, Idaho*

... after being rushed to the emergency room, undergoing more surgery and receiving blood, I was told by a different, very concerned doctor that I was lucky to be alive. –Julie Thomas, Georgia

I want America to know that abortion hurts women. Women are created to love and nurture their children, not have them ripped from their wombs and thrown away. –Karen Bodle, Pennsylvania[158]

The word "abortion" is often used without much thought as to what it really entails. The more information a woman is given regarding abortion—including the actual procedure itself, the development of her baby, what the baby may feel, the potential complications, etc.—the less likely it is that she will choose to abort her child. The abortion industry knows this and works tirelessly to ensure that women are not given relevant information.

There are many types of abortions that cause pain and trauma—not only to the baby, but to the woman as well. Be warned that in the next section, I will describe some common abortion procedures. I have done this not to condemn women who already have had abortions, but rather to give you another tool to dissuade women who are considering abortion. Accurate information will help women make an informed decision and hopefully choose life for her own sake as well as her child's.

A friend of mine was pressured by her husband into having an abortion. I realize she may read this chapter one day. She deeply regrets her abortion, and some family members believe it is a contributing factor in the mental illness she has suffered since the abortion. The following descriptions may be very disturbing to her and to others who have aborted their babies. If you are a woman who has aborted your baby and you would like to get help, please go to www.RachelsVineyard.org or www.SilentNoMoreAwareness.

---

[158] More testimonies of women who have been harmed by abortion can be found at www.operationoutcry.org.

org or call the National Helpline for Abortion Recovery at 1-866-482-LIFE. There is help available!

Abortion Procedures and Complications[159]

> **Warning: This section contains graphic and disturbing descriptions of some abortion procedures. If you would prefer not to read them, please skip to the next section.**

As you read the following abortion procedures, keep in mind that "the highest density of pain receptors per square inch of skin in human development occurs in utero from 20 to 30 weeks of gestation."[160]

Suction Curettage Abortion—Usually done during the first trimester, a sharp tool attached to a suction catheter or tube is used to dismember the baby in the womb, and the body parts are suctioned out. (Note: A baby's heart begins beating about three weeks after conception.)

Abortionist Dr. Martin Haskell testified that sometimes when the fetus is small enough, it passes through the catheter and dies in transit. In other cases the fetus "dies in the suction bottle after it's actually all the way out."[161]

Dilation and Extraction (D & E)—The transcript of a U.S. Supreme Court case provides a description of a D & E procedure:

> *The doctor grips a fetal part with the forceps and pulls it back through the cervix. ... The friction causes the fetus to tear apart. For example, a leg might be ripped off the fetus as it is pulled through the cervix and out of the woman. The process of evacuating the fetus piece by piece continues until it has been completely removed.*[162]

Another abortionist, Dr. Warren Hern, explains why a D & E may be necessary for second trimester abortions: "The procedure changes

---

[159] I used several sources to document abortion procedures and the complications arising from abortion, including: National Right to Life (www.nlrc.org); United Families International's *Guide to Family Issues: Abortion*, retrieved June 13, 2009, from http://unitedfamilies.org/downloads/Abortion_GuidetoFamilyIssues.pdf; and *Safety of Abortion*, retrieved June 13, 2009 from The National Abortion Federation Web Site: http://www.prochoice.org/about_abortion/facts/safety_of_abortion.html

[160] Testimony of Dr. Kanwaljeet S. Anand, before U.S. Federal Court, 2003.

[161] Sworn testimony given by abortionist Martin Haskell, M. D., in U.S. District Court for the Western District of Wisconsin (Madison, WI, May 27, 1999, Case No. 98-C-0305-S).

[162] *Gonzales v. Carhart*, 127 S. Ct. 1610, 550 U.S. (U.S. Sup. Ct. 2007).

significantly at 21 weeks because the fetal tissues become much more cohesive and difficult to dismember." He then suggests that long, curved scissors should be used to "decapitate and dismember the fetus."[163]

Warning: I need to issue another warning here. If you feel you've read enough, skip past the next three abortion procedure descriptions, as the worst is yet to come.

Saline Amniocentesis (salt poisoning)—Although a variety of chemicals are used to abort babies, in a saline amniocentesis procedure, the chemical of choice is a concentrated saline solution that is infused into the amniotic sac. As the baby breathes in the solution, the salt slowly burns its lungs and eats away the baby's skin. A shriveled, dead baby is delivered shortly thereafter.

Hysterotomy—This abortion procedure is similar to a Cesarean section, except the purpose is to take a life rather than save one. An incision is made in the mother's abdomen, and the baby, placenta and amniotic sac are removed. Sometimes the extracted baby is still alive and is left to die, usually by slow suffocation because the lungs are not fully developed.

Partial Birth Abortion—This is the most controversial abortion procedure because it usually involves killing a live baby (sometimes at, or very near, full term) just before it is born. It really cannot be considered anything other than a form of infanticide.

First, ultrasound is used to help the doctor locate the baby's feet. Forceps are then used to grasp the feet, pulling the baby into the birth canal. At this point, the baby is completely delivered, except for the head. The doctor then inserts blunt-tipped scissors in a closed position into the base of the baby's skull. He opens the scissors to enlarge the wound (there is no anesthesia for the baby). A manual or electric vacuum tube then extracts the baby's brain, causing the skull to contract or collapse; and the dead baby is delivered.

Partial birth abortions are performed legally in many parts of the world. They also were performed legally in the United States until 2007 when the U.S. Supreme Court finally upheld the constitutionality of a federal

---

[163] Hern, W. (1984). *Abortion Practice*. Philadelphia: J. B. Lippincott Company.

legislative ban on the procedure. Several previous attempts to outlaw the procedure had been struck down. At the time I wrote this chapter, some members of the U.S. Congress were considering enactment of The Freedom of Choice Act (FOCA), which would strike down the ban on partial birth abortion and nullify any laws which restrict abortion (including parental consent laws). It will also force doctors who oppose abortion to perform them anyway or risk losing their license.

Except for partial birth abortion, all of the other abortion procedures described here are still legal in the United States and in many parts of the world. If, by the time you read this, FOCA has not been passed, we can keep you apprised of any developments so you can help us try to prevent its passage. If it has passed, our priority should be to rescind this policy, as FOCA is one of the most draconian, pro-abortion bills in existence.

It is ironic that the same nation that finds it "cruel and unusual" to painlessly execute murderers continues to subject its most innocent and helpless members to legally protected, painful deaths.

The Multiple and Serious Consequences of Abortion for Mothers

Every woman considering abortion should be informed that approximately 1 out of every 10 women who have a legal abortion will experience physical complications, 20 percent of which will be life threatening.[164]

The list of abortion complications below is not exhaustive but certainly informative. Accurate information can save lives.

Abortion Complications that can Cause Death

Incomplete Abortion—The abortionist accidentally leaves behind body parts of the fetus or fails to completely remove the placenta, which causes bleeding and serious infections.

Sepsis—A serious infection in the bloodstream caused by contaminated abortion instruments.

---

[164] Frank, P. I., et al., (1985). Induced abortion operations and their early sequelae. *Journal of the Royal College of General Practitioners, 35*(73), 175-180; Grimes, D. A. & Cates, W. Abortion: Methods and complications. In Hafez, E. S. E. (ed) *Human Reproduction, Conception and Contraception.* Hagerstown: Harper & Row.

Hemorrhage—Rapid loss of blood due to heavy bleeding either during or after the procedure.

Amniotic Fluid Embolism—May be caused by an allergic reaction to the cells of the baby, causing the mother's heart to stop, resulting in coma or death.

Intra-abdominal Injury—The abortionist accidentally cuts or punctures the mother's bowel, bladder, cervix, uterus, ovaries, fallopian tubes, or intestines. This can cause internal bleeding that may go undetected until it is too late. Pregnant mothers are advised to "hold still" during the abortion to reduce the risk of injury.

Breast Cancer—During pregnancy, the mother's breasts prepare to produce milk. When this process is abruptly interrupted due to abortion, the milk-producing cells are more susceptible to becoming cancerous.

Missed Abortion—When the doctor thinks he has aborted the baby, but has not—e.g., in the case of a missed twin, a tubal pregnancy, or a double uterus—a number of complications such as those listed above can result.

Suicide—Women who abort their babies have much higher rates of suicide.[165]

Additional Physical Complications from Abortion

Additional complications have been well documented, including:

- Sterility
- Vomiting
- Fever
- Infection
- Endotoxic Shock
- Bleeding
- Nausea
- Cramping
- Hepatitis
- Convulsions
- Intestinal Problems
- Embolism

---

[165] Gissler, M., et al. (2005). Injury deaths, suicides and homicides associated with pregnancy, Finland 1987-2000. *European Journal of Public Health, 15*(5), 459-463.

- Second Degree Burns
- Endometritis
- Pelvic Inflammatory Disease (PID)
- Chronic Abdominal Pain
- Peritonitis

Mental Complications from Abortion

Research shows that abortive mothers have much higher rates of the following:

- Suicidal Ideation
- Self-Hate
- Low Self-Esteem
- Remorse
- Sleep Disorders
- Sexual Dysfunction
- Change in Personality
- Nervous Disorders
- Increased Promiscuity
- Social Regression
- Anniversary Date Grief
- Harm to Future Children
- Need for Prescribed Psychotropic Drugs
- Anxiety Attacks
- Depression
- Guilt
- Flashbacks
- Substance Abuse
- Relationship Problems
- Psychiatric Complications
- Aversion to Males
- Decreased Sex Drive
- Regrets Later in Life
- Suicide

Abortive mothers experience much higher rates of the following problems with future pregnancies and births:

- Sterility
- Miscarriages
- Bleeding
- Babies with Disabilities
- Early Death
- Placenta Previa
- Abnormal Development of Placenta
- Labor and Delivery Complications
- Difficulty Conceiving
- Ectopic Pregnancies
- Premature Babies
- Low Birth Weight Babies
- Cervical Incompetence

Studies show that abortive mothers also are more likely to physically abuse subsequent children[166] and have difficulty bonding to them.

Many abortive women have found healing through working with pro-life organizations and helping to prevent other women from making the same mistake they did. In fact, Norma McCorvey, the "Roe" in the landmark Supreme Court case *Roe v. Wade* that legalized abortion in the United States, later came to deeply regret her role in making abortion legal. She has since publicly confessed that she lied when she said she had been raped because she thought that would make the judges more sympathetic. In recent years, she has worked diligently to try to overturn *Roe v. Wade* and to persuade women not to abort their babies. She is now a powerful spokesperson for the pro-life movement.[167]

Profiting from Abortion

Hundreds of millions of tax dollars are used to fund abortions. In 2007 alone, Planned Parenthood, a nonprofit organization and one of the largest abortion providers in the world, received $336 million from the U.S. government, a third of its record $1 billion in revenues. The founder of Planned Parenthood, Margaret Sanger, once said, "The most merciful thing that a large family does to one of its infant members is to kill it."[168] And this is the organization being funded by U.S. tax dollars.

Let's just set aside for a minute the fact that Planned Parenthood reported aborting 289,650 babies in 2007 alone. Let's forget that abortion is one of the most controversial issues of our time and that nearly half of Americans (and more in some polls) oppose unlimited abortion, yet their tax dollars are being used against their will to subsidize businesses that profit from abortion.

And let's ignore for a moment the fact that Planned Parenthood is being investigated for fraudulently taking millions of tax dollars and has welcomed a donation specifically limited to aborting "black babies." (They are also under investigation for refusing to report pregnancies of minors who have been sexually abused by adults.)

Let's just forget all of that and focus on a financial decision to use tax dollars to fund any "nonprofit" group that cleared about $300 million

---

[166] Coleman, P. K., et al. (2005). Associations between voluntary and involuntary forms of perinatal loss and child maltreatment among low-income mothers. *Acta Paediatrica, 94*(10), 1476-1483.

[167] *Norma McCorvey.* (n.d.). Retrieved June 16, 2009 from Wikipedia: http://en.wikipedia.org/wiki/Norma_McCorvey

[168] Sanger, M. (1920). *Woman and the new race.* New York: Eugenics Publishing Company.

in excess revenue and that has assets of over $1 billion The amount they cleared in 2007 is about the same amount of federal funding they received that year. Certainly, there are better uses for our tax dollars.

Recently, my nephews in California had two very sick beloved pet rats that needed to be put to sleep. Their parents were surprised when they were told by the vet that the law required each rat to receive a checkup from a veterinarian first. If the rats could reasonably be healed, an effort must be made to find an adoptive home first. There was a mandatory waiting period, then if the vet determined that it was in the best interest of the rats to be put to sleep, it had to be done painlessly. In many areas, human life at its earliest stages does not even have the same protection as the life of an animal such as a rat.

The good news is that the tide is turning in our favor. Support for protecting life in the United States is at the highest it has ever been in 15 years. A 2009 Gallup Poll found that 51 percent of Americans considered themselves "pro-life," while 42 percent considered themselves "pro-choice." This increase may be due in part to technological developments that show stunningly detailed images of unborn children, thereby revealing the true nature of abortion.[169]

While working to overturn *Roe v. Wade* and to prevent laws such as FOCA from being enacted, pro-life advocates also should work to establish laws requiring:

- Prohibition on use of tax dollars to fund organizations like Planned Parenthood that promote or perform abortions.
- Doctors to inform mothers of all the potential physical and psychological complications of abortion.
- Consent of the other spouse/partner when one spouse/partner wants an abortion.
- Mandatory waiting periods for women contemplating abortion.
- Doctors to inform mothers of the ability of the fetus to feel pain and of the specific effects of abortion procedures on her unborn child and offer anesthesia for late term babies about to be aborted.

[169] Saad, L. *More Americans "Pro-Life" Than "Pro-Choice" for First Time.* Gallup's annual Values and Beliefs Survey. Results are based on telephone interviews with 1,015 national adults, aged 18 and older, conducted May 7-10, 2009. Margin of sampling error is ±3 percentage points. Retrieved June 13, 2009, from http://www.gallup.com/poll/118399/more-americans-pro-life-than-pro-choice-first-time.aspx

- Restrictions that specifically and more narrowly define the circumstances under which a child can be aborted.
- All abortions to be performed by licensed doctors.
- Abortion clinics to offer pregnant mothers the opportunity to see an ultrasound of their baby before performing an abortion.
- Criminal penalties for coercing a woman into having an abortion.
- Parental consent for teens seeking abortions.

Stand for the Family—What You Can Do

While this issue may seem overwhelming, there *are* things that can be done to help save lives. Two important things you can do to help are to:

1. Pass on the information in this chapter to anyone you know who may be contemplating abortion.

2. Pass on the Web site address for Operation Outcry (www. operationoutcry.org) to anyone you know who has had an abortion and encourage her to file a declaration on how abortion has hurt her. These efforts make a difference. A "friend of the court" brief filed by the Justice Foundation on behalf of 180 women hurt by abortion was quoted in the U.S. Supreme Court decision upholding the federal ban on partial-birth abortion in the United States.

3. Subscribe to *The Family Watch* e-newsletter and respond to our action alerts asking you to e-mail or call lawmakers to support laws protecting life. We will keep you updated on legislative action on FOCA and the movement to overturn *Roe v. Wade*.

I am certain there would be far fewer abortions if women were more informed. Please disseminate this information far and wide, and perhaps together we can save some lives as well as help women and their families avoid unnecessary pain and suffering.

For More Information: You can access our Family Policy Brief on abortion on our Web site at www.familywatchinternational.org.

"As for my people, children are their oppressors ..."

—Isaiah 3:12

Chapter 8

The Assault on Parental Rights

Anti-family activists working to undermine parental rights insist that children should be autonomous. They define "children's rights" to include, among other things, the right to abortion and sexual experimentation. And they insist that these "rights" of children, in essence, supersede the rights of parents to guide and direct their children.

In a UN speech, I once heard a Danish gentleman argue that because children represent approximately 50 percent of the world's population, they should have 50 percent of the power in government. He was serious. Imagine affirmative action for children, with quotas for placing them in government and policymaking positions.

A German speaker proposed that since 10-year-olds can have higher IQs than some adults, children should be allowed to vote at a very early age. Another speaker declared that children must be free to "experience, experiment and decide" without parental interference.

These comments represent a troubling development at the international level to give children "the right to participate" in government on equal footing with adults and to give them autonomous rights from their parents.

Child rights activists demand that governments "hear the children," but, in reality, they want governments to hear only those children who have been pre-selected and indoctrinated with anti-family views. Any time children are invited to participate at the UN, it is very difficult to get floor time for those who might support abstinence before marriage and protection of the unborn.

UNICEF Promotes Radical Rights for Children

In 2002, I participated in the UN Special Session on Children. The conference was chaired by UNICEF—the United Nations International Children's Emergency Fund—an organization known by most people for the humanitarian assistance they provide to needy children throughout the world. Few people are aware, however, that UNICEF departed significantly from an exclusively humanitarian focus during the 10 years Carol Bellamy led the agency. Though Ms. Bellamy's 10-year term expired several years ago, some UNICEF bureaucrats are still working to promote radical rights for children and have pushed countries, such as Columbia, to make abortion legal.

In 2004, Richard Horton, editor of *The Lancet*, a prestigious medical journal, summarized UNICEF's agenda:

> *UNICEF clearly has a pivotal role to lead the world's efforts to make children a global priority. Under Bellamy's leadership UNICEF is presently in a poor position to do so. Her distinctive focus has been to advocate for the rights of children ... But a preoccupation with rights ignores the fact that children will have no opportunity for development at all unless they survive. The language of rights means little to a child stillborn, an infant dying in pain from pneumonia, or a child desiccated by famine. The most fundamental right of all is the right to survive. Child survival must sit at the core of UNICEF's advocacy and country work. Currently, and shamefully, it does not.*[170]

At the 2002 UN Special Session, UNICEF encouraged children's participation, even designating some children as part of official government delegations. In addition, agency staff used this session to push for abortion and sexual rights for children. It was very disturbing to see young children, "representing" organizations from around the world, walking the halls of the UN wearing green T-shirts that said, "I Support Sexual Rights and Services for Everyone."

Children representing organizations from around the world were wearing green T-shirts that said, "I Support Sexual Rights and Services for Everyone."

Glaringly absent from the conference agenda was any real focus on desperately needed basic health care, clean water, shelter, and food. Millions of children around the world will continue to die of disease

[170] Horton, R. (2004). UNICEF leadership 2005-2015: a call for strategic change. *The Lancet, 364*(9451), 2071-2074.

and starvation every year, and more than 150 million orphans languish while activists squander funding in pursuing radical sexual rights for children.

At the 2002 session, UNICEF established a youth caucus in order to allow children they had carefully groomed to have input into a UN document being negotiated. The caucus claimed to represent the views of all of the world's youth, yet they were promoting sexual rights and abortion rights for children. Members of our pro-family contingent decided that if the UN must "hear the children" they should hear from children on both sides of the issues.

At the final negotiation session, members of the pro-family coalition brought a group of children to quietly join the youth caucus. A young lady who hadn't previously mentioned her pro-life views was voted by the youth to represent them in a speech on the UN floor. Adult organizers of the youth caucus were aghast when, rather than promoting their radical views, the young lady called upon member states to protect life before as well as after birth.

We also launched a new youth caucus to promote respect for the family, abstinence education, protection of the unborn, and families for orphans.[171] My daughter, who was 16 at the time, co-chaired this Child Advocacy Caucus.[172] We were fortunate to attract some UN delegates to our caucus meeting, and we gave them talking points on our issues.

Also at this special session we visited with two teenage South African girls who were sponsored by UNICEF. We discussed with them our view on abstinence before marriage. They wondered why the UNICEF program in their country had never taught them about abstinence. They had relatives and friends dying from AIDS, while UNICEF was promoting condoms without disclosing their failure rates.[173] "We have come so far to let the world know the needs of the children in our country," the girls exclaimed. "What good are these 'rights' when our basic needs are not being met?"

---

[171] Visit our Web site at www.familiesfororphans.org to learn more about this project and how you can help some of the 150 million orphans around the world.

[172] This Caucus was officially registered at the World Summit on Children and organized by Susan Roylance, a co-founder of United Families International (www.unitedfamilies.org).

[173] A comprehensive chart on contraceptive failure rates can be found at The Concerned Parent Report Web Site: http://www.concernedparents.com/Abstracts/Why%20Contraception%20 is%20not%20the%20Answer/Contraceptive%20Failure%20Rate%20Chart.htm

Protection Rights vs. Choice Rights for Children

At one point during this session, I met the Ambassador from Mali in the hall. She was the chair of the conference negotiations. I expressed my frustrations that in all of the discussion no one was differentiating between "protection rights" (survival and protection) for children and "choice rights" (for example, the right to participate in government or to have an abortion without parental consent). She encouraged me to get on the speaker's list to clarify these differences. Unfortunately, the feminists were able to keep me off the list, but we were allowed to distribute my printed speech on the UN floor.

We need to help policymakers carefully distinguish between fundamental human rights and those "rights" that social engineers invent to implement their own agendas.

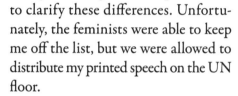

Calling something a "right" is a common tactic used to try to shield policies from careful scrutiny. After all, if something is a "right," then that is the end of the discussion. We need to help policymakers carefully distinguish between fundamental human rights and those "rights" that social engineers invent to implement their own agendas.

Radical NGOs Bemoan Pro-Family Victories

In order to stay informed, I am on the e-mail distribution lists of a number of anti-family organizations that assert influence at the UN. After the negotiating session for the children's conference, I received an e-mail action alert from an NGO called Canada for Population and Development—one of many NGOs across the world with the mission to "liberate children from their parents' oppressive sexual teachings." The NGO's action alert gave their assessment of the negotiations up to that point, saying, "Among [the document's] many weaknesses is the lack of attention given to sexual and reproductive rights." (Remember, this was a conference about children.)

One section of the alert, titled "The Return of the Right-wing Organizations," noted that the pro-family groups had been "more disruptive than ever before." (We were having an impact!)

Here is how our activities at the conference were portrayed in the alert:

> The youth caucus had a large group of youth from the so-called "pro-family" and "pro-life" groups who wanted to focus the discussion on issues relating to the family, parental rights, and chastity. Once again, the right-wing is promoting the concept of the "ideal" family as the nuclear family based on a man and woman united by marriage and their children.
>
> Right-wing governments and groups are also attempting to insert language in the outcome document that would strengthen parental authority and control to the detriment of established children's rights. For instance, they are calling for language to be included to the effect that HIV/AIDS counseling for children and adolescents would only be available with the "knowledge of parents," and generally oppose providing information, education and services to adolescents with respect to their sexual and reproductive health and rights, without parental consent. Clearly, the adoption of such language must be fought against as it could result in significant damage to young people's access to reproductive health services.
>
> Of great concern is the fact that right-wing organizations are aggressively promoting the idea that "instead of teaching children how to protect themselves from HIV/AIDS, we should teach them the culture of chastity and self-control."
>
> Furthermore, right-wing organizations are also demanding specific protection for the fetus to be included in the outcome document, accompanied by a recognition that the "fetus is a basic phase of childhood."[174]

We plead guilty as charged. All this and more was exactly what our pro-family coalition was doing and, happily, we were very successful at that conference.

---

[174] *Return of the right-wing organizations.* (n.d.). Retrieved March 14, 2008, from Action Canada for Population and Development Web Site: http://www.acpd.ca/acpd.cfm/en/section/ActionAlert/ articleID /80#return

The UN Convention on the Rights of the Child

One of the greatest assaults on parental rights is the UN Convention on the Rights of the Child, commonly known as the CRC, which went into effect in 1990. At the time of the printing of this book, every country except the United States and Somalia has ratified the CRC. One reason the United States has not ratified the CRC is because it pits children against their parents by prematurely granting them unwarranted autonomous rights. This is unfortunate because most of the CRC treaty establishes laudable goals.

At the Special Session on Children in 2002, U.S. Ambassador Michael Southwick protested efforts by other UN member states to pressure the United States to ratify the CRC. He announced, despite its positive aspects, "We believe the text goes too far."[175]

Ambassador Southwick went on to say, "The United States does not accept obligations based on [the CRC], nor do we accept that it is the best or the only framework for developing programs and policies to benefit children." Ambassador Southwick placed "the erosion of parental authority" on par with HIV/AIDS, sexual exploitation and war-affected children; and he called for emphasis on "the vital role the family plays in the upbringing of children."[176]

"The United States does not accept obligations based on [the CRC], nor do we accept that it is the best or the only framework for developing programs and policies to benefit children."
—*Ambassador Michael Southwick*

To our delight, after his speech the mood of the conference immediately changed. Children's rights activists quieted as pro-family countries began to speak out, requesting that references to the importance of the family be included in the document under review. The draft document was thrown out and the delegates prepared a new document for further negotiations, which included more pro-family provisions.

---

[175] Press Release #82, U.S. Mission to the United Nations, Statement by Ambassador E. Michael Southwick, Deputy Assistant Secretary of State for International Organization Affairs, Preparatory Committee for the General Assembly Special Session on Children, June 12, 2001.

[176] Ibid.

So What's Wrong with the CRC?

There is plenty that is right with the Convention on the Rights of the Child. In fact, the preamble makes the following pro-family statement:

> *Convinced that the family, as the fundamental group of society and the natural environment for the growth and well-being of all its members and particularly children, should be afforded the necessary protection and assistance so that it can fully assume its responsibilities within the community ...*

Then the Convention recognizes:

> *... the child, for the full and harmonious development of his or her personality, should grow up in a family environment, in an atmosphere of happiness, love and understanding. ...*

With regard to parental rights, the Convention states in Article 5:

> *States Parties shall respect the responsibilities, rights and duties of parents or, where applicable, the members of the extended family or community as provided for by local custom, legal guardians or other persons legally responsible for the child, to provide, in a manner consistent with the evolving capacities of the child, appropriate direction and guidance in the exercise by the child of the rights recognized in the present Convention.*

The problem with Article 5, however, is with the last phrase. It only allows member states to respect parental rights "in a manner consistent with the evolving capacities of the child, appropriate direction and guidance in *the exercise by the child of the rights recognized in the present Convention.*" (Emphasis added.) To understand why this is a concern requires an understanding of the rights the Convention recognizes.

Article 13 of the CRC states:

> *The child shall have the right to freedom of expression; this right shall include freedom to seek, receive and impart information and ideas of all kinds, regardless of frontiers, either orally, in writing or in print, in the form of art, or through any other media of the child's choice.*

This "right" could be interpreted to include unrestricted access to violent entertainment, pornography or the Internet. Imagine a home where parents cannot monitor media choices.

Article 14 says:

This "right" could be interpreted to include unrestricted access to violent entertainment, pornography or the Internet. Imagine a home where parents cannot monitor media choices.

States Parties shall respect the right of the child to freedom of thought, conscience and religion.

Imagine what happens when a 6-year-old child doesn't feel like going to church with the family. Could the child sue his parents?

Article 15 of the CRC is also troublesome because it gives the child the right to "freedom of association." This means it might be illegal for you, as a parent, to prevent your child from associating with friends or even adults that may be a bad influence on them. Under this provision parents might not even be able to forbid their child to join a gang.

Article 16 provides that:

> *No child shall be subjected to arbitrary or unlawful interference with his or her privacy, family, home or correspondence. ...*[177]

This could be interpreted to mean that parents cannot limit or monitor e-mail, cell phones or Internet chatroom communications.

These possible interpretations are not without precedence. For example, in Canada (which is a party to the CRC), a teenager sued her father for grounding her from a weekend-long school field trip. The father had disciplined his daughter for disobeying him when she posted images of herself on the Internet. The Canadian court ruled that the father's punishment was too severe and ordered him to let his daughter go on the field trip. The father also lost on appeal.

Since it is one of only two countries that has not ratified the CRC, the United States is under great international pressure to do so. Depending on the makeup of Congress, the U.S. position on the CRC changes. The

---

[177] Convention on the Rights of the Child, adopted and opened for signature, ratification and accession by General Assembly Resolution 44/25 of 20 November 1989. The text of the Convention is available at http://www.unhchr.ch/html/menu3/b/k2crc.htm

Obama administration announced its intention to get the U.S. Senate to ratify the CRC, and there are many children's rights activists currently working toward U.S. ratification. If the CRC is ratified by the United States by the time you read this book, we will need to work toward withdrawing ratification.

Other countries are using the CRC as "the" basis for all laws and policies regarding children. My friend, Dr. Abdul Carimo of Mozambique, was tasked by his government to reform Mozambique's child welfare laws. He explained that his team first looked at all of the international treaties and agreements Mozambique has signed as the key framework or basis for all of their new laws and policies. Since Mozambique has ratified the CRC, their new child welfare laws are based on it. Many other countries have also based their laws on CRC principles. This is good news and bad news. As I mentioned before, many of the CRC provisions are constructive; however, most governments do not recognize the problems inherent with granting children the autonomous rights noted above.

The Assault on Parental Rights in the United States

Parental Consent Laws

In the United States, battles continue to rage in many states over parental consent laws that allow parents to prohibit their children from receiving sexually explicit information, contraceptives, or abortions without their parents' knowledge or approval. In some states, my daughter, who could not go to the dentist to have her teeth cleaned or even take cold medicine at school without my written permission, would be allowed to have an abortion without my consent or even my knowledge. This just doesn't make sense.

> *In some states, my daughter, who could not even take cold medicine at school without my written permission, would be allowed to have an abortion without my consent or even my knowledge.*

The National Education Association

The National Education Association (NEA) is the largest teachers' union in the United States. In an article titled *The NEA Spells Out Its*

Policies, Phyllis Schlafly, founder and president of Eagle Forum, outlines the NEA's radical agenda, which constitutes an assault on parental rights:

> NEA resolutions cover the waterfront of all sorts of political issues that have nothing to do with improving education for schoolchildren ...
>
> NEA resolutions include all the major feminist goals such as "the right to reproductive freedom" (i.e., abortion on demand) ... and "the use of non-sexist language" (i.e., censoring out all masculine words such as husband and father). The NEA even urges its affiliates to work for ratification of the Equal Rights Amendment.
>
> The influence of the gay lobby is pervasive in dozens of NEA resolutions adopted by 2008 convention delegates. Diversity is the code word used for pro-gay indoctrination in the classroom.
>
> The NEA's diversity resolution makes clear that this means teaching about "sexual orientation" and "gender identification," words that are repeated in dozens of resolutions. The NEA demands that "diversity-based curricula" even be imposed on preschoolers.
>
> The NEA urges its members to offer "diverse role models" by the "hiring and promotion of diverse education employees in our public schools." The NEA puts "domestic partnerships, civil unions, and marriage" on an equal footing.

The NEA wants all sex education courses, textbooks, curricula, instructional materials and activities to include indoctrination about sexual orientation.

> The NEA wants every child (i.e., regardless of age) to have "direct and confidential access (i.e., without notification to parents) to comprehensive health (i.e., including learning how to use condoms for premarital sex), social, and psychological programs and services."

The NEA wants public schools to take over the physical and mental care of students through school clinics that provide services, diagnosis, treatment, family-planning counseling, and access to birth control methods "with instruction in their use." Family planning clinics are called on to "provide intensive counseling."

The NEA wants all sex education courses, textbooks, curricula, instructional materials and activities to include indoctrination about sexual orientation and gender identification plus warnings about homophobia ...

The NEA is strong for "multicultural education," which the resolution makes clear does not mean studying facts about different countries and cultures. It means "the process of incorporating the values" and influencing "behavior" toward the NEA's version of "the common good," such as "reducing homophobia."

Will parents be silent about the radical goals of their children's teachers?[178]

As parents and concerned citizens, we need to organize ourselves to ensure that the NEA does not implement its radical agenda in our local schools or state legislatures.

The U.S. Courts' Increasing Assault on Parental Rights

In 2007, Chief Judge Mark Wolf of the U.S. district court in Massachusetts declared that parents have no right to shield their children from pro-homosexual indoctrination in public schools in that state.[179] We briefly discussed this case in Chapter 2, but it bears repeating in more detail.

Chief Judge Mark Wolf of the U.S. district court in Massachusetts declared that parents have no right to shield their children from pro-homosexual indoctrination in public schools in that state.

Judge Wolf's landmark ruling addressed a lawsuit filed by two couples, the Parkers and the Wirthlins, who were attempting to protect their children from homosexual indoctrination in their elementary school. One of the books at issue in the case, titled *King*

---

[178] Schlafly, P. (2008, July 30). *The NEA spells out its policies.* Retrieved June 13, 2009, from the Eagle Forum Web site: http://www.eagleforum.org/column/2008/july08/08-07-30.html
[179] *Parker v. Hurley*, 474 F. Supp. 2d 261 (D. Mass. 2007).

and King, was read during class. The story is about a prince looking for a spouse. After rejecting several princesses, the prince finally finds his true love—another prince. The book ends with an illustration of the two princes kissing. The Parkers and Wirthlins were not seeking to stop the schools from promoting homosexuality; rather, they simply sought to opt their children out of such teachings.

Judge Wolf made the following statements to support his outrageous decision:

> "The [U.S.] Constitution does not permit [parents] to prescribe what [their] children will be taught [in public schools]."

> "Under the Constitution, public schools are entitled to teach anything that is reasonably related to the goals of preparing students to become productive citizens in our democracy. Diversity is a hallmark of our nation. It is increasingly evident that our diversity includes differences in sexual orientation."

> "The conduct at issue [teaching about homosexuality through children's books] is rationally related to the goal of ... eradicating what the Massachusetts Supreme Judicial Court characterized as the 'deep and scaring hardship' that the past ban on same-sex marriage imposed 'on a very real segment of the community for no rational reason.'"

> "Parents have a right to inform their children when and as they wish on the subject of sex; they have no constitutional right, however, to prevent a public school from providing its students with whatever information it wishes to provide, sexual or otherwise, when and as the school determines that it is appropriate to do so."

> "As it is difficult to change attitudes and stereotypes after they have developed, it is reasonable for public schools to attempt to teach understanding and respect for gays and lesbians to young students in order to minimize the risk of damaging abuse in school of those who may be perceived to be different."

In rejecting the simple request of the Parkers and Wirthlins to exempt their children from class when the teacher is discussing homosexuality or same-sex marriage, Judge Wolf stated: "An exodus from class when issues of homosexuality or same-sex marriage are to be discussed could send the message that gays, lesbians, and the children of same-sex parents are inferior and, therefore, have a damaging effect on those students."[180]

Judge Wolf also claimed that parents do not have a constitutional right "to prevent a public school from providing its students with whatever information it wishes to provide, sexual or otherwise" because parents can send their children to private schools or home school them if they do not like the curriculum in their public school. Even if parents could afford to send their children to private schools, should that really be necessary and the only way to protect children from such indoctrination?

On appeal, the U.S. Court of Appeals for the First Circuit reaffirmed the lower court's dismissal of the case, noting that public education prepares students for citizenship. As an example of such preparation, the appellate court cited a U.S. Supreme Court precedent stating that schools have a right to prohibit lewd speech. Ironically, the court then relied in part on that precedent to rule that parents cannot prohibit the promotion of homosexuality in public schools. Of most significance, the appellate court reasoned that since "Massachusetts has recognized gay marriage under its state constitution," the state's schools have the right to "educate their students regarding that recognition."[181]

This ruling means that where same-sex marriage is legalized, public schools have the right (and some would claim the responsibility) to educate their students about homosexuality and same-sex marriage.

If the government will not leave our children alone, then we cannot afford to leave the government alone. Parents must understand that they can no longer abide by a "live and let live" philosophy when it comes to same-sex marriage. Parents have a critical, vested interest in ensuring that same-sex marriage is not legalized where they live.

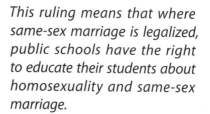

This ruling means that where same-sex marriage is legalized, public schools have the right to educate their students about homosexuality and same-sex marriage.

---

[180] Ibid (quoting *Goodridge v. Department of Health*, 440 Mass. 309, 341 (2003)).
[181] *Parker v. Hurley*, 2008 U.S. App. LEXIS 2070 (1st Cir. Mass., Jan. 31, 2008).

The *Parker* case is just one case in a series of rulings undermining parental rights. Judge Wolf relied on two other cases to justify his ruling against the Parkers and the Wirthlins. The first case, *Brown v. Hot, Sexy and Safer Productions*, held that high schools could force students to attend AIDS awareness events that use minors in sexually explicit skits, in spite of their own wishes (or those of their parents) to opt out according to existing school procedure. Judge Wolf found *Brown* indistinguishable from the *Parker* case. The second case, *Fields v. Palmdale*, ruled that an elementary school could distribute an offensive and sexually explicit survey to young children because parents' right to control the upbringing of their children "does not extend beyond the threshold of the school door."[182]

> *Fields v. Palmdale, ruled that an elementary school could distribute an offensive and sexually explicit survey to young children because parents' right to control the upbringing of their children "does not extend beyond the threshold of the school door."*

The Parkers and Wirthlins appealed their case to the U.S. Supreme Court, which declined to hear it. This means that the decision stands as is.

Phyllis Schlafly of Eagle Forum suggests that since "the federal government gives about $60 billion a year to public schools," we should seek to elect a presidential candidate that will:

> ... promise to sign school appropriation bills only if they contain language to protect parents' rights to protect their children against such things as nosy questionnaires about sex, drugs and suicide; mental health screening; forcing school children to be put on psychotropic drugs; courses that promote ... homosexuality; ... classroom materials that parents consider pornographic; giving birth control to 6th grade girls without parents' knowledge or

---

[182] *See Brown v. Hot, Sexy and Safer Prods., Inc.*, 68 F.3d 525 (1st Cir. 1995); *Fields v. Palmdale Sch. Dist.*, 427 F.3d 1197 (9th Cir. 2005), *aff'd per curiam*, 447 F.3d 1187 (9th Cir. 2006). To understand how corrupt some of this sexual education can be, see the background section of the *Brown* opinion available at http://www.ca1.uscourts.gov/cgi-bin/getopn.pl?OPINION=95-1275.01A

consent; and sex education and sexual orientation courses even if they are masquerading as "diversity" courses.[183]

Phyllis Schlafly's suggestion is sound. We should also work to enact legislation that prohibits funding of school programs that insist on indoctrinating our children in radical theories of sexuality.

In summary, your right to raise your children according to your own values is slowly being eroded by others who are trying to "save" your children from you. These activists are using the courts, legislatures and schools to instill their anti-family, anti-moral, anti-life values in the young minds and hearts of your children and grandchildren. If we do nothing, they will prevail. If we act collectively and decisively, we can stop their assaults and firmly reestablish the right and responsibilities of parents to guide, protect and nurture their children.

Stand for the Family—What You Can Do

Experience demonstrates that laws intended to protect our children in the schools must use very precise and comprehensive language or schools will find ways to get around them. Massachusetts, for example, has a statute which requires parental notification and the right to exempt children from any curricula that primarily involve human sexual education or human sexuality issues. However, the school declined to apply this statutory exemption to the Parkers and Wirthlins on the grounds that the books at issue in the case did not "primarily" involve human sexual education or human sexuality issues. Indeed, the school superintendent explained that it would not even notify parents of any "discussions, activities or materials that simply reference same-gender parents or that otherwise recognize the existence of differences in sexual orientation."[184]

When my children received some homosexual indoctrination materials in our public schools in Gilbert, Arizona, I did some research and found an Arizona statute that prohibits our state's public schools from promoting homosexuality as healthy or normal. I thought I had the legal tool to have these materials removed, but the school board was not impressed. They

---

[183] What We Want in a Presidential Candidate. Speech given October 19, 2007, printed in *The Phyllis Schlafley Report*. (2007, November). *41*(4).Retrieved June 13, 2009 from the Eagle Forum Web site: http://www.eagleforum.org/psr/2007/nov07/psrnov07.html

[184] Statement by Paul Ash, Superintendent of Lexington, Massachusetts Schools, *Lexington Minuteman* Thursday, September 22, 2005.

responded that since the provision I found was under the sex education section of the Arizona statutes governing schools, it only prohibited such teachings in "sex education" classes.

Homosexuality had been promoted to my children and their friends in a history class, a speech and debate class, and a science class. The school decided it was perfectly legal to promote homosexuality in these other classes, and neither I nor anyone else could do anything about it.

The remedy is to work to pass new state legislation that clearly and unambiguously prohibits the indoctrination of children about homosexuality or the promotion of promiscuous sex in *any* class and in any manner. To protect our children from such teachings, parents need to band together to pass clearly worded legislation in every state and at the federal level.

For More Information: To read our free Family Policy Brief on the Convention on the Rights of the Child referred to in this chapter, go to the Family Policy Resource Center on our Web site, www.familywatchinternational.org.

If you need help in drafting clear, unambiguous wording for legislation to protect your children from "sexual rights" indoctrination in your public schools or you need more information on any issue discussed herein, please visit the Family Watch Web site to contact us.

Chapter 9

The Assault on Our Children's Sexuality

On March 1, 2010, while I was participating in the Commission on the Status of Women (CSW) at the UN, I was asked to leave a closed-door, "Girls Only" meeting sponsored by Girl Scouts of the USA (GSUSA). As soon as the meeting ended, I entered the room, and from a stack on the back table, picked up a booklet, "Healthy, Happy, and Hot," produced by the International Planned Parenthood Federation (IPPF)[185]. I was stunned as I flipped through the pages.

This offensive booklet promotes sexual pleasure to teens and states, *"Many people think sex is just about vaginal or anal intercourse. But, there are lots of different ways to have sex and lots of different types of sex."*[186] The booklet encourages masturbation and talking "dirty" and depicts both same-sex and opposite-sex couples. It also tells HIV-infected teens that they do not have to inform their sexual partners they are infected.

This same day I reported in *The Family Watch* (the official e-newsletter of Family Watch International) that this vulgar booklet was available to the girls in the meeting. Various news sources picked up the story, and GSUSA promptly issued an official statement in which they denied that the booklets were distributed and suggested that they had been left by a previous group using the same room. However, this is unlikely as it was the first day of the conference, and the few groups that had used the room before the Girls Scouts had addressed topics completely unrelated to those in the booklet.

It is important to note that GSUSA did not state that they believe the booklet is unsuitable and highly inappropriate, just that they did not actively pass them out. The GSUSA response also denied any official association with Planned Parenthood, but it seems someone forgot to tell Kathy Cloninger, CEO of GSUSA, who admitted on NBC's Today Show in 2004 that GSUSA partners with "Planned Parenthood organizations

---

[185] International Planned Parenthood Federation. (2010). *Healthy, Happy and Hot.* January 2010. Retrieved March 23, 2010 from http://www.ippf.org/NR/rdonlyres/B4462DDE-487D-4194-B0E0-193A04095819/0/HappyHealthyHot.pdf
[186] Ibid at page 7.

across the country to bring information-based sex education programs to girls."[187]

In fact, the local Girl Scout council in Waco, Texas, has regularly co-sponsored sex education conferences with Planned Parenthood. During one such conference, a sex book was distributed to 700 girls that condones masturbation and contains explicit drawings of couples having sex and of a boy putting on a condom. American Life League's STOPP International conducted a study of Girl Scout councils throughout the United States. At the time, they found that about 20 percent of local councils had some type of relationship with Planned Parenthood.[188]

A few days after the Girls Only meeting, Family Watch UN representatives, Carol Nixon and Lynn Douglas (Family Watch had a team of 30 volunteers monitoring UN meetings at CSW), attended another UN Girl Scout meeting. This meeting was organized by the World Association of Girl Guides and Girl Scouts (WAGGGS), of which Girl Scouts of the USA is an official member. WAGGGS, which is an official member of the European Youth Forum, included a panel discussion as part of their UN meeting. During this discussion, one of the panelists from the European Youth Forum boasted about how they partner with International Planned Parenthood to reach children though non-formal education programs (such as the Girl Scouts) to teach acceptance of gays, lesbians and transgenders at an early age.

Even more concerning, the WAGGGS Web site proudly states that for this UN conference they brought in "young people from more than 20 countries and every continent" and that their UN delegation at this conference included a support team of "10 Girl Scouts from Connecticut and Vermont."[189]

The WAGGGS Web site also reported that their UN delegation demanded "sexual and reproductive rights," which they defined to include "access to comprehensive sexuality education [The "Healthy, Happy, and Hot" booklet certainly would satisfy this demand] and sexual and reproductive health services, including . . . safe abortions."[190]

---

[187] John Pisciotta of Pro-Life in Waco and Girl Scout CEO Katy Cloninger discuss boycott of Girl Scout cookies. Retrieved May 7, 2010 from http://www.lightoftruth.info/transcript.html

[188] *Planned Parenthood and Girl Scout Relationships.* Retrieved May 7, 2010 from http://www.stopp.org/scouts/

[189] *"WAGGGS at the Commission on the Status of Women.* Retrieved May 7, 2010 from http://www.wagggsworld.org/en/CSW54

[190] *Young people advocating for sexual and reproductive rights.* Retrieved May 7, 2010 from http://www.wagggsworld.org/en/CSW54/Day6

In a written statement submitted by the World Association of Girl Guides and Girl Scouts to the UN, WAGGGS called on governments to ensure (among other things) that 1) non-formal education programs be instituted for the "sexual development of girls and young women"; 2) young women be provided with "opportunities to be involved in the planning, delivering and evaluation of sexual education"; and 3) that support be given to organizations that "provide safe spaces for girls and young women to discuss sex and sexuality free from discrimination."[191]

Please note that I am a reluctant witness against the Girl Scouts. I was a Girl Scout myself, and I know of many honorable women who have devoted years of service to this program. But leaders, parents, supporters and concerned citizens need to know that something has gone very wrong with the Girl Scouts. These activities and statements would indicate that Girl Scouts of the USA has made a seismic shift and is now promoting the radical feminist agenda, which includes advocating for abortion and unrestrained sex.

It's very clear that the Girl Scouts have much more on their minds these days than cookies and campfires. Instead, the Girl Scouts have joined the ranks of many other individuals and organizations whose underlying agenda is to sexualize our children. Parents beware.

Many sexual activists and far left academicians believe that children are sexual from birth, and sexual experimentation is a normal and healthy part of a young child's development. Planned Parenthood's Web site, for example, encourages teaching children as young as five about masturbation, homosexual relations, and gender identities (i.e., transgender or transsexual relations).

Planned Parenthood also advocates teaching young children that it is "normal to touch one's sex organs for pleasure" and that "people experience sexual pleasure in a number of different ways." This is clearly intended to encourage adults to sexualize children at a very early age.

Early Sex is Harmful to Children

The assault on our children's sexuality is promulgated by the sex industry. They know that if they can sexualize children or even turn them into sexual addicts, the children eventually will become lifelong customers and revenues will continue to flow. (The tobacco industry has been accused of doing the same type of thing with advertisements aimed at teenagers.)

A child's sexuality is very fragile during their formative years. Sexually exploited or abused children suffer negative effects that can haunt them for the rest of their lives. Many find it difficult to form healthy, loving relationships. Too often they become promiscuous and abusers themselves. When sexuality is exploited, especially during childhood, chaos can ensue.[192]

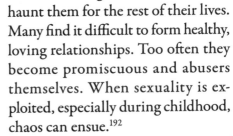

They know that if they can sexualize children or even turn them into sexual addicts, the children eventually will become lifelong customers and revenues will continue to flow.

Sadly, much of the sexualization of children occurs at school and through other programs paid for by our tax dollars.

Students from a Boulder, Colorado, high school were required to attend a World Affairs Conference. A conference transcript includes this telling statement by an "expert" clinical psychologist from UCLA:

> *I'm going to encourage you to have sex and encourage you to use drugs ... and I don't care if it's with men and men, women and women, men and women—whatever combination you would like to put together.*[193]

There is a worldwide, adult-driven movement that is gathering steam, which seeks to liberate children from their parents' oppressive views regarding sexuality and grant sexual rights to children as young as 10 years old.

In an interview about her book *Harmful to Minors: The Perils of Protecting Children from Sex*, author Judith Levine stated, "My book says

---

[192] Dominquez, R. Z., Nelke, C. F., & Perry, B. D. (2002). Child Sexual Abuse in: *Encyclopedia of Crime and Punishment Vol 1*.(David Levinson, Ed.) Thousand Oaks: Sage Publications, 202-207; Finkelhor, D., & Browne, A. (1986). Impact of child sexual abuse: a review of the research. *Psychological Bulletin, 99*(1), 66-77; Trocme, N., & Wolfe, D. (2001). Child maltreatment in Canada: Canadian incidence study of reported child abuse and neglect: Selected results. Ottawa: National Clearinghouse on Family Violence, Health Canada.

[193] Statement by Joel Becker, professor of Clinical Psychology at the University of California, Los Angeles. The full transcript of the panelists' speeches can be found at http://www.bvsdwatch.org/content/view/91/1/

that sexuality is a fact of life, and a potentially wonderful part of growing up for children *at all stages of their lives.*" (Emphasis added.)[194] Levine claims that the real danger to children is the "conservative religious agenda that would deny minors all sexual information and sexual expression." She continues:

> *The fact is, most kids will say yes to sexuality at some point during their childhood or teenage years. Our choice as adults is whether or not we will help make those experiences safe, consensual and happy.*[195]

People like Levine and the psychologist from UCLA and organizations like Planned Parenthood are driving the sex education programs in many public schools, and they must be stopped.

Pushing Sex in U.S. Public Schools

Several years ago, an excellent bill was introduced in the Arizona legislature that was designed to eliminate references to sexuality in the public schools outside of sex education courses. Some believed the bill was unnecessary, but our family's experience showed otherwise.

For example, *The Storm*, a short story read aloud in my daughter's high school English class, is about an adulterous encounter. The story includes an explicit description of a man's sensations as he looked at a naked woman's body which "aroused all the old-time infatuation and desire for her flesh" and of the woman's "sensuous desire."

Unbelievably, after this detailed account of an adulterous affair was read aloud to boys and girls sitting in the same class, the students were asked to talk about how the story made them feel. My daughter was mortified.

It is not only morally irresponsible, but it is inexcusable for teachers to present material intended to sexually arouse children. Public schools have no business allowing sexually erotic material of any kind in any class for any reason.

---

[194] *Q and A with Judith Levine, the author of Harmful to Minors: The Perils of Protecting Children from Sex.* Retrieved March 24, 2007, from University of Minnesota Press Web site: http://www.upress.umn.edu/BookExtras/HarmfultoMinors/HarmfultoMinorsQandA.html
[195] Ibid.

Another blatant example comes from a European history textbook also used in our local high school. The textbook is riddled with inappropriate sexual material, such as the following:

WARNING: The following italicized excerpts are quite explicit.

The term homosexuality was coined only in 1892, but what it designates today—manual, oral, or anal erotic activity with a person of the same sex—goes back very far in human history.[196]

... the strongly preferred erotic practice, anal relations, involved adult males usually between nineteen and forty years of age in the active or penetrating role and adolescents under eighteen years of age as the passive partner.[197]

Most parents I know would be stunned to discover that their high school students taking this history class are required to know the preferred sexual position of early European homosexuals and pedophiles.

The following excerpt teaches students that, historically, European teens allegedly have enjoyed being sexually abused by older men:

... When interrogated, fifteen-year-old Bartolomeo di Jacopo confessed that Piero had sodomized him many times, saying, "This he did out of great love and good brotherhood, because they are in a confraternity together, and he did as good neighbors do." Bartolomeo di Jacopo understood their relationships as being based on the emotional bonds between members of their confraternity and neighborhood associations. Their sexual relationship, though forbidden, was woven into the entire fabric of their community life. He perceived his sexual acts as part of traditional male bonding. ... Homoerotic relationships played an important role in defining stages of life, expressing distinctions of status, and shaping masculine gender identity.[198]

---

[196] McKay, J., Hill, B., & Buckler, J. (1999). *A History of Western Society*, 6th Edition, Boston: Houghton Mifflin, 434.
[197] Ibid at page 435.
[198] Ibid.

This next excerpt from the textbook was clearly intended to convince students that early Christians accepted homosexuality:

> Early Christians, as we have seen ... displayed no special prejudice against homosexuals. ... Beginning in the late 12th century, however, a profound change occurred in public attitudes toward homosexual behavior. Why did this happen if prejudice against homosexuals cannot be traced to early Christianity?[199]

These excerpts provide chilling examples of what is being presented in many schools across the country, unbeknownst to most parents.

Please note: The legalization of same-sex marriage accelerates the trend toward more permissive sex education in public schools. After same-sex marriage became legal in Massachusetts, that state's Brookline High School distributed copies of a sex education booklet, titled *The Little Black Book—Queer in the 21st Century*, to hundreds of students. The booklet contains explicit and graphic instructions for performing "safe gay sex" and explicit photo instructions showing how to use condoms. The book includes a list of homosexual bars and clubs in the Boston area "for the discerning queer boy." It mentions abstaining from sex, then asks, "But how much fun is that?"

Accurate Medical Information?

Several years ago, a bill was proposed by the Arizona legislature that would have required state-funded sex education programs to "... provide accurate medical information that is in accordance with current public health data and information provided by the American Medical Association or the National Centers for Disease Control and Prevention."

Sounds good, until you dig deeper. Lynn Allred wrote the following report regarding this seemingly positive proposed legislation:

> The Arizona State Board of Education Administrative Code currently allows local school districts to design their own sex education programs requiring in part that the instruction be appropriate to the grade level, promote abstinence, and be medically accurate.

---

[199] Ibid at page 349.

So what was wrong with this bill? All youth are certainly entitled to the most current and most medically accurate scientific data available—and who better to dispense it than the American Medical Association or the federal government's Centers for Disease Control and Prevention (CDC)? Surely, both of these agencies are more than qualified to determine the information that our youth need to remain free from sexually transmitted diseases.

Not so fast.

The CDC has approved and recommends graphic sex education programs that most parents would find extremely offensive. Below are some examples from the CDC's "Programs that Work" that I found on the CDC Web site:

> **WARNING: Some sexually explicit information follows. Skip to the next section if you prefer not to read the actual examples. Remember, this is a federal agency recommending these programs.**

CDC's 4th to 9th Grade Program—"Focus on Kids"

Condom Race Activity. Divide youth into two teams and give everyone a condom. Have the teams stand in two lines and give the first person in each line a cucumber. Each person on the team must put the condom on the cucumber and take it off. ... The team that finishes first wins.

Brainstorming Activity. *Ask youth to brainstorm ways to be close to a person and show you care without having sexual intercourse. ... The list may include ...* [We have excluded the list of suggested erotic activities for teens.]

Suggested CDC Parental Permission Slip. "I understand that all discussions that my child will have with the group leaders of this project will be confidential and will not be reported to me or anyone else."

CDC's 7th to 12th Grade Program—"Be Proud! Be Responsible!"

Brainstorming Activity. Think up a sexual fantasy using condoms. Hide them on your body and ask your partner to find it. Tease each other manually while putting on the condom.

Summarize by saying: Once you and a partner agree to use condoms, do something positive and fun. Go to the store together. Buy lots of different brands and colors. Plan a special day when you can experiment. Just talking about how you can use all those condoms can be a turn on.

This program also recommends a role-playing activity between two homosexuals, Gerald and Allen. The goal of this role play is for Gerald to negotiate condom use with Allen (before a sexual encounter) without damaging the relationship.

Please note the span of grades targeted for these programs and the CDC's request that parents of children as young as 10 years old (4th grade) waive their rights to be informed. Fortunately, after this information was exposed and the public became aware of the blatant attempts of the CDC to lower the natural modesty and inhibitions of our children, the outcry put an end to the proposed Arizona legislation. But this doesn't stop other state sex education programs from adopting CDC-recommended programs.

The bad guys were even sneakier with their next bill, which would have required that sex education in Arizona be recognized as accurate and objective by "leading professional organizations and agencies with relevant expertise in the field."

The American College of Obstetricians and Gynecologists (ACOG) claims to be "the nation's leading group of professionals providing health care for women."[200] However, the ACOG opposed national legislation requiring condom labels to state the scientifically proven fact that human papillomavirus (HPV) can cause cervical cancer

---

[200] American College of Obstetricians and Gynecologists. Retrieved March 24, 2008, from http://www.acog.org/from_home/acoginfo.cfm

and that condoms do not prevent the transmission of HPV. They have stated that it would be "medically inappropriate" to warn the public that condoms do not provide adequate protection for HPV transmission. They hold this position even though they know that HPV is the most common sexually transmitted disease (STD) in the country—estimated to be up to five times more common than all other STDs combined.

The cost of ignorance each year is an estimated 12,000 cases of invasive cervical cancer in the United States, with a medical bill approaching $2 billion. An estimated 4,000 American women will die from cervical cancer each year—roughly the same number of women that will die of AIDS.[201]

According to the National Cancer Institute (NCI), the evidence that condoms do not protect against HPV is so definitive that "additional research efforts by the NCI on the effectiveness of condoms in preventing HPV transmission is not warranted."[202] Yet the American College of Obstetricians and Gynecologists, a "leading professional organization," believes it would be "medically inappropriate" to warn the public about HPV?

Unfortunately, the Centers for Disease Control, an agency "with relevant expertise," instructs teachers to teach that "Condoms are very effective because they don't break easily and they don't leak. They are also good protection against sexually transmitted disease (STD)."[203]

Since HPV is transmitted by skin-to-skin contact, nothing short of a full-body condom would prevent the transmission of HPV. Such blatantly false "medically accurate" information is uncon-scionable. Please pay close attention to the legislation in your own

[201] *Cervical Cancer.* (n.d.). Retrieved June 15, 2009, from Centers for Disease Control and Prevention Web site: http://www.cdc.gov/cancer/cervical/
[202] Letter from Richard D. Klausner, Director of National Cancer Institute to Tom Bliley Jr., Chairman of the House Commerce Committee, February 16, 1999. Retrieved November 24, 2008 from Library of Congress Web site: http://www.congress.gov/cgi-bin/query/R?r109:FLD001:H59257
[203] *CDC Fact Sheet.* Retrieved March 24, 2008, from Centers for Disease Control and Prevention Web site: http://www.cdc.gov/about/resources/facts.htm

state which may open the door for "safe sex" or "reduced risk" sex-ed programs—code words for "anything goes as long as you use a condom." This elastic language is about as safe as a sheath of latex. It may work if you're lucky. But if it doesn't, the end result could be devastating.

Your local school system may not need legislation to allow it to teach the CDC programs and activities. State legislation or policies promoting such things as "tolerance" and "diversity" may be enough to enable schools to adopt the CDC curriculum—or something worse.

Do you know what YOUR kids are being taught?

(End of Lynn Allred's report)

Is "Anytown" in Your Town? You Better Find Out!

In addition to examining the curricula in your schools, be wary of programs such as the "Anytown" program. "Anytown" is a weekend-long, overnight, out-of-town workshop that purports to help students learn the public virtues of tolerance and acceptance in order to prevent discrimination in public schools.[204] However, under the guise of teaching "leadership skills," this program promotes promiscuity and homosexuality to schoolchildren.

Every child should have the right to attend school without encountering cruelty or harassment. Yet this program, though laudable in its purported goals, crosses the line of appropriate public instruction. The program creates a fundamental bias in favor of homosexuality. It encourages homosexual youth to define themselves primarily by their sexual preferences. It equates homosexuals with religious and ethnic groups that have historically been denied legitimate civil rights.

During our high school's program, student groups—including the self-labeled "BLT with a G" group (bisexuals, lesbians, transgenders and gays)—were instructed to list all the positive attributes of their group. All

---

[204] The Anytown program is a national program run by a nonprofit organization called The National Conference of Community and Justice, formerly, The National Conference of Christians and Jews. When the organization began, the focus was primarily on bringing together people of various races and religions. The Anytown motto is "Building Leaders. Embracing Diversity." Their camps are called by a variety of names. Our high school Anytown program is called "Tiger Town." If this program is in your school it could be established under the name of Anytown Jr, Anytown, Powertown, Empowertown, Unitown, or Minitown.

the students then joined together to share the positive attributes of each group. This, and other similar activities, creates a supportive environment, so students attending Anytown have felt empowered to "come out" as openly homosexual.

I challenge the idea that youth should define themselves by their sexual urges, particularly if those urges lead them to behavior that is destructive. In Chapter 3, I presented research showing that homosexual behavior is associated with much higher rates of sexually transmitted diseases (especially AIDS), suicide, and lower life expectancy. Why would a public school encourage behavior that can lead to such negative outcomes?

"Tolerance" and "showing respect" for an individual should not be equated with condoning behavior that is harmful.

"Tolerance" and "showing respect" for *an individual* should not be equated with condoning *behavior* that is harmful. Historically, "tolerance" has been a rather passive word for "allowance given to that which is not wholly approved."[205] However, tolerance now is being redefined by many to mean active support for, approval of, and respect for any sexual behavior regardless of its impact on individuals, families or society.

Sexualization of Children Hits Close to Every Home

I know of countless examples that hit close to home and show just how our children are being sexualized at school. While many of the examples come from my local school, I doubt that your school district is much different than mine. For example:

- Our schools have shown a biology video that explains how homosexual couples can become parents.
- A friend of mine reported that her 11-year-old son ended up cowering in the bathroom, traumatized by an extremely graphic and vulgar lesson on sex and condom use that was presented in his sixth-grade class.

---

[205] *The Webster's Encyclopedic Dictionary of the English Language.* (1969). Chicago: Consolidated Book Publishers. 879.

- In another state, a student was forced by her substitute teacher to watch *Brokeback Mountain*, a graphic movie about homosexual lovers.

- In Arizona, a state university offered a class on pornography for which viewing XXX-rated films was part of the curriculum.

I could go on and on, as there are many more examples. The examples themselves are disturbing, and even more so when you remember that it is your tax dollars that fund these schools and their programs.

Your taxes also are used internationally to sexualize children worldwide.

UNFPA Promotes Explicit Graphic Sexual Education

Each year, population control advocates pressure the U.S. government to appropriate millions of dollars for the United Nations Population Fund (UNFPA), an agency that has been implicated in facilitating forced abortions and the forced sterilization of women in Peru and China. Thankfully, for eight straight years during the Bush administration, that funding was withheld. However, when Obama became president, he vowed to ensure funding for UNFPA again.

In March 2009, Congress appropriated $50 million to UNFPA at the request of President Obama. This was done in a time of economic crisis when the U.S. government was scrambling to bail out banks and businesses to save the economy.

In addition, one of President Obama's first official acts following his election was to rescind the Mexico City Policy which prevented U.S. international aid from being given to organizations that promote or perform abortions.

We need to be vigilant, and the next time funding for UNFPA is proposed by Congress, which happens every year, we need to make sure that we oppose it. We also need to raise awareness of UNFPA's little-known, blatant promotion of sexual promiscuity to children.

Several years ago, individuals from Nicaragua, Honduras and El Salvador sent me a variety of UNFPA-published sex education manuals distributed in their countries, all of which are inappropriate for children. Here are excerpts from some of these manuals:

> **Homosexuality**—*"It is common for boys to have frequent sexual intercourse with other boys, and to look at each other to compare the size of different parts of the body."*[206]

> **Bisexuality**—*"Women and men with a full sexual identity have erotic preferences for people of the opposite sex, of their own sex and of both sexes."*[207]

> **Pornography**—*"Sometimes we can be sexually stimulated while watching erotic pictures or movies."*[208]

> **Masturbation**—I've chosen not to quote the manuals directly here. The manuals teach children that sexual fantasies, bisexual feelings and masturbation are normal characteristics in early adolescence. Children are also instructed on various methods of masturbation.[209]

> **Children's Sexual Rights**—*"Every person has reproductive and sexual rights irregardless of sex, age, race, ethnicity, nationality or economic and social condition."*[210]

> **Sexualizing Children**—In activity number eight in the "Rainbow Workbook," youth ages 10 through 14 are presented with an outline drawing of a male and female body, titled *"Qualities of the Ideal Boyfriend and Girlfriend."* Children are instructed to draw in the physical qualities of their ideal boyfriend or girlfriend.[211]

---

[206] Manual de Consejeria Para Adolescentes. Copyright Fondo de Poblacion de las Naciones Unidas (FNUAP). (2000, December). [English Translation: Manual for Counseling Adolescents. Copyright UNFPA]. Managua, Nicaragua. 33.

[207] Ibid at page 59.

[208] De Adolescentes Para Adolescentes: Manual de Salud Sexual y Reproductiva, Ministerio de Salud Publica y Asistencia Social, apoyado por el Fondo de Poblacion de las Naciones Unidas (FNUAP). (1999, December). [English Translation: From Adolescents to Adolescents: Manual of Sexual and Reproductive Health. Ministry of Public Health and Social Assistance. Supported by UNFPA]. San Salvador, El Salvador. 78.

[209] Supra note 15, at page 74.

[210] Derechos sexuales y reproductivos, un enfoque para adolescentes. Copyright Fondo de Poblacion de las Naciones Unidas (FNUAP). (2000, November). [English Translation: Manual for Counseling Adolescents. Copyright UNFPA]. Managua, Nicaragua. 3.

[211] El Arco Iris. Cuaderno de trabajo para adolescentes de 10 a 14 anos, Fondo de Poblacionde las Naciones Unidas (FNUAP). (1999, December). [English Translation: Rainbow Workbook for Adolescents from 10 to 14 Years Old. Supported by UNFPA], San Salvador, El Salvador. 82, 100.

UNFPA knows they would likely run into more resistance with this type of graphic sexual education in the United States. Instead, the agency is exploiting developing nations by promoting its sexual agenda where strong opposition is least likely to be encountered.

The following is an excerpt from a letter that a representative of the Nicaraguan Women's Association faxed to me outlining the abuses of UNFPA in Nicaragua:

Dear Sharon,

The Minister of the Family in Nicaragua requested I send to you UNFPA publications in our country which are against our laws.

I am sending to you a copy of a manual published by UNFPA for the Ministry of Health. It is a guide for counselors and is directed to adolescents. It includes promotion of homosexuality (which is penalized by Nicaraguan law), the promotion of masturbation, and the promotion of risky sexual conduct teaching them that responsibility is wearing a condom or using contraceptives.

I am also sending you a copy of a booklet on "sexual and reproductive rights" for an adolescent which has recently been published by UNFPA and Procuraduria de Derechos Humanos, and which is being distributed to teenagers throughout the country. The booklet tells teenagers that they have the right to engage in whatever sexual conduct. [sic] UNFPA has also funded a soap opera with other organizations including USAID [United States Agency for International Development] *that promotes homosexuality, abortion, sexual freedom for adolescents, and has a strong anti-family propaganda. Its name is "Sexto Sentido." It is an expensive production and is aired on Nicaragua's most popular TV channel. At the end of every episode you can see the USAID logo and in some episodes, the UNFPA logo.*

I also called my friend from El Salvador, and she will send you the copy of the UNFPA manual, which promotes emergency contraception, and which is against El Salvador's law. Honduras must also have proof of UNFPA's wrongdoings.

Thank you for trying so hard to stop the funding for an organization that is doing so much harm to our countries.

Yours truly,
Evangelina Guirola
Associacion Nicaraguense de la Mujer

Our contacts in Africa and Latin America have told us that this kind of curriculum continues to be promoted today. Unfortunately, most Americans have never even heard of UNFPA, even though millions of their tax dollars have funded it in past years.

> *Unfortunately, most Americans have never even heard of UNFPA, even though millions of their tax dollars have funded it in past years.*

Citizens Must Get Involved!

Sometimes, all that is needed to get a bad school policy or program changed is for one parent to speak out. Of course, there is power in numbers as well. The pornography class at our state university was cancelled due to public outcry after we conducted an e-mail campaign alerting the public about the class. The Anytown program at our own high school was altered to remove the parts that supported homosexuality. And, because parents took action, the elementary school teacher who presented sixth graders with explicit and inappropriate sexual information was fired.

Do you know what your tax dollars are funding? Do you know what the public schools are teaching? Do you know what your children and grandchildren are reading, watching and listening to?

It is not possible to screen everything that the world throws at our children, but we must do what we can. And we certainly must stop the government from spending our tax dollars to sexualize our children through the public school systems.

Stand for the Family—What you can do:

Especially if you are a parent or if you have direct responsibility for children in your home, do what you can to get involved in the schools. Please don't suppose that your schools are different from mine. Rather, assume that there are problems, then work to identify and eliminate them. In particular:

- Know the laws and policies that affect your children's education.
- Make it a practice to review all of the books your children are given at school. You don't necessarily have to read textbooks from cover to cover, but be sure to at least look through the list of topics in the table of contents and the index and review any that look suspicious. You should specifically look up the words "sex" and "homosexuality" in the index.
- In addition to checking textbooks, ask to see the curricula being used in your children's classrooms, especially materials used in sex education or "life skills" classes. Some schools will have materials you can borrow to take home, while others may want you to review the materials onsite. Either way, schools should readily provide the curricula when asked.
- Talk to your children. I would never have known about some of the inappropriate materials our schools were promoting unless my children had reported them to me. I taught them not to assume that if it comes from a teacher it must be okay. We have encouraged them to independently watch for and inform my husband and me of inappropriate information and activities.

To help us at Family Watch help other parents, please inform us of any objectionable activities or materials you find in your schools by contacting us through our Web site at www.familywatchinternational. org. We are compiling a list of troublesome textbooks that will be posted on our site.

If you sign up for our free Family Watch e-newsletter, *The Family Watch*, you will be informed when the list is posted or updated. Our newsletter will also inform you when funding proposals for UNFPA come up. You will be invited to help stop the funding by calling or e-mailing legislators.

Note: In March 2010, Family Watch International issued an invitation to concerned citizens and parents to join them in calling upon Girl Scouts of the USA to denounce the "Healthy, Happy and Hot" booklet, renounce their association with Planned Parenthood and withdraw from WAGGGS. For further information and updates about this issue, please visit: www. standforthefamily.org.

Chapter 10

Who Could be Against the Traditional Family and Why?

"I am against the family! I am against what you represent! Down with the family!" a woman yelled at me from the crowd.

I was in Mesa, Arizona, riding in the back of a convertible in the Veterans Day parade and holding a sign that read "Will You Stand for the Family?"

Having been selected by American Mothers, Inc., as the 2007 Arizona Mother of the Year, I was expected to participate in several parades and other events, and I had decided to take every opportunity I could to promote the traditional family. After all, I had agreed to represent American Mothers (the official sponsor of Mother's Day and the organization that chooses Mothers of the Year in every state annually) because that organization supports the same family values I am passionate about.

Obviously, the woman at the parade was not too happy about my message and I was not prepared for such vehement opposition to the family in such a family-oriented community.

A few days later at another parade in my hometown of Gilbert, Arizona, I had another disturbing experience. During the long, two-hour wait for the parade to begin, I gathered signatures for Family Watch International's "I Stand for the Family" petition. (A copy of the petition is included at the back of this book.) I approached three women standing next to their children's soccer float and asked them if they would like to sign the petition, explaining it was a pledge to support efforts to promote the family by protecting marriage between a man and a woman, life before as well as after birth, religious freedom, and parental rights.

Two of the women began to sign the petition, but the third "soccer mom" exclaimed, "I will not sign that petition! This view does not belong in this community, and I will not stand to have you here. You must stop right now!" Then in an attempt to put an emphatic end to the discussion, she pointed to the crowd and shouted, "There are children here!" as if somehow my message of marriage and family was going to corrupt the children. I wondered how she thought all of the children got here in the first place.

To most people, the word "family" immediately engenders good feelings. In fact, positive feelings about family are so instinctive, that it is hard for many people to believe that that family is under attack. Those of us who work together in this cause have on occasion had trouble convincing some people that there are those who are diametrically opposed to the institution of "the family."

Yet the incidents at these parades—along with other numerous experiences at the local, national and international level—have shown to me that the concerted attack on the traditional family is not only real, but is widespread and unrelenting. A single visit to any United Nations meeting when a social topic is being discussed[212] is all you would need to understand how pervasive and serious the attacks are at the international level.

Eminent family scholar Dr. Patrick Fagan warned:

> *Few Americans are aware that agencies within the United Nations system are involved in a campaign to undermine the foundations of society; the two-parent married family, religions that espouse the primary importance of marriage and traditional sexual morality, and the legal and social structures that protect these institutions.*[213]

Many Anti-Family Activists Have Dysfunctional Families

Consider carefully the following: "The complete destruction of traditional marriage and the nuclear family is the revolutionary or utopian goal of feminism."[214]

One of my goals in this chapter is to convince you that the above quote cannot be simply dismissed as the ranting of a crazy person. Rather, it reveals the driving force of radical feminists, who, along with a number of other groups, are currently influencing government policies at all levels.

During a United Nations NGO meeting on children, a UNICEF official raised her hand and suggested that the document under negotiation

---

[212] The UN holds conferences on a variety of topics, including food security, sustainable development, shelter, property rights, disabilities, diseases, etc.

[213] Fagan, P. (2001). *How UN Conventions on Women's and Children's Rights Undermine Family, Religion, and Sovereignty.* Retrieved March 25, 2008, from Heritage Foundation Web site: http://www.heritage.org/Research/InternationalOrganizations/BG1407.cfm

[214] Millett, K. (1970). *Sexual Politics.* Garden City: Doubleday.

should mention "the family." This had an immediate chilling effect in the room, and the official was quickly taken aside and quietly reprimanded by a colleague. "Family," she was told, "is an inflammatory term that is very upsetting to many people."

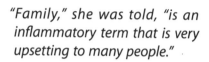

Later, I asked one of the feminists participating in the conference why the word "family" was so controversial. She responded that "the family" is a patriarchal institution which oppresses women.

"Family," she was told, "is an inflammatory term that is very upsetting to many people."

As I walked through the UN hallways at another UN conference on women,[215] I noticed a flyer advertising an NGO presentation titled "The Decriminalization of Prostitution." The topic sounded interesting, so a few members of our pro-family contingent decided to attend.

A panelist from Australia presented her case for legalizing prostitution. Although I did not agree with her conclusion, she made some very good points. She described how rich Westerners (usually from America) charter planes to go to brothels and hire prostitutes in Third World countries. She portrayed these prostitutes as impoverished victims, with no other way to feed themselves and their children but to sell their bodies. She explained that where prostitution is illegal it is these poor women who are thrown in jail and punished while their rich patrons return to their countries with no repercussions.

After the presentation, I thanked her for the new perspective she had given me. Then I asked, "Wouldn't it be better for us to focus on strengthening families and marriages and on developing economic programs for poor women so they will not be forced into prostitution to survive?"

She immediately screamed at me, "I am a lesbian, and in the depths of my heart I believe that the only safe place for a child is in a lesbian home being raised by two women!"

She immediately screamed at me so everyone in the room could hear, "I am a lesbian, and in the depths of

---

[215] The outcome documents that are produced at major UN conferences are generally reviewed by member states every five years. This 2000 conference on women's rights, known as Beijing +5, was the five-year review of the UN Beijing Declaration and Platform for Action from the Fourth World Conference on Women that was held in September, 1995, in Beijing, China.

my heart I believe that the only safe place for a child is in a lesbian home being raised by two women!"

Then another woman, wagging her finger in my face yelled, "You! You! You are the cause of all these problems! The U.S. has not paid its dues to the UN and you should be ashamed!" She continued, "I was sexually abused by my grandfather! My sister was sexually abused by my grandfather! You cannot tell me that the family is a safe place!"

I was stunned. But I finally had another piece of the puzzle. For the life of me, I had been unable to understand until that moment why so many women at the UN were promoting the lesbian, anti-family agenda and why they *hated* men. I finally realized that at least some of these women had been abused by a male family member. For them, the family had failed, and men were the perpetrators. They hated anything to do with the family and traditional marriage.

How sad that their own families had failed them so miserably. How sad for the rest of the world that these embittered women have so much influence and power over UN negotiations. Dysfunctional, abusive families are a breeding ground for anti-family activists. Now the dysfunction these activists experienced in childhood is affecting international social policy. As more families disintegrate, the ranks of the anti-family forces will grow, and the attacks against the traditional family will increase.

Dysfunctional, abusive families are a breeding ground for anti-family activists. As more families disintegrate, the ranks of the anti-family forces will grow, and the attacks against the traditional family will increase.

So Why do Radical Feminists Seek to Destroy the Family?

Prominent feminist Charlotte Bunch, a spokesman for the campaign to establish a new UN super office on women's issues, wrote a revealing paper back in the 1970s. Had the UN delegates seen this paper before they passed a General Assembly resolution to establish the office, it might have given them pause. It is almost certain that the women who campaigned for the creation of the office will be nominated by their colleagues to run the office and that should concern us all.

Consider the following excerpts from Charlotte Bunch's paper:

"The development of Lesbian-feminist politics as the basis for the liberation of women is our top priority."

"Lesbians must become feminists and fight against woman oppression, just as feminists must become Lesbians if they hope to end male supremacy."

"The only way oppressed people end their oppression is by seizing power."

"As long as straight women see Lesbianism as a bedroom issue, they hold back the development of politics and strategies which would put an end to male supremacy."

"Being a Lesbian means ending your identification with, allegiance to, dependence on, and support of heterosexuality."

"Lesbianism is the key to liberation."[216]

The author was promoting sex between women as a way to rebel against men and destroy "male supremacy" in our society. In the view of many feminists, marriage and the family are patriarchal institutions that exist to oppress women.

Unfortunately, lesbians are not the only anti-family activists who have infiltrated the UN and negatively influenced its policies.

Limiting Humans in a Misguided Attempt to Save the Planet

There are generally two views about human life: either people are valuable and useful natural resources, or they are the enemy of the planet and we should limit human populations and activities for the good of "Mother Earth." We espouse the former view, while most anti-family activists advocate the latter.

Environmentalists have joined forces with the population control activists to try to convince the world that we need to limit the number of people on the earth to save the planet. This worldview (which is debunked

---

[216] Bunch, C. (1972, January). Lesbians in revolt. *The Furies: Lesbian/Feminist Monthly*, 1, 8-9. Retrieved July 9, 2009 from http://scriptorium.lib.duke.edu/wlm/furies/

in the Assault on Life chapter) is the driving force behind many anti-family policies.

One group which espouses the anti-human view is the Optimum Population Trust, a think tank headquartered in the United Kingdom. They claim:

> *... humans—the prime cause of all shortages of resources—may cause parts of the planet to become uninhabitable, with governments pushed towards coercive population control measures as a regrettable but lesser evil than conflict and suffering.*
>
> *... The condom, the Pill, and the intrauterine device ought to be as powerful symbols for the green movement as the bicycle.*
>
> *A "stop at two" children or "one child less" guideline for couples ... should be introduced by the government, promoted in schools and in the media and backed by environmental groups. This should be promoted as part of a greener lifestyle and as an example to couples worldwide, encouraging them to limit their own family size to protect the environment.*[217]

Again, the Assault on Life chapter clearly shows that there are plenty of resources to go around. The real problem is proper allocation. Many economies, especially in Europe and parts of Asia (e.g., Japan), are in a serious crisis because not enough children are being born to support and replace aging populations.

Saving "Mother Earth"

Those who believe there are too many humans on the earth are driving anti-family policies. They have established a UN agency (i.e., The United Nations Fund for Population Activities, UNFPA) with a multi-million dollar budget to limit human populations through birth control and sterilization. As noted earlier, UNFPA has been implicated in the sterilization of women in developing countries without their knowledge or consent. Population control activists have created multiple organizations

---

[217] Guillebaud, J. (2007). *Youthquake: Population, fertility and environment in the 21st century.* Retrieved March 25, 2008, from Optimum Population Trust Web site: http://www.optimumpopulation.org/Youthquake.pdf

(e.g., Planned Parenthood) that promote abortion and contraception as the key to sustainable development especially in third world countries.

Abortion is an important part of population control because no matter how hard activists try to get people to use contraceptives, many pregnancies still occur due to unprotected sex and contraceptive failure. They promote homosexuality because same-sex unions cannot produce children, and if more people choose homosexuality, there will be fewer heterosexual breeders.

Activists also push the feminist agenda because they know if they can get women into the workforce and focused on their careers, they will not have time to bear and raise children, and will self-limit their families.

And since millions of people from various faiths believe in maintaining strong families and hold that one of God's commandments is to "multiply and replenish the earth,"[218] the destruction of religion is a prime objective of population control activists.

Sexual Rights Activists

Population control activists often are also sexual rights activists and seek to sexualize young children, which can make it difficult for children to form healthy marriage relationships and stable families in the future. They seek to take away parental rights to guide their children's education and create school curriculums that teach children that "responsible sexual behavior" does not mean confining sex to marriage; it means using a condom. They do this even though they know that studies show sexually active children (and even many adults) will not always use condoms (especially in the heat of the moment) even when condoms are readily available and even when children know why and how to use them.

These activists don't just teach children that it is okay to satisfy their sexual urges outside of marriage, they encourage them to engage in premarital and homosexual sex. Then they demand that governments pick up the tab for out-of-wedlock pregnancies and all of the well-documented, negative outcomes that go along with promiscuous sex and single-parent families.

---

[218] Holy Bible, Genesis 1:28.

Who Is Working to Destroy the Family?

International Level

At the UN, radical feminists, extreme environmentalists, sexual rights activists, heads of some UN agencies, NGOs (especially International Planned Parenthood Federation), and some UN member state delegations work together to promote an anti-family agenda.[219] It is hard to clearly categorize specific delegations at the UN as being for or against the traditional family because governments are constantly changing. Also, member state delegates do not always represent the views of their government and, at times, they promote their personal political agendas on the UN floor. In fact, one of our major strategies at UN conferences is to inform governments when their delegates are promoting anti-family provisions contrary to their countries' laws or policies. We have been successful several times in getting governments to reprimand their delegates and instruct them to reverse their anti-family positions in UN negotiations.

The countries that have been fairly consistent in strongly pushing for anti-life and anti-family policies are Canada, the European Union (EU), Australia and New Zealand. Sometimes the United States falls into that category, depending on who is in the White House. Brazil recently has become a leader in promoting anti-family provisions. At the June 2006 UN General Assembly High Level Meeting on HIV/AIDS in New York, a spokesman for Brazil's delegation was a transvestite (a man dressed as a woman). We learned from another UN delegate that, in a closed meeting, the Brazilian delegate announced that Brazil would never accept a UN recommendation encouraging abstinence as he could not practice abstinence and did not believe anyone else could either.

Generally, the most valiant, family-friendly UN delegations include the Muslim countries, many African and Latin American countries, and the United States when the president in power supports family values. When the U.S. president is more liberal on family policies, as is the case at the time this book went to print, the United States occasionally leads

---

[219] Chapter 3 discussed a plan developed in Glen Cove, New York, by NGOs and UN officials to promote sexual rights that are detrimental to the family. A report of how that plan has been successfully implemented by manipulating the UN system to promote abortion has been outlined in *Rights by Stealth, The Role of Human Rights Treaty Bodies in the Campaign for an International Right to Abortion*, Sylva. D., & Yoshihara, S. The International Organizations Research Group, The Catholic Family and Human Rights Institute. Electronic version available at http://www.c-fam. org/docLib/20080425_Number_8_Rights_By_Stealth.pdf

the charge in promoting anti-family provisions and programs at the UN. This makes it difficult for us as Americans and members of the pro-family contingency because we find ourselves in the ironic position of having to rally other nations to oppose our own delegation to the UN on family issues.

Occasionally, an Eastern European country with strong pro-family traditions, like Hungary, Poland or Malta will break off from the EU's common position and bravely support family issues. The Vatican holds observer status at the UN, and its delegates consistently speak out in favor of traditional family values. Many times, when family issues are being debated, the Vatican delegates have led the charge to block bad policies or promote policies that protect the family, but, in the end, the Vatican has no vote.

In addition, at times, individual UN delegates demonstrate heroic pro-family stances. Some have done so even at the risk of their countries losing essential development monies from liberal, rich countries or international institutions like the World Bank. At one UN conference, a delegate from an African country, who had been fearless in speaking out in favor of pro-family policies, left a closed negotiating session shaking her head. She reported that a delegate from the EU had approached her and threatened to cut off funding to her country if she did not agree to a "reproductive health services" provision that would likely be used to promote abortion.

This delegate has since been removed from her position at the UN, reportedly because of the pressure exerted by nations that fund development in her country and that were opposed to her vocal support of the family in UN negotiations.

National/State/Local Level

At the national level, attacks on family values usually come from feminists, liberal politicians, activist judges, and rights-based groups seeking to promote "personal liberty," defined in this context as freedom from any moral restraints or from the natural consequences of poor choices.

> *At the national level, attacks on family values usually come from feminists, liberal politicians, activist judges, and rights-based groups seeking to promote freedom from any moral restraints or from the natural consequences of poor choices.*

Consider the following quote from Linda Gordon, a prominent feminist and history professor at New York University:

The nuclear family must be destroyed, and people must find better ways of living together. ... Whatever its ultimate meaning, the break-up of families now is an objectively revolutionary process. ... Families will be finally destroyed only when a revolutionary social and economic organization permits people's needs for love and security to be met in ways that do not impose divisions of labor, or any external roles, at all. [220]

Higher institutions of learning are notorious for promoting anti-family ideologies, especially in the departments of family or women's studies and in the field of social work. One study showed that 72 percent of those teaching at U.S. colleges and universities are self-described as "liberal," while only 15 percent are "conservative." Of those surveyed, 84 percent favor abortion rights and 67 percent believe that homosexuality is acceptable.[221] The general population is far more conservative. Yet these socially liberal teachers are carefully shaping the minds and hearts of the rising generation.

At the local level, the greatest anti-family assault occurs through public school curricula. I have given many examples of inappropriate material used to teach our children in other chapters.

Of course, there is the media, the pornography industry,[222] and others who make billions of dollars promoting sexual promiscuity that destroys children and families. "Family planning" industries make huge profits from condom distribution and abortion.[223] Finally, many businesses, NGOs and wealthy philanthropists also have supported anti-family policies largely because they have bought into the overpopulation worldview.

Feminists and Homosexual Activists Took Their Cause to the UN

Women's rights activists in the United States, reeling from their failure to pass the Equal Rights Amendment (ERA) to the U.S. Constitution in the

[220] Gordon, L. (1969). Functions of the family. *Women: A Journal of Liberation.*

[221] Rothman, S., Lichter, S. R., & Nevitte, N. (2005). Politics and Professional Advancement Among College Faculty. *The Forum, 3*(1).

[222] It is difficult to get an exact figure on annual worldwide pornography revenues. Estimates vary widely and range from several billion dollars to almost $100 billion.

[223] The 2005-2006 annual report issued by the Planned Parenthood Federation of America reports revenues of $902.8 million, with a $55.8 million profit. Of this revenue, $305.3 million (34 percent) comes from U.S. taxpayer dollars. Together with the International Planned Parenthood Federation, over $1 billion in revenue is generated for reproductive services (abortion and other birth control methods).

1970s, took their cause to the United Nations. These women have worked diligently for 30 years to implement their agenda through UN treaties and documents and have partnered with activists from other countries.

They load UN documents with radical anti-family provisions, then these documents are negotiated and signed by UN member states who commit to implement them in their respective countries. Under the banner of "sexual rights," feminists have joined with homosexual activists, "sex workers" (prostitutes), and child sexual rights advocates (one of these groups was associated with NAMBLA, the North American Man/Boy Love Association), to create a formidable international sexual rights movement.

These groups have managed to amass considerable power and influence by seeking and obtaining appointments to leadership positions in UN agencies, on panels, and as members of UN treaty monitoring committees. Some have even managed to get themselves appointed to official UN delegations of member states so they can directly influence UN negotiations. Since sexual rights activists know they cannot get much of their agenda passed by the popular vote in their own countries, they see the UN as an alternative and, frankly, easier mechanism to impose their sexual rights agenda on countries through treaties, conventions and resolutions.

Since sexual rights activists know they cannot get much of their agenda passed by the popular vote in their own countries, they see the UN as an alternative and, frankly, easier mechanism to impose their sexual rights agenda on countries through treaties, conventions and resolutions.

The Family Considered an Obstacle to "Gender Equality"

Since mothers and fathers often assume different roles in traditional marriage, many feminist activists see the traditional family as an obstacle to true "gender equality." For example, at the 2003 UN Commission on the Status of Women (CSW),[224] the document to be negotiated essentially was a radical feminist wish list titled "The Role of Men and Boys in Achieving Gender Equality." One proposal called for the revision of textbooks and curricula in member states to eliminate gender stereotypes. Another

---

[224] The UN Commission on the Status of Women 48th Session, March 26, 2003.

proposal called for "changing harmful attitudes and traditional perceptions of male and female roles."

These proposals were acceptable to most when viewed through the lens of women's rights. However, members of the pro-family coalition pointed out to the UN delegates that when interpreted through the lens of homosexual rights, the proposals took on an entirely new meaning.

At one point, the chairperson interjected that school curricula should not show girls playing with dolls. The delegate from Sudan responded, "But girls *do* play with dolls in my country." We could hardly believe that UN delegates were actually trying to dictate how children should play.

> *We could hardly believe that UN delegates were actually trying to dictate how children should play.*

We also distributed materials showing the delegates that the proposal "to eliminate gender stereotypes" could be used to attack motherhood by citing examples where the UN CEDAW committee had already identified motherhood as a negative gender stereotype. Our materials initiated a debate on the UN floor, and after heated discussions the controversial wording was removed.

Also, to help flush out the activists' agenda, we distributed information to pro-family delegations asking them to demand definitions for several new terms being proposed, such as "masculinities" and "sexualities." To show pro-family delegations the potential for abuse if key terms in documents are left undefined, we provided them with the Oxford Dictionary definition of sexualities: "Identifying one's sexuality, sexual desire, sexual appetite, sexiness, carnality, physicalness, eroticism, sensuality, sexual orientation, or sexual preferences." Our efforts were rewarded when the delegate from Sudan read this definition from our talking points[225] on the UN floor, and a number of delegates then demanded that the term be deleted.

Delegations promoting "reproductive rights" and "sexual rights" for women and girls deceptively insisted that none of the proposed terms included abortion. So we distributed statements from the UN

---

[225] Marcia Barlow and I, representing United Families International (www.unitedfamilies.org) at this particular conference, created the talking points for the UN delegates.

CEDAW committee that define "reproductive rights" to include abortion. As is so often the case, simply exposing the real agenda at issue led to its defeat.

Same-Sex Marriage and the Disappearance of Mothers and Fathers

The light really came on for me when I saw the staunch opposition to a U.S. proposal to "promote the understanding of the importance of both fathers and mothers to the well-being of women and girls."

What could possibly be wrong with that recommendation? The delegate from Ireland, speaking on behalf of the EU, opposed the language because he believed the terms "mothers" and "fathers" were "too limiting."

When several delegates suggested the addition of "legal guardians" and "caregivers" to make the language more inclusive, it still did not satisfy the EU. They also asked to have the word "both" removed when modifying the word "parents." They insisted on replacing the words "mothers" and "fathers" with "women" and "men," and this became a point of contention throughout the negotiations.

Why the contention? If the UN recognizes the essential role of both parents—a father and a mother in raising their children—then they "discriminate" against same-sex partners who can never provide a child with both a father and a mother.

These UN negotiations are a microcosm of what is now happening in various countries around the world. If we don't act, respect for the unique and complementary roles played by mothers and fathers in family and society may eventually be lost. In fact, now that same-sex marriage is legally sanctioned in some areas of the world (and it is spreading), it may eventually become illegal to publicly promote motherhood and fatherhood without risking accusations of discrimination.

Unless we stop this trend, just as surely as references to God are being systematically removed from the public

Unless we stop this trend, references to the importance of both mothers and fathers in the life of a child will be systematically removed so as to not offend same-sex couples.

square so as not to offend atheists, references to the importance of both mothers and fathers in the life of a child will be systematically removed so as to not offend same-sex couples.

Responsible Citizens are Making a Difference!

Let's put the world back in perspective. Most people in the world believe in traditional marriage and family and want to protect these critical institutions. Yet these people have largely been silent. Why? While they may have realized the family was under attack, they haven't understood how successful those attacks have been, how many things are being affected, and how close to home and personal these attacks really are. In other words, they haven't been aware that, as those who are pro-family fail to take a stand, the radical views of the small, but vocal, group of attackers will prevail and eventually have an impact in their backyard. However, as more good people become aware and join the fight, we will have a stronger voice and can take back critical institutions like local public schools and even the UN.

Upon returning from a major UN conference, one of our volunteers commented, "I wasn't sure what impact a mom from Gilbert, Arizona, with fishy crackers and baby wipes in her purse could have on international policy." Then she saw the effect that just our presence had at the UN. It has been amazing to watch what can be accomplished locally, nationally and internationally when concerned citizens become involved and learn how to be effective.

At one particularly difficult UN conference, during the heat of contentious negotiations, a delegate representing Slovakia approached us and broke down into tears as she told us:

> You just don't know what a difference it makes to have you here. We go into those closed-door sessions, and the rich, developed nations put pressure on us to accept language validating their anti-family policies. When we don't agree, they make us feel like we are weird or that there is something wrong with us. Then we come out and see normal people like you supporting us, and we know we are doing the right thing.

As Family Watch combines our strength with other pro-family individuals and groups in our communities and nations, our voices are heard by reasonable policymakers. We are then able to protect families from bad social policies and laws. At the international level, we join with pro-family groups in other countries at the World Congress of Families[226] conferences to network and strategize how to protect the family. At the UN, we participate in a pro-family coalition, which, although grossly outnumbered by anti-family groups (sometimes 100 to 1), has been very successful in stopping many anti-family policies from being adopted. At the national and local level, we network with many good groups who are working at the grassroots level to protect the family. Yet all of these efforts need help and support.

Etched in one of the remnants of the fallen Berlin Wall in Germany is this quote: "Many small people, in many small places, doing many small things can change the face of the world." If we all work in our spheres of influence, whether it be in our own homes, neighborhoods or communities, we can turn back the tide that is working to destroy our families. It will take our combined best efforts.

Stand for the Family—What You Can Do

An important way you can help right now is to sign the "I Stand for the Family" petition and join the global movement for the family. Our goal is to rally one million people across the world to protect and defend marriage and the family, with a minimum of one thousand people in each state in the United States and in every country. You can go to our Web site at www.familywatchinternational.org and sign the petition electronically. Your e-mail address will serve as your signature. People in more than 80 countries have already signed the petition. You can also find a hard copy of the petition in the back of this book.

By signing the petition, you will be linked with people across the world who have committed to do what they can in their sphere of influence to preserve and protect the family. You will also begin receiving email updates on emerging family issues and occasionally will be asked to act, with a click

---

[226] As noted in an earlier footnote, The World Congress of Families (WCF) is a biennial conference chaired by Dr. Allan Carlson of the Howard Center for Family, Religion and Society. The WCF brings together government, religious and community leaders, scholars, and experts in family issues as well as concerned citizens who are working to preserve the family around the world. Information on the WCF can be found at www.worldcongress.org.

of a mouse, to make your voice heard on an important family issue at the international or national level. You can also help by sending others to our Web site to sign the petition.

Chapter 11

The Assault on Gender

Lynn Allred attended the UN Commission on Human Rights in 2004 and wrote the following report.

The Infamous Brazilian Resolution *(Report by Lynn Allred)*

At the UN Commission on Human Rights,[227] Brazil introduced a controversial resolution seeking to establish the "expression of sexual orientation" as an international human right. International policy experts generally agreed that if this resolution were to pass, it could very likely pave the way for the legalization of same-sex marriage across the world. That was likely the intent of those who drafted it.

Yet, this move to establish rights to express one's sexual orientation goes beyond same-sex marriage, opening possibilities for a wide range of destructive behavior, all of which is detrimental to the family.

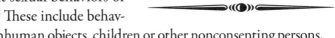

According to the American Psychiatric Association's (APA) Diagnostic and Statistical Manual, there are at least 23 different sexual behaviors or orientations.

According to the American Psychiatric Association's (APA) Diagnostic and Statistical Manual, there are at least 23 different sexual behaviors or "orientations."[228] These include behaviors involving nonhuman objects, children or other nonconsenting persons, and sadomasochistic sex. Although many people define sexual orientation as only including heterosexuality, homosexuality or bisexuality, it is within the realm of possibility that some of the sexual behaviors currently

---

[227] In 2004, the UN Commission on Human Rights (CHR) was made up of 53 UN member states elected by the Economic and Social Council of the United Nations. Delegations gathered in Geneva, Switzerland, annually for six weeks during March and April to negotiate and adopt about 100 resolutions on human rights—including civil and political rights, economic rights, cultural rights, children's rights, women's rights and social rights. The resolutions cover everything from racial discrimination to health, torture, execution and violence against women and indigenous peoples. The CHR has since been reformed and renamed and is now called the UN Human Rights Council.

[228] American Psychiatric Association. (2000). Paraphilias. *Diagnostic and statistical manual of mental disorders* (4th ed. text revision, pp. 566-582). Washington, D.C.: American Psychiatric Association.

considered abnormal by the APA eventually could be considered normal sexual orientations.

It wasn't that long ago that the APA considered homosexuality and bisexuality abnormal. Currently, there is a movement to promote transgenderism and transsexuality as normal orientations as well. Who knows what will be next. This is the reason that "rights" based on "sexual orientation" is such a dangerous concept, especially when "sexual orientation" has not been defined in a negotiated UN document. Certainly all 23 sexual behaviors identified by the APA should not be entitled to special legal protections.

While we feel great compassion for those who struggle with same-sex attraction or any other sexual orientation issue, granting special rights based on sexual behavior does not make sense. Although *every* individual is entitled to the same fundamental rights regardless of fixed characteristics such as race, color, sex or national origin, rights should never be granted based on sexual behavior or sexual preference.

Our pro-family contingent adamantly opposed the Brazilian proposal for a number of reasons. First, the UN was not established or designed to dictate sexual norms to member states. If the UN had passed this provision, it clearly would have overstepped its charter. Of even greater concern, if passed, the provision could have been cited by courts across the world (including the United States)[229] to (1) overturn laws protecting traditional marriage; (2) challenge constitutional provisions defining marriage as a union between a man and a woman only; and (3) establish the right to almost any kind of sexual behavior no matter how harmful.

Not only that, but since sexual orientation has not been defined by UN member states, it would be difficult to restrict this newly proposed right to just homosexual men and lesbian women. For example, it could open the door for pedophiles to demand protection under this clause by simply claiming that their "sexual orientation" is toward children.

(End of Lynn Allred's report.)

At the time of these Human Rights Commission negotiations, I was serving as president of United Families International (UFI). Based

---

[229] U.S. courts increasingly are looking to international norms as a basis for their decisions. In 2002, for example, the majority opinion written by Supreme Court Justice John Paul Stevens in *Atkins v. Virginia* favorably cited the European Union's position in striking down a law allowing the execution of mentally retarded individuals. Then, in 2003, a majority opinion in *Lawrence v. Texas* cited to the European Convention on Human Rights and the Wolfenden Report from Great Britain as support for granting constitutional protection to homosexual sodomy.

on what Lynn shared with us in her report, another colleague, Sheldon Kinsel I created an action alert. The alert was sent out through UFI and asked people to e-mail the UN delegations of the 53 member countries of the Human Rights Commission and express their strong opposition to the sexual orientation proposal.

The response to this action alert was overwhelming. More than 350,000 e-mail messages were generated to these UN delegations![230] No one had ever done anything like that on such a large scale before, and the e-mails were very effective.

Citing a lack of international support, the Brazilian delegation tabled its resolution. An Egyptian delegate to the UN, told us that these e-mails likely were responsible for the withdrawal of the Brazilian resolution.

Dueling UN Statements on Sexual Orientation and Gender Identity

Four years later, in December 2008, a newly formed UN coalition led by France issued a statement to the UN General Assembly calling upon all nations to protect sexual orientation (read: homosexuality) and gender identity (read: transsexuality), and repeal all laws restricting these sexual behaviors. The statement was signed by 66 member states.

Although the statement was nonbinding, this was the first time an official UN statement claimed that homosexual and transsexual behaviors are human rights. This was a very dangerous development.

Family Watch drafted a counterstatement, which was redrafted by some pro-family UN delegates and distributed to other UN delegations to gather support. Family Watch sent faxes to over 90 member states encouraging them to sign on to the counterstatement. A number of organizations in the UN pro-family coalition worked together to gather support as well.

France had had several months to gather their signatories on the UN statement they authored. In about two weeks, 57 UN member states had signed the counterstatement we helped initiate. The signed counterstatement was then introduced to the UN General Assembly after the French statement was presented. This was a significant victory for the pro-family coalition, as this official statement counteracted the false impression that the whole world was in favor of promoting and protecting homosexuality and transexuality.

---

[230] The term "mission" is a common way to refer to either the physical office or the actual delegation of a UN member state. There are 192 UN member states.

The counterstatement cited Article 16 of the Universal Declaration on Human Rights (UNDR) reaffirming that the family is "the natural and fundamental group unit of society" and challenged the claim that *any* binding UN documents included a right to the sexual behaviors listed in the French-authored document. The counterstatement also reaffirmed Article 29 of the UNDR, which establishes the right of UN member states to enact laws that meet "just requirements of morality, public order and the general welfare in a democratic society." Finally, it noted with concern, attempts to misinterpret the UNDR to create "new rights" that were never agreed upon by member states.

Although some would pretend otherwise, these duelling statements made it very clear that, as of yet, there is no international consensus on protecting sexual orientation or gender identity. In fact, these issues are among the most controversial social issues at the UN, next to abortion.

Subsequently, at the UN Commission on the Status of Women conference in 2009, a presentation was given by the groups that initiated the French-authored statement on sexual orientation. They announced their plans to spend the next three years pressuring more nations to sign their statement and to gather enough support to present it as a UN resolution rather than a statement. In March 2009, the U.S. government announced their plans to sign the sexual orientation statement, despite the fact that the Bush administration had refused to sign it just prior to President Obama taking office.

We will be working with family-friendly UN member states to add signatures on a new counterstatement to try to prevent the French-led statement from becoming a UN resolution.

Radical Gender Theories

A common myth is that gender is merely a "social construct." Some claim we can thus choose our gender because it is fluid, changeable and determined by our feelings about ourselves, not by our biology. In other words, under this radical definition, there are no fixed categories such as male and female.

A good example of an attempt to hijack the meaning of the word "gender" to reflect this "social construct" model was when the UN Office of the Special Advisor on Gender Issues and the Advancement of Women issued a statement seeking to define gender as:

> ... *The social attributes and opportunities associated with being male and female and the relationships between women and men and girls and boys, as well as the relations between women and those between men. These attributes, opportunities and relationships are socially constructed and are learned through socialization processes. They are context/time-specific and changeable.*[231]

This was a sneaky attempt to force countries to retroactively reinterpret all UN documents containing the term "gender." No UN office has the right to redefine gender for the entire world! Even if it were the business of the UN, gender already has been defined more than once by the UN member states in consensus UN documents. For example, Article 7(3) of the Rome Statute of the International Criminal Court states:

> *For the purposes of this Statute, it is understood that the term "gender" refers to the two sexes, male and female, within the context of society. The term "gender" does not indicate any meaning different from the above.*

Another official UN conference document states that "the term 'gender' refers to the two sexes, male and female."[232]

Consensus language in official UN documents should always trump statements issued by UN bureaucrats who are there only to support or carry out mandates by UN member states. Unfortunately, many UN bureaucrats believe otherwise and are part of the sexual rights movement discussed in detail in Chapter 4.

One goal of the sexual rights movement is to make "gender" mean, in laws and policies, something that one *feels* or *chooses* rather than what

---

[231] Gender Mainstreaming: Strategy For Promoting Gender Equality. (2008). Office of the Special Advisor on Gender Issues and Advancement of Women. Retrieved March 31, 2008, from United Nations Inter-Agency Network on Women and Gender Equality: http://www.un.org/womenwatch/osagi/pdf/factsheet1.pdf

[232] Outcome Document of the 2001 World Conference against Racism, Racial Discrimination, Xenophobia and Related Intolerance. This document includes the following formal note: *Notes 1. For the purpose of this Declaration and Programme of Action, it was understood that the term "gender" refers to the two sexes, male and female, within the context of society. The term "gender" does not indicate any meaning different from the above.*

someone *is* (i.e., male or female). So how should society deal with gender confusion?

One goal of the sexual rights movement is to make "gender" mean, in laws and policies, something that one feels or chooses rather than what someone is (i.e., male or female).

There are two opposing approaches. One is to consider gender confusion abnormal or unhealthy and try to help the person who wants to change through therapy and intervention. This was the standard approach until it became politically incorrect. The new approach is to call behaviors tied to gender confusion normal, remove these behaviors from the official lists of mental disorders, and claim that people struggling with gender confusion are entitled to special "rights," including the right to express themselves as the opposite gender. Under this paradigm, rather than helping the individual to change, society must change to accommodate and enable their confusion. The latter approach is beginning to prevail and is being taught in many colleges nationwide.

Family Watch International led a panel at a board meeting of community colleges in Arizona to debate this very issue. The person heading up the diversity office of the Maricopa County Community College District (the largest district of community colleges in the United States) gave testimony before the board. She claimed that some people are born in the body of the wrong gender and need affirmation as they transition from their biological gender to the opposite gender. She was promoting a policy that would force teachers and students to affirm people as the opposite gender or face charges of discrimination.

The policy she was proposing would have given students and faculty an unlimited right to "express" themselves as the opposite gender on campus, thereby allowing men who claim they feel like they are women to use the women's bathrooms and showers.

Fortunately, our panel gave strong testimony against this new policy, and it was pulled from the agenda. However, I am sure it will be proposed again when its promoters feel they have enough support to pass it.

Dr. Nancy Felipe Russo, a professor of psychology at Arizona State University, claims that gender is completely independent from the physical characteristics that make someone either male or female. So, she opines, "We should conceptualize gender as a structural variable, that it depends on the situation, and that is in 'the eye of the beholder' and not 'in' the person."[233]

This type of thinking can directly affect laws and policies. For example, the California state penal code defines gender this way:

> *"Gender" means the victim's actual sex or the defendant's perception of the victim's sex, and includes the defendant's perception of the victim's identity, appearance, or behavior, whether or not that identity, appearance, or behavior is different from that traditionally associated with the victim's sex at birth.*[234]

Can you imagine what happens when this confusion is taught to children through sex education programs in schools? Remember that it is normal for adolescents to have lots of questions related to their sexuality, so youth are especially vulnerable.

Please understand that the drive for "sexual rights" is not limited to homosexuality. The movement for sexual rights, including nondiscrimination provisions protecting "gender identity and expression," broadly encompasses rights for lesbians, gays, bisexuals and transgenders (LGBT). Sometimes a "Q" is added to LGBT for "queers" or those who are "questioning."

To understand just how confusing sexuality choices have become, here are two examples that Canadian sociology professor Aaron H. Devor describes:

> **Example 1**—*A male crossdresser in a long-term sexual relationship with a woman who loves the woman in her partner. When effectively crossdressed, the first individual is a male who acts as a woman. The partner changes neither gender nor sex, she remains female and a woman. However, when they have sexual relations they are one male and one female, hence heterosexual, and both are acting as women. Therefore, they are heterosexual on the basis of their sexes, but they are lesbian on the basis of their genders. Thus the male could be described as a male heterosexual crossdresser lesbian woman, whereas the female would be a female heterosexual lesbian woman.*

---

[233] "Sex" versus "Gender," (1993, April). Women's Studies E-mail Forum. Retrieved June 15, 2009, http://userpages.umbc.edu/~korenman/wmst/sex_v_gender.html
[234] California Penal Code Section 13519.4.

Example 2—A male crossdresser married to a female crossdresser. Both crossdressers keep their sex statuses but switch their genders. Thus, the male's gendered sexuality would be male heterosexual crossdresser straight woman, whereas the female's would be female heterosexual crossdresser straight man.[235]

It is difficult to keep track of all of the evolving "genders." Internationally, there is a movement to legally recognize and protect seven genders—namely male, female, homosexual male, homosexual female, transgender male, transgender female and bisexual.

The International "Gender" Agenda

If you repeat radical ideas loud enough and often enough, and if they are not adequately refuted, *they will take root* no matter how crazy or farfetched they are.

A group of "sexual rights" activists produced a dangerous document that could take root if we let it. The document, titled "The Yogyakarta Principles on the Application of International Human Rights Law in Relation to Sexual Orientation and Gender Identity,"[236] was created by a group of 30 activists—self-proclaimed "experts" on sexuality and human rights. They call themselves "The International Commission of Jurists and the International Service for Human Rights." Their goal was to gather and interpret all "existing international human rights law" relating to human sexuality and dictate to countries what their obligations are under those laws.

The Yogyakarta Principles claim to "affirm binding international legal standards," which require all nations to accept, protect, endorse and promote sexual promiscuity and homosexuality. But these particular "sexual rights" have been at the center of many heated UN debates (several which I have personally witnessed), and each time they have been flatly

---

[235] Devor, A. (1996). *How many sexes? How many genders? When two are not enough.* Retrieved March 31, 2008, from University of Victoria Web site: http://web.uvic.ca/~ahdevor/HowMany/HowMany.html

[236] The entire text of the Yogyakarta Principles can be found at www.yogyakartaprinciples.org.

rejected. Fortunately, up until the writing of this book, the UN pro-family coalition has provided help to UN delegates that has enabled them to keep broad "sexual rights," or protections based on "sexual orientation," out of binding UN documents.

When looked at closely, it's easy to see that the Yogyakarta Principles are a poorly disguised wish list promoted largely by those seeking legal and societal endorsement of promiscuous lifestyles. The next section will show you how dangerous this document is and why we need to make sure it does not get any traction.

The Broad Reach of the Yogyakarta Principles

The Yogyakarta Principles loftily declare that "human sexual orientation and gender identity are integral to every person's dignity and humanity and must not be the basis for discrimination or abuse." This sounds nice; however, consider their definitions of the following terms:

> ***"Sexual Orientation"***—*Sexual orientation is understood to refer to each person's capacity for profound emotional, affectional and sexual attraction to, and intimate and sexual relations with, individuals of a different gender or the same gender or more than one gender.*

> ***"Gender Identity"***—*Gender identity is understood to refer to each person's deeply felt internal and individual experience of gender, which may or may not correspond with the sex assigned at birth, including the personal sense of the body (which may involve, if freely chosen, modification of bodily appearance or function by medical, surgical or other means) and other expressions of gender, including dress, speech and mannerisms.*

According to the Yogyakarta Principles, a government would violate a person's "human rights" if it limited in any way one's sexual expression or sexual preferences. Furthermore, the Yogyakarta Principles allege that this expression, which can include sex-change operations, is integral to a person's "dignity and humanity."

"Sexual Orientation"—The Trojan Horse for Sexual Anarchy

Keep in mind, the term "sexual orientation" does not always just connote a homosexual orientation. The term may actually be used as a Trojan Horse to eventually sneak in protections for all sorts of sexual orientations that would never be accepted otherwise. As mentioned earlier, the American Psychiatric Association recognizes 23 different sexual behaviors or orientations, including pedophilia, transgenderism, transsexuality, voyeurism, sexual masochism, sexual sadism, and many other "orientations" that I will not mention out of sensitivity to the reader.[237]

Try this quick exercise to see how the term "sexual orientation" could be used deceptively to promote sexual anarchy. Take the statement below from the Yogyakarta Principles and replace the term "sexual orientation" with the term "pedophilia" (the behavior of an individual who is sexually oriented toward children). Here is how it would read:

> [Pedophiles are] entitled to enjoy all human rights without discrimination on the basis of [their pedophilia] or gender identity. [Pedophiles are] entitled to equality before the law *and the equal protection of the law without any such discrimination whether or not the enjoyment of another human right is also affected.* (Emphasis added.)

Sounds pretty shocking, doesn't it? An overwhelming majority would not consider pedophilia a human right. But liberal social scientists and groups like the North American Man/Boy Love Association (NAMBLA) have promoted pedophilia for years and advocate the legalization of sex between children and adults. They are using the same successful strategy that homosexual advocates have followed for three decades.

Because the drafters of the Yogyakarta Principles do not exclude *any* sexual behaviors from their definition of sexual orientation, they in essence are claiming that the expression of all sexual orientations (not just homosexuality) is a human right protected by international law.

---

[237] The list of 23 sexual behaviors and orientations recognized by the APA can be found in the Policy Resource Center on our Web site at www.familywatchinternational.org.

Abolishing Traditional Gender Roles

The Yogyakarta Principles also mandate that nations "eliminate prejudices *and customs* based on the idea of ... stereotyped roles for men and women." (Emphasis added.) Translation: Nations must eliminate not just laws, but also traditions like Mother's Day and Father's Day.

Remember, the United Nations CEDAW committee, has already criticized countries for recognizing Mother's Day.

The United Nations CEDAW committee has already criticized countries for recognizing Mother's Day.

U.S. Constitution First Amendment Trampled

Consider this mandate from the Yogyakarta Principles: "Ensure that the exercise of freedom of opinion and expression does not violate the rights and freedoms of persons of diverse sexual orientations and gender identities."

The Yogyakarta Principles could make it illegal to hold a negative opinion or express a negative belief about a specific sexual orientation. Censorship of religious texts, speech or even scientific research that says anything negative about any sexual orientation could follow.

Though they have been unsuccessful, there have already been lawsuits against Bible publishers in the United States because Bibles contain statements denouncing homosexuality (e.g., Leviticus 18:22). If the Yogyakarta Principles are enacted, however, such lawsuits would likely succeed. Indeed, the Principles would give force to broad hate crimes legislation already enacted.

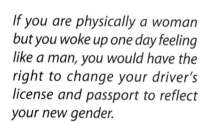

If you are physically a woman but you woke up one day feeling like a man, you would have the right to change your driver's license and passport to reflect your new gender.

A Right to Change One's Gender

The Yogyakarta Principles require nations to ensure that "identity papers ... reflect the person's profound self-defined gender identity." In other words, if you are physically a woman but you woke up one day feeling like a man, you would have the right to change your driver's license and passport to reflect your new gender.

And what if a person desired to surgically alter their appearance but lacked the resources or support to do so? Governments should facilitate "access by those seeking body modifications related to gender reassignment to competent, nondiscriminatory treatment, care and support" and "undertake targeted programmes to provide social support for all persons experiencing gender transitioning or reassignment."

Government may have to pay for sex change operations under this provision. In fact, this has already happened in Canada. The Canadian government has been funding sex change operations for those who desired them. Facing a budget shortage, the government attempted to eliminate financial support for these procedures. The backlash from individuals desiring this procedure caused the government to reinstate the funding at the expense of funding for a program to prevent teen suicide.

Treatment Prohibited for Unwanted Same-Sex Attraction

According to the Yogyakarta group, a "person's sexual orientation and gender identity ... are *not* to be treated, cured or suppressed." (Emphasis added.)

What does that say about the man who has a sexual orientation toward children or any of the other 22 sexual orientations or behaviors recognized by the APA?

And what about those who struggle with unwanted same-sex attraction? The Yogyakarta group wants these people to be denied help.

And what about those who struggle with *unwanted* same-sex attraction? The Yogyakarta group wants these people to be denied help.

They want to "ensure that any medical or psychological treatment or counseling does not, explicitly or implicitly, treat sexual orientation and gender identity as medical conditions to be treated, cured or suppressed." (Emphasis added.)

Going After Our Children

The Yogyakarta group wants to liberalize the sexual expression of children, declaring that "a child who is capable of forming personal views has the right to express those views freely" and that "the best interests of the child shall be a primary consideration" and "that the sexual orientation or gender identity of the child or of any family member or other person may not be considered incompatible with such best interests." This could override a parent's right to direct a child away from homosexuality and open the door for homosexual adoption.

The Principles also require governments to ensure that education promotes "respect" for "diverse sexual orientations and gender identities." This is much broader than just promoting homosexuality, as problematic as that is.

The Yogyakarta group also is attempting to eliminate dress codes, demanding that children have the "right to express identity or personhood, including through speech, deportment, dress, bodily characteristics, choice of name or any other means." Most teens could benefit from some parental guidance in all these areas.

Advancement of the Yogyakarta Principles at the United Nations

The Office of the UN High Commissioner for Human Rights

In November 2007, the Yogyakarta Principles were formally launched at the UN by a panel sponsored by a coalition of NGOs and the governments of Argentina, Brazil and Uruguay. Participants on the panel included Mary Robinson, the former UN High Commissioner for Human Rights. Her successor, Louise Arbour, also wrote a statement in support of the Principles for the occasion.

In addition, in conjunction with the 60th anniversary of the Universal Declaration of Human Rights, the UN High Commissioner issued a written statement calling it "unthinkable" to discriminate against people on the basis of "sexual orientation or gender identity" and referenced the Yogyakarta Principles as support for her statement.

UN Granting Consultative Status to Homosexual Groups

In recent years, the UN, under great pressure from homosexual activists, granted consultative status[238] to homosexual rights groups despite the protest of several countries. This development was the result of an aggressive campaign launched by the International Lesbian and Gay Association (ILGA), urging all of the Association's more than 600 affiliates to apply for consultative status with the UN.

Shortly after the Yogyakarta Principles were released, Beto de Jesus, a member of the Board of the Brazilian LGBT Federation (one of the homosexual groups granted consultative status), delivered a speech at the UN Human Rights Council encouraging the Council to use the Yogyakarta Principles to frame a future debate on sexual orientation and gender identity. Shortly thereafter, the leader of another homosexual group that had just been granted consultative status declared that the group would use their new status at the UN to advance homosexual rights in the countries of UN member states that had voted against them being accredited.

UN Rapporteurs

Although the task clearly was outside of their assigned mandates, nine UN rapporteurs[239] were part of the team of 30 "experts" who drafted the Yogyakarta Principles. In an October 2009 report to the UN General Assembly, one of these rapporteurs, Martin Scheinin, tried to advance the Yogyakarta Principles that he had helped draft. He also had the audacity to attempt to redefine gender for the whole world in his report.

Fortunately, due to the efforts of a number of UN delegates led by the African voting bloc and supported by Islamic countries and some of the Caribbean states, Scheinin's report was successfully rejected by a majority vote of the UN member states.

A statement by the representative from St. Lucia, made just before the final General Assembly vote to reject Scheinin's report, expressed her country's "opposition to the incorporation of the Special Rapporteur's personal ideas about what a 'gender perspective' means in the context of his mandate" and lamented the fact that the rapporteur had "(a) exceeded

---

[238] Consultative status allows an organization special access to UN meetings and UN delegations.

[239] UN rapporteurs are supposed to be nonbiased experts that provide reports to the UN on various human rights issues that they are assigned to study and report on.

his mandate, (b) unilaterally attempted to change the definition of a universally accepted term, [and] (c) based his definition on premises which do not exist in international human rights law."

We are grateful to the UN delegates who were willing to push back against these UN "experts" who are seeking to manipulate the UN system to advance their sexual rights agenda.

Universal Periodic Reviews

Sexual rights activists are also using the UN Universal Periodic Reviews (UPRs)[240] to advance the Yogyakarta Principles. A number of these groups submit complaints to the UPR Committee outlining what they consider to be human rights violations relating to sexual orientation and gender identity. Many of the NGOs are relying on the Yogyakarta Principles to justify their grievances to the UPR Committee.

Pushback Against the Principles

As previously mentioned, activists claim that the Yogyakarta Principles are universal legal standards that have obtained the status of customary international law because of their alleged widespread acceptance. This can easily be refuted by the fact that most UN member states have laws that run counter to one or more of the provisions of the Principles. The fact that sexual rights activists are fighting to get the Principles recognized as internationally accepted norms also indicates that they are not the norm.

However, the Principles could soon become the norm if sexual rights activists can convince enough countries to accept them as binding legal standards that they are obligated to enforce or even if the activists can convince countries to adopt part or all of the Principles as national policy.

According to the UN Charter, all UN agencies, employees, staff, special rapporteurs, committees, etc., are supposed to be accountable to UN member states. Yet, somehow, the tables have turned, and many of these UN-created or UN-affiliated entities are trying to make UN member states accountable to them as they overstep their mandates to promote the sexual rights agenda. In fact, sexual rights activists aggressively seek appointments to all of these UN entities so they can manipulate various

---

[240] All UN member states are reviewed periodically by the UN and are called to account for any supposed human rights abuses in their respective countries.

parts of the UN system to pressure UN member states into adopting laws and policies that advance their agenda.

Conclusion

Remember: If radical ideas are repeated often enough, in enough venues, and over a sufficiently long enough period of time without being adequately refuted, they eventually take hold. This holds true no matter how crazy or farfetched the ideas are. In fact, as we already have learned, radical ideas can become "customary international law" when they are continually repeated in written documents at the UN and in other international forums.

In summary, the people behind the Yogyakarta Principles are after nothing less than governmental and societal recognition, respect, endorsement and promotion of any kind of sexual behavior, no matter how harmful.

> *The people behind the Yogyakarta Principles are after nothing less than governmental and societal recognition, respect, endorsement and promotion of any kind of sexual behavior, no matter how harmful.*

The Yogyakarta Principles represent one of the most dangerous assaults on the family to date. You can bet that sexual rights advocates will repeatedly use and refer to them in whole or in part to promote sexual anarchy at the international, national, state and local level.

The assault on gender strikes at the roots of the traditional family. Gender confusion destabilizes families and nations. Imagine being a child in a home with "parents" whose "gender" is "time-specific and changeable." Yogyakarta Principles supporters demand the right to indoctrinate our children into sexual promiscuity and to use the law to silence any who oppose them. We owe it to children throughout the world to make sure that these Yogyakarta Principles never take root.

For More Information: Family Watch International has published a free Family Policy Brief on the Yogyakarta Principles, which can be accessed by going to the Family Policy Resource Center on our Web site at www.familywatchinternational.org.

Chapter 12

Defending Traditional Marriage

Since marriage is the glue that cements the family together, the fight to preserve marriage is, in reality, a fight to preserve the family.

In the fall of 2008, I received an e-mail from a friend who took his family to an event to show support for Proposition 8, which called for a California Constitutional amendment defining marriage as between one man and one woman. My friend describes what happened when they joined others along a busy road during the morning commute to wave signs in support of the proposition.

> *As we were sign waving, a young woman came up and was standing behind my family. We invited her to hold a banner with us. I did not pay much attention, when suddenly, she took out a pair of scissors and started slashing at the banner. At one point, she held [the scissors] up to my daughter's face. We wrestled with her to get her to let go, and she ran off, taking a couple of our signs, and jumped in a car and sped off. My younger daughters were in tears. Fortunately, no one was injured. I cannot for the life of me understand why people are so full of hate. I am probably more shaken than my family.*

It is no secret that same-sex marriage is one of the most controversial issues of our time. This is just one example of the many attacks against those who were peacefully exercising their constitutional right as citizens to express support for man/woman marriage. Another friend reported that at a similar rally in California people were stopping their cars and screaming obscenities at the families, even those families that had their young children with them.

My sister, who lives in California, was interviewed and her family featured in a front-page story in *The Sacramento Bee*, because of their support for Proposition 8. Quotes from her interview were picked up by numerous media sources, including *Time* magazine.

Newsweek called the article featuring my sister's family the "low point" for the campaign pushing same-sex marriage, meaning that the magazine felt *The Sacramento Bee* article had a major impact in getting people to support Proposition 8. Due to the backlash created by their front-page story, my sister had to transfer her children to a private school to protect them. Here are some excerpts from comments her husband posted on the newspaper's Web site:

> *I have put my money where my beliefs and mind are. I have risked my good name and put at risk many things—career, safety, etc. As a person asked, "Why would I ever choose to be gay?" I ask the same question: "Why would I ever choose to have done something like this?"*

> *It is simple. This isn't about hate, bigotry or the rest. We have had many things written about us, spoken at us, and my children abused and slandered. I find it interesting that this is from the side screaming for "tolerance" and "love everyone" and "accept people."*

> *The family has existed since the beginning of time. It is the foundation of civilization. It has outlasted everything here on earth—kingdoms, empires, catastrophes, holocausts—everything. ... If the family fails, then all is lost.*

Marriage Ping Pong

Those who want to legalize same-sex marriage are not content to let the voice of the people decide this issue. For example, in 2000, a majority of people in California voted to pass Proposition 22, a state statute defining marriage between a man and a woman. Same-sex marriage advocates then successfully challenged the statute in court. The California Supreme Court ignored the will of the people and, in 2008, overturned Prop 22 in a decision that established by judicial fiat a constitutional right for homosexuals to marry.

Pro-marriage Californians went back to the polls later that year and passed Proposition 8, an amendment to the state Constitution that overturned the Court's decision by defining marriage as between a man and woman only. Same-sex marriage advocates then went back to the California courts with another lawsuit seeking to have judges yet again negate the will of the people by overturning Prop 8.

Fortunately, the California Supreme Court upheld Prop 8 as constitutional; so, for the time being, man/woman marriage is still protected in California. But that could change yet again. Same-sex marriage activists have vowed to try to pass yet another state constitutional amendment to reverse Prop 8. And, even more concerning, a few days before the California high court upheld Prop 8, same-sex-marriage advocates filed suit in federal court to overturn Prop 8 claiming that denying same-sex couples the right to marry is a violation of the U.S. Constitution. The case may seem weak, as everyone knows the U.S. Constitution does not establish a right to same-sex marriage. But we also know the U.S. Constitution does not establish a right to sodomy or to abortion, yet the Supreme Court has ruled that it does.

If this suit challenging Prop 8 makes its way to the Supreme Court, which is highly probable, some experts who have analyzed the current make-up of the Court say there may be enough votes to invent a new right to same-sex marriage even if majority opinion is still against it. Not only that, but since several judges will likely retire before the case reaches the Supreme Court, appointments of more liberal replacements could make such a ruling even more probable. So the battle over the meaning of marriage in California and in the rest of the country is just warming up.

These battles are like a high stakes ping pong game, a power struggle between the majority of the people and the courts. Same-sex marriage advocates undoubtedly will continue to challenge marriage protection laws in state and federal courts until a case makes its way to the U.S. Supreme Court.

With one bad decision, the U.S. Supreme Court could overturn all 30 of the state constitutional protections for marriage, all other state marriage protection laws, and the federal Defense of Marriage Act (DOMA) by finding that the U.S. Constitution gives homosexuals the right to marry.

As current U.S. Supreme Court justices retire and are replaced, the nature of the court will change in unpredictable ways. Same-sex marriage advocates are counting on new appointees to provide enough votes to enable the Supreme Court to strike down all federal and state laws protecting man/woman marriage. Indeed, with one bad decision, the U.S. Supreme

Court could overturn all 30 of the state constitutional protections for marriage, all other state marriage protection laws, and the federal Defense of Marriage Act (DOMA) by finding that the U.S. Constitution gives homosexuals the right to marry.

In Massachusetts, Connecticut, California and Iowa, same-sex marriage was thrust upon those states, not by the will of the people, but by unelected judges. Iowa's Supreme Court decision is most disturbing as it found that "equal protection can only be defined by the standards of each generation." This was the court's way of suggesting that each generation gets to redefine their Constitutional rights. In other words, fundamental rights are not fixed but evolve in meaning every single generation depending on cultural changes, etc.; and judges can decide the standard of this generation regarding same-sex marriage.

Unfortunately, these judges were dead wrong on what this generation of Americans believes regarding same-sex marriage. A CBS News poll that was released the week after Iowa's highest judges forced same-sex marriage on their state showed that only 33 percent of Americans believe that same-sex couples should be allowed to marry.

So these Iowa judges were using their own personal views to redefine the meaning of marriage. As with the U.S. Constitution, the constitutions of Massachusetts, Connecticut, California and Iowa are silent on the right of same-sex couples to marry. All four state high court decisions were based, in large part, on the faulty assumption that a person's sexual orientation is like race or gender, and therefore government cannot deny people marriage rights. According to these judges, not allowing homosexuals to marry (even if all legal rights associated with marriage already are available to homosexuals, as they are in California) relegates them to "second class citizen" status and impacts their "dignity."

The courts are not empowered to make laws, only to interpret them. Inventing a supposed "constitutional right" to same-sex marriage is judicial activism at its very worst.

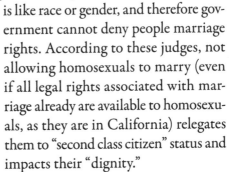

We now have a classic "slippery slope" situation. Under the line of reasoning used in the four state court cases, any group of individuals (e.g., multiple adults, children with adults, etc.) who felt their dignity was impacted by not being allowed to marry could argue they had a constitutional right to do so. This overreaching of the courts in blatant acts of judicial activism threatens our very form of government. The courts are not empowered to *make* laws, only to *interpret* them. Inventing a supposed "constitutional right" to same-sex marriage is judicial activism at its very worst.

The week after Iowa legalized same-sex marriage, Vermont did so as well but with a significant difference. This time it was the legislature that established same-sex marriage by statute. The Vermont governor vetoed the bill, but the legislature then was able to override the veto by a single vote in the House. Does this mean that, at least in Vermont, a slim majority of the people of that state support same-sex marriage? Not really. Interestingly, a *New York Times* article reported that one of the Vermont legislators changed his position against same-sex marriage and voted to override the governor's veto "after 228 of his constituents reached out and urged him to support the override, compared with 198 who urged him to oppose it."[241] In other words, if 31 more people had called his office asking him to vote against same-sex marriage he might not have changed his vote, and Vermont may not have same-sex marriage today. A single additional vote in the House to sustain the governor's veto is all it would have taken.

This should be a lesson to all of us working to protect marriage. If people do not get involved and make their voices heard, the other side will win by default—even if there are more people on our side.

It also should be noted that Vermont has the lowest fertility rate in the nation as well as the one of the lowest levels of reported religiosity amongst its people. So I guess you could say that Vermont is one of the most anti-child, anti-God states in the nation which makes the legislature's decision much easier to understand. Once a people devalue God and children it is much easier to devalue marriage and to deconstruct it by saying that any combination of people will do.

Marriage defenders must become more effective in presenting the case for man/woman marriage and demanding that it be responsibly and thoroughly considered by their elected representatives. After the loss in Vermont, the lessons learned in that state were starting to be applied in other Northeastern states that also were being targeted by the anti-marriage

---

[241] Goodnough, A. (2009, April 7). Gay rights groups celebrate victories in marriage push. *The New York Times*. Retrieved April 8, 2009 from http://www.nytimes.com/2009/04/08/us/08vermont. html?_r=1&th&emc=th

forces.[242] At the printing of this book, battles over same-sex marriage legislation were occurring in New Hampshire, New Jersey, New York, Maine and Washington, D.C.

The Solution: A Federal Marriage Amendment

So, in light of the actions of activist state judges and legislators, how can we preserve traditional marriage? And how can we guard against a future U.S. Supreme Court striking down all of the state marriage amendments and marriage laws, thus legalizing same-sex marriage across the United States against the will of the majority of Americans? (Remember the U.S. Supreme Court already has had an indirect impact on same-sex marriage through its infamous opinion in the *Lawrence v. Texas* case.)

The answer is quite simple. It is to pass a federal marriage amendment to the United States Constitution. If the Constitution were amended to define marriage as a legal union of a man and a woman only, this would trump any attempts by the Supreme Court to establish a right to same-sex marriage. Of course, amending the Constitution is easier said than done. An amendment to the U.S. Constitution has to pass both the House and the Senate with a two-thirds vote and then be ratified by three-fourths of the states. That is a tall order.

A number of legislators in Congress already have attempted on two occasions to gather sufficient support to propose a marriage amendment to the states for ratification and failed on both occasions. With the outcome of the 2008 elections, Congressional support for a federal marriage amendment is now even lower.

However, there is another way to amend the Constitution—one which has been largely ignored—and that is to have the state legislatures convene a Constitutional Convention. As provided for in Article V of the Constitution, a Constitutional Convention may be called if applications are made by two-thirds of the state legislatures. Over 400 separate applications from individual states for a Constitutional Convention have been made over

---

[242] Note that the same day Vermont legalized same-sex marriage, the Washington, D.C., City Council voted to recognize same-sex marriages performed in other states. See Stewart, N., & Craig, T. (2008, April 8). D.C. Council Votes to Recognize Gay Nuptials Elsewhere. *The Washington Post*. Retrieved June 15, 2009 from http://www.washingtonpost.com/wp-dyn/content/article/2009/04/07/AR2009040702200.html

the years on a variety of issues,[243] but for various reasons, no convention has ever been successfully convened since the Constitution was adopted.

I want to be very clear that I am not advocating for a Constitutional Convention at this point. Since the Constitution does not define the procedures for convening a Convention, nor how the delegates would be chosen, nor if a Convention can be limited to just one issue, for now there are too many unanswered questions. However, since this alternative may be the only option left for protecting man/woman marriage in the United States, I think it bears further examination.

If there were a way to limit a Convention to just the marriage issue and to pass legislation defining a prudent process for convening a Convention, it could become a viable option. Calling for a Convention is a tall order because at least 34 states must submit calls to Congress for it to happen. However, given that some 38 or so states already have defined marriage between a man and a woman and more are seeking to do so, the political support at the state level might be strong enough if the kinks could be worked out.

If the process can be safeguarded against a runaway convention that would delve into other issues, a Constitutional Convention convened to preserve marriage may be an idea whose time has come. After all, if the Founding Fathers did not intend for this amendment process to ever be used, then why did they put it in the Constitution? Indeed, could it be that the procedure to amend the Constitution via a Constitutional Convention was inserted in Article V for such a time as this? If not to save marriage, or for a similar issue of overwhelming importance, then what else for?

Ten Reasons to Defend Man/Woman Marriage

The assault on marriage is one of the greatest threats not only to the family, but also to religious and civil freedoms. Below I have provided talking points that can be used in efforts to preserve the legal and cultural support for the institution of man/woman marriage. Some of the support

---

[243] A number of states applied for a Convention over the issues of a balanced budget and abortion. In addition, because the states were so close to convening a Convention over the issue of allowing U.S. Senators to be elected directly by the people, Congress decided to give in and proposed the amendment themselves. The states then ratified the proposal which became the 17th Amendment. More recently, in the 1990s, the movement to limit Congressional terms resorted to Convention calls, but never obtained the required number of calls. So, the idea of a Constitutional Convention is not new. The main reason we have never had one before on a critical issue with broad support is because, in the end, Congress has given in and voted on the proposed amendment.

and examples for the talking points come from other chapters in this book, but they are repeated here so you have the strongest possible points and support to use in defending marriage.

1. Legalizing same-sex marriage severs children from their right to know and be raised by their biological parents.

Whatever a government legalizes, it encourages and, therefore, fosters its development. Policymakers know this all too well.

If same-sex marriage is legalized, more children will be raised without a mother or a father. That is inevitable. As shown by the studies cited in Chapter 3, social science research overwhelmingly proves that children do best on all measures of health, wellbeing and development when they are raised by their married biological parents. Man/woman marriage optimizes the chances of children being raised and cared for by both biological parents, while same-sex marriages establish unions that will always deny the child the opportunity to be raised by either a mother or a father.

Research shows that mothers and fathers, by nature of their different genders, make unique contributions to the development of their children and that these contributions cannot be replaced by two "parents" of the same sex. If society sanctions marriages that make it impossible for children to be raised by both a mother and father, children will suffer.

To use an analogy: You could pass a law that says oranges now are apples. But oranges will never look like apples or taste like apples or be apples no matter how many laws we pass, nor will they ever produce the same seeds as apples. Just because we recognize this reality does not mean we have animosity toward oranges. In fact, we can like both oranges and apples and still hold an opinion that they are different. While this example may seem simplistic, it illustrates that the proposed experiment with same-sex marriage attempts to achieve the impossible. Same-sex marriage is radically different and will never bear the same fruit as man/woman marriage—no matter how many laws are passed.

2. Legalizing same-sex marriage encourages the creation of children through reproductive arrangements that are not in their best interest.

Biology dictates that same-sex couples cannot have children naturally. Hence, legal approval of same-sex marriages further encourages the use of sperm banks, surrogate mothers, and a number of other artificial reproductive technologies. The "products" of these technologies (i.e., children) too often find themselves at the center of court battles to determine their legally recognized parents.

Troubling testimonies have begun to emerge from children created through donated sperm about the negative impact their environments have had on them. For example, a woman raised by two lesbian parents from birth stated, "I have still felt an empty space in my life, the lack of a father, and no matter the love that I have had from both of my mothers and the rarity of their compassion for me, there is a balance that comes from a mother and a father that can create the most stable and lasting family. I would not keep the blessings a father can give from any child."[244]

3. Against their parents' wishes, more children will be taught that homosexuality is healthy and normal.

Wherever same-sex marriage is legalized, parents will have no legal basis to object to books read in schools that promote homosexuality, like *Heather Has Two Mommies*.

This is what David Parker found out after same-sex marriage was legalized in Massachusetts. His experience bears repeating. He was arrested and indefinitely banned from school property for refusing to leave a public elementary school until the school administrators would agree to opt out his six-year-old child from being exposed to homosexual "education." His arrest led to a night in jail.

Mr. Parker and his wife along with another couple, the Wirthlins, then filed a lawsuit in U.S. federal district court in Massachusetts

---

[244] The Supreme Council for Family Affairs, State of Qatar, & The World Family Policy Center, Brigham Young University. (2004). *The World Unites to Protect the Family*. Retrieved June 15, 2009 from http://www.yearofthefamily.org/PDF%20Files/The_World_Unites_to_Save_the_Family_Reports.pdf

to try to stop their school from indoctrinating their children on homosexuality. They lost. When they appealed the lower court decision, the U.S. Court of Appeals for the First Circuit also ruled against them, declaring that parents cannot prohibit the promotion of homosexuality in the schools of Massachusetts. The federal appellate court reasoned that since "Massachusetts has recognized gay marriage under its state constitution," the state's schools have the right to "educate their students regarding that recognition."[245] The U.S. Supreme Court turned down their appeal, so the decision against them stands.

4. When rights for same-sex couples are expanded, freedom of speech and religion are threatened as citizens and business owners are coerced to act against conscience and belief.

We can already see examples of the clash between "same-sex rights" and the core constitutional freedoms of speech and religion occurring in the United States and around the world:

- After same-sex marriage was legalized in Massachusetts, Catholic Charities, the largest facilitator of adoptions in that state, had to drop their adoption program because it was required by law to facilitate adoption of children to same-sex couples and it did not want to face lawsuits.

- A photographer in New Mexico was fined $6,500 for politely declining to photograph a "commitment ceremony" of two lesbians because same-sex relationships violated her religious beliefs.

- A church in New Jersey lost its tax-exempt status for some of its property because it refused to rent out its pavilion for a lesbian "commitment ceremony."

- Due to a settlement agreement, the largest adoption advertising company on the Internet can no longer advertise *any* couples from California as potential adoptive parents because the company's owners, as a matter of conscience, refused to advertise homosexual California couples in its service.

---

[245] *Parker v. Hurley*, 2008 U.S. App. LEXIS 2070 (1ˢᵗ Cir. Mass., Jan. 31, 2008).

- Pastors in Sweden and Canada were prosecuted for speaking out publicly against same-sex marriage based on their reading of biblical scripture.
- A U.S. Bible publisher has been sued for publishing a Bible which has a verse condemning homosexuality.
- Doctors in California were sued for declining to artificially inseminate a lesbian woman because it was against their religious beliefs. The court ruled that the doctors illegally discriminated against the lesbian and ordered them to pay damages.
- Several individuals who donated to the Proposition 8 campaign to protect marriage in California had to quit their jobs after homosexuals protested and staged boycotts against the businesses where they worked.
- The largest dating service on the Internet, eHarmony, has been forced to provide dating services for homosexuals.

5. Wherever same-sex marriage is legalized, promoting motherhood and fatherhood could be deemed discriminatory.

In some countries, it already is considered discriminatory to honor mothers and fathers due to the fear of offending children who have single parents, lesbian mothers or homosexual fathers. For example, some schools in Scotland have banned the making of Father's Day cards in their schools.

Mothers and fathers are no longer recognized on birth certificates in some places where same-sex marriage has been legalized. For example, in Massachusetts and Spain, parents can no longer be referred to as mother and father on birth certificates. They must be designated as "Party A and B" and "Progenitor A and B," respectively. (The latter example ignores the biological fact that only one member of a same-sex couple can possibly be the "progenitor.")

Since legalizing same-sex marriage will create more officially sanctioned families without mothers or fathers, it is certain to fuel the current effort to remove all references to mothers and fathers in our society under the guise of eliminating "discrimination."

6. Same-sex marriage opens up a Pandora's box of problems.

Legalizing same-sex marriage not only radically changes the sexual norms of society (which obviously impacts our children), it also opens the door for polyamory (multiple people "married" to each other) and other "marriage" arrangements to become accepted or legalized.

Noted scholar Elizabeth Marquardt warned: "[R]ecent events make clear that successes in the same-sex marriage movement have emboldened others who wish to borrow the language of civil rights to break open the two-person understanding of marriage and, with it, parenthood." Such individuals include polyamorists who believe in polyamory (meaning, "many loves"), which involves relationships of three or more people. According to Marquardt, polymorists argue that "being poly is just who they are [and] if two parents are good for children, then three or more 'parents,' spread among one or more households and sharing a sexual relationship with one another, is even better."[246]

7. Promiscuity in marriage will become more generally accepted.

Some homosexual activists claim "monogamous" same-sex couples behave like monogamous heterosexual couples. The research in the previous chapter refutes this claim. The homosexual lifestyle is generally highly promiscuous.

Many male homosexuals readily admit that monogamy and fidelity for them mean something entirely different than what most of society accepts the term to mean. Monogamy, especially for male partners (as lesbians are generally more faithful), can mean remaining "emotionally monogamous" as a couple while still having multiple sexual relations with other men, including casual encounters with strangers.

An article in the *New York Times* four years after same-sex marriage was legalized in Massachusetts highlighted the widely accepted promiscuous nature of many "monogamous" same-sex marriages:

---

[246] Marquardt, E. (2008, January 30). How redefining marriage redefines parenthood. Speech given at the Iona Institute, Dublin, Ireland. Retrieved April 18, 2008 from the Iona Institute for Religion and Society Web site: http://www.ionainstitute.ie/pdfs/Marquardt_talk.pdf

> *While many* [homosexual] *couples want conventional marriages, some are drawing on a creative definition of family forged while living "outside mainstream society," said Joyce Kauffman, a family lawyer and gay activist.... Eric Erbelding and his husband, Michael Peck, both 44, see each other only every other weekend because Mr. Peck works in Pittsburgh. So, Mr. Erbelding said, "Our rule is you can play around because, you know, you have to be practical." Still, Mr. Erbelding said, most married gay couples he knows are "for the most part monogamous, but for maybe a casual three-way."*[247]

Contrary to the assertion of some gay activists, there is no evidence indicating that allowing same-sex marriage diminishes the generally promiscuous lifestyle of homosexuals.

8. Disturbing social impacts already exist where same-sex marriage has been legalized.

The Netherlands was the first country to legalize same-sex marriage in 2001. Several years later, a group of Dutch professors warned in an open letter "about the wisdom of the efforts [in the Netherlands] to deconstruct marriage in its traditional form."[248] The Dutch "increasingly regard marriage as no longer relevant" because they have been persuaded that "marriage is not connected to parenthood and that marriage and cohabitation are equally valid 'lifestyle choices.'"[249]

In 2005, the parliament of France established a commission to study the needs of children and families. The commission considered, among other things, the potential impact of legalizing same-sex marriage in France based on the experience of countries such as Belgium and the Netherlands that had done so. After commission members traveled to these countries and held extensive hearings in France, they strongly recommended that France *not* legalize same-sex marriage, *not* allow same-sex adoptions and *not* encourage or support French same-sex couples to have children by artificial means. Their primary

---

[247] Belluck, P. (2008, June 15). Gay Couples Find Marriage Is a Mixed Bag. *The New York Times*. Retrieved June 15, 2009 from http://www.nytimes.com/2008/06/15/us/15marriage.html
[248] An unofficial translation of this letter can be found at http://www.heritage.org/Research/Family/netherlands statement.cfm.
[249] Ibid.

reason for making these recommendations was to protect children and French society.[250]

9. Societies that have deviated from monogamous man/woman marriage are weakened.

Back in 1935, renowned anthropologist Joseph Daniel Unwin, seeking to prove that man/woman marriage was an irrelevant and harmful cultural institution, was surprised to find exactly the opposite. In an address to the British Psychological Society, Unwin stated:

> ... *If we know what sexual regulations a society has adopted, we can prophesy accurately the pattern of its cultural behavior. ...In human records, there is no case of an absolutely monogamous society failing to display great* [cultural] *energy. I do not know of a case on which great energy has been displayed by a society that has not been absolutely monogamous.*

> ... *If ... a society modifies its sexual regulations, and a new generation is born into a less rigorous* [monogamous] *tradition, its energy decreases. ... If it comes into contact with a more vigorous society, it is deprived of its sovereignty, and possibly conquered.*[251]

Similarly, after studying the history of hundreds of cultures, Pitirim Sorokin, founder and first chair of the Sociology Department at Harvard, found several decades later that virtually all political revolutions that brought about societal collapse were preceded by a sexual revolution in which marriage and family were devalued. He stated:

> *Any considerable change in marriage behavior, any increase in sexual promiscuity and illicit relations, is pregnant with momentous consequences. A sex revolution drastically affects the lives of millions, deeply disturbs the community, and decisively influences the future of society.*[252]

---

[250] Parliamentary Report on the Family and the Rights of Children, (2006, January 27). Retrieved April 18, 2008, from the Institute for the Study of Marriage, Law and Culture Web site: http://www.marriageinstitute.ca/images/PARLIAMENTARY%20REPORT%20ON%20THE%20FAMILY%20AND%20THE%20RIGHTS%20OF%20CHILDREN.pdf

[251] Unwin, J. D. *Sexual regulations and cultural behavior*. Address given to the Medical Section of the British Psychological Society, Library of Congress No. HQ12.U52.

[252] Sorokin, P. A. (1956). *The American Sex Revolution*. Boston: Porter Sargent.

History repeatedly has shown that societies which have deviated from monogamous man/woman marriage are weakened and eventually fall if they do not correct their course.

10. Legalizing same-sex marriage will not eliminate the negative consequences of homosexual behavior.

Polls show that many well-intentioned people support legalizing same-sex marriage because they mistakenly believe homosexuality is genetic, fixed and immutable. Again, research documented in Chapter 4 clearly proves that it is not.

These well-meaning people also believe that by granting homosexual marriage rights we will help homosexuals be less marginalized by society. In other words, they see legalizing same-sex marriage as the compassionate response. However, by legalizing same-sex marriage, we may be exacerbating the very problems we are seeking to solve for adults, while at the same time creating new ones for children.

Researchers studying homosexuality agree that homosexuals experience a disproportionate amount of negative outcomes. These outcomes, which were documented in Chapter 3 (e.g., high rates of domestic violence,[253] suicidal tendencies,[254] lower life expectancy,[255] drug and alcohol problems,[256] etc.), are well-recognized by the gay community and are not generally in dispute. What is being disputed, however, is how to best help homosexuals avoid these negative outcomes.

---

[253] Brand, P. A., & Kidd, A. H. (1986). Frequency of physical aggression in heterosexual and female homosexual dyads. *Psychological Reports, 59*(3), 1307-1313; Waterman, C. K., Dawson, L. J., & Bologna, M. (1989). Sexual coercion in gay male and lesbian relationships: Predictors and implications and support services. *The Journal of Sex Research, 26*(1), 118-124; Owen, S., & Burke, T. W. (2004). An exploration of the prevalence of domestic violence in same-sex relationships. *Psychological Reports, 95*(1), 129-132.

[254] Saunders, J. M., & Valente, S. M. (1987). Suicide risk among gay men and lesbians: A review. *Death Studies, 11*(1), 1-23; Saghir, M. T., Robins, E., Walbran, B., & Gentry, K. A. (1970). Homosexuality. IV. Psychiatric disorders and disability in the female homosexuals. *American Journal of Psychiatry, 127*(2), 147-154; King, M., et al., (2008). A systematic review of mental disorder, suicide, and deliberate self harm in lesbian, gay and bisexual people. *BMC Psychiatry, 18,* 70.

[255] Cameron, P., Cameron, K., & Playfair, W. (1998). Does homosexual activity shorten life? *Psychological Reports 83,* 847-866.

[256] Lewis, C. E., Saghir, M. T., & Robins, E. (1982). Drinking patterns in homosexual and heterosexual women. *Journal of Clinical Psychiatry, 43*(7), 277-279; Craig, R. J. (1987). MMPI-derived prevalence estimates of homosexuality among drug dependent patients. *The International Journal of Addictions, 22*(11), 1139-1145; Fifield, L., Latham, J. D., & Phillips, C. (1977). *Alcoholism in the gay community: The price of alienation, isolation, and oppression.* Los Angeles: The Gay Community Services Center; Fenwick, R. D. & Pillard, R. C. (1978). *Advocate guide to gay health.* New York: E. P. Dutton.

As mentioned earlier, while some claim these outcomes are the result of society's refusal to accept homosexuality as healthy and normal, in European countries where same-sex relations have been more accepted or legalized there is no measurable difference in these negative statistics.[257] This indicates that societal attitudes toward same-sex relations are not likely a significant cause of these negative outcomes, and that marriage rights for homosexuals does not and will not resolve them.

The truly compassionate response is to avoid affirming a lifestyle that carries with it multiple negative outcomes and, instead, offer support to ameliorate these outcomes and to help people change who want to do so.

Suppose a good friend of yours had a smoking addiction. A true friend would encourage him to discontinue his unhealthy behavior. Just because you believe smoking is unhealthy and harmful does not mean you hate people who smoke. You can genuinely care for your friend while at the same time (1) work to ensure the public is protected from secondhand smoke, and (2) encourage him to change. So it is with opposing same-sex marriage. If you are concerned about those who engage in homosexual behavior, it would be better to affirm them as valued individuals rather than affirm their unhealthy lifestyle.

Conclusion

Legalizing same-sex marriage will do much more than simply allow same gender individuals to "marry." By putting an official governmental stamp of approval on same-sex marriage, it will mainstream homosexuality into all aspects of society—including our schools, businesses and churches—and back it up with the force of law.

Legalizing same-sex marriage may not benefit the very group it is intended to help. And history indicates it will harm future generations as well.

---

[257] Sandfort, T. G., et al. (2001). Same-sex sexual behavior and psychiatric disorders: Findings from the Netherlands Mental Health Survey and Incidence (NEMESIS). *Archives of General Psychiatry, 58*(1), 85-91.

Defending traditional marriage is not mean-spirited. It is the legitimate response of the majority of people who want what is best for individuals (including homosexuals), children and our society, and thus want to preserve the proven and essential institution of man/woman marriage. The many negative consequences that would result from legalizing same-sex marriage clearly provide strong reasons for preserving man/woman marriage.

Stand for the Family—What You Can Do

- Become active in supporting laws and policies in your state that strengthen marriage and/or protect the man/woman definition of marriage.
- Work to elect politicians that will stand for man/woman marriage.
- Sign the petition on our Web site in the Family Watch Action Center calling for a federal Constitutional marriage amendment. Invite your personal contacts to sign the petition as well.
- Check out the curriculum in the schools in your area and make sure the schools are not promoting homosexuality or alternative family structures to students.
- Use the talking points in this chapter to promote man/woman marriage in your conversation with others.
- Oppose appointments by our President of any justices to the U.S. Supreme Court who do not support protecting man/woman marriage.
- If you are married, strengthen your marriage, thereby establishing a stable foundation for your children.
- Teach your children the benefits of marriage to them and to society. You may want to share with them the research section on "Outcomes According to Family Structure" in Chapter 3 to help them see the benefits of choosing to marry and stay married.
- Keep informed on the marriage issues by regularly reading *The Family Watch* e-newsletter and respond to any action alerts to support marriage we may send you.

For More Information: To access our free Family Policy Briefs, Ten Reasons to Defend Man/Woman Marriage, Traditional Marriage is Essential for a Healthy Society, and Why the U.S. Must Pass a Federal Amendment, go to the Family Policy Resource Center on our Web site at www.family-watchinternational.org.

Chapter 13

Pornography's Assault on the Family

A while ago, I received a startling phone call from a friend. She asked me if we could shelter her and her children. She feared for her life. She explained that her husband had been addicted to pornography for many years, but that his addiction had escalated to viewing violent pornography. He had just told his wife that he had drawn a picture of her being violently killed.

We took her in and helped her obtain a restraining order against her husband. Outwardly, this man appeared to be a great husband and dad. It would have been difficult for anyone who knew him (other than his wife) to see that he had a serious sexual addiction. His pornography addiction tore apart his family, creating catastrophic consequences for his wife and children. He lost everything.

Another woman did not learn of her husband's pornography addiction until he left her and their child for another woman. She then found out that he had been involved in pornography since he was 14. There had been no pornography in his home growing up; he had accessed it at a friend's house.

One woman recounted that her father-in-law sent her husband pornography before they married, telling him it would help him be faithful to her. Her husband then developed a pornography addiction that became so severe that she had to leave him.

Finally, another friend of ours, after 30 years of marriage, confessed to his wife in tears that he had a pornography addiction, which had escalated to the point that he was compulsively promiscuous. His wife wondered if he had infected her with the HIV/AIDS virus since he confessed he had had sex with numerous prostitutes over the years. Fortunately he sought treatment and the marriage was saved, but not until after much pain and hard work.

It is virtually certain that some of your friends or family members also have been impacted by pornography. Many claim that viewing pornography is a harmless activity that carries no negative consequences to anyone. Victims know differently, and the data show otherwise.

Pornography destroys lives, dreams, marriages and families. It does not discriminate based on race, culture, age, gender, political affiliation, religion or financial status. It is a leading cause of marital and family breakdown today and generates serious problems for individuals, families and societies.

Pornography is Big Business

Virtually every country in the world has been inundated by a steady increase in the availability of pornographic materials in the form of magazines, films and electronic images on the Internet.

By one estimate, worldwide pornography revenues in 2006 alone exceeded $97 billion—more than the revenues of many of the top technology companies combined (e.g., Microsoft, Google, Amazon, eBay, Yahoo! and Apple) and more than the combined revenues of ABC, CBS and NBC.[258] Obviously the sex industry has an enormous interest in legally protecting pornography.[259]

Could there be an undetected pornography problem in your home?

Consider these compelling statistics:

- There are 4.2 million pornographic sites on the Internet (about 12 percent of the total number of existing Web sites).[260]
- There are 68 million daily search engine requests for pornography (25 percent of total search engine requests).[261]
- Thirty-one percent of men surveyed said they had visited sex sites. Eighteen percent of the married men surveyed and 17.8 percent of those who claimed to be Christians had visited sex sites.[262]

---

[258] Pornography statistics. (n.d.). Retrieved June 15, 2009, from Family Safe Media Web site: http://familysafemedia.com/pornography_statistics.html#anchor1

[259] "Forbes Magazine breaks down the global profits this way: adult videos, $20 billion; sex clubs, $5 billion; magazines, $7.5 billion; phone sex, $4.5 billion; escort services, $11 billion; cable, satellite and pay-per-view TV, $2.5 billion; CD-ROMs and DVD ROMs, $1.5 billion; Internet (sales and memberships), $1.5 billion; novelties, $1 billion; and others, $1.5 billion." LaRue, J. (2002). Concerned Women for America. Retrieved June 15, 2009, from http://www.cwfa.org/articledisplay.asp?id=2909&department=LEGAL&categoryid=pornography; With regard to U.S. profits, Internet sales account for a much higher percentage (second only behind adult videos) probably due to the wider availability of computers. See Pornography statistics. (n.d.). Retrieved June 15, 2009, from Family Safe Media Web site: http://familysafemedia.com/pornography_statistics.html#anchor2

[260] Pornography statistics. (n.d.). Retrieved June 15, 2009, from Family Safe Media Web site: http://familysafemedia.com/pornography_statistics.html#anchor4

[261] Pornography statistics. (n.d.). Retrieved June 15, 2009, from Family Safe Web site: http://familysafemedia.com/pornography_statistics.html#anchor4

[262] *Zogby/Focus Survey Reveals Shocking Internet Sex Statistics*, (2000, March 30). Legal Facts: Family Research Council Vol. 2. No. 20.

In 2007, researchers at Brigham Young University surveyed 813 college students and their parents from six schools across the country. Of those surveyed:

- An astounding 86.2 percent reported viewing pornographic material in the past 12 months.
- Of the men surveyed, 48.4 percent reported viewing pornography at least weekly.
- One in five young adult men reported viewing pornography every day or nearly every day.
- Two-thirds of male students said pornography use is acceptable.
- Surprisingly, nearly half of the female students surveyed said viewing pornography is an acceptable way to express one's sexuality.[263]

Dr. Patrick Carnes, a renowned psychologist and expert on sex addiction, estimates that 3 percent to 6 percent of Americans (up to 18 million people) have sex addictions.[264] Other researchers estimate that the total is even higher. Many of these sex addictions are fueled by pornography. It also is becoming more common for girls and women to develop pornography problems.[265] For some, a single exposure can lead to an addiction. For others, it may take repeated exposure.

It is difficult to uncover pornography problems because, as with other addictions, pornography users will go to great lengths to keep their addiction a secret. Denial is common. Facing the truth can be devastating and can cause pain to close family members, especially spouses. Ironically, many involved in pornography do so against their own personal convictions and religious beliefs. This causes serious self-worth and shame issues. Other addicts rationalize that viewing pornography is not harmful.

---

[263] Carroll, J. S., et al. (2008). Generation XXX: Pornography acceptance and use among emerging adults. *Journal of Adolescent Research, 23*(1), 6-30.

[264] *Frequently asked questions.* (n.d.). Retrieved May 16, 2005, from SexHelp.com Web site: http://www.sexhelp.com/addiction_faq.cfm

[265] According to a survey by Zogby International, women represent one out of every three visitors to adult Web sites; 41 percent of women surveyed said they have deliberately viewed or downloaded pornographic pictures and movies; and one out of every six women (including Christians) struggles with an addiction to pornography. Prince, T. (2007, August 9). *Though pornography use skyrockets among lay leaders, pastors in United States, gospel offers hope.* Retrieved June 15, 2009, from the Alabama Baptist Web site: http://www.thealabamabaptist.org//print-edition-article-detail.php?id_art=3316

Family members can become pornography enablers by ignoring signs of addiction and denying a problem exists. To remain in denial is to risk pornography's intrusion in your home and allow its destructive forces to take root.

Pornography Changes its Victims

In a paper published in the *Journal of Family Issues*, researchers reported that after six weeks of viewing pornography, their subjects:

- Developed a "greater acceptance of premarital and extramarital sex."
- Developed "greater tolerance" for multiple sexual partners.
- Enhanced their "belief that male and female promiscuity are natural and that the repression of sexual inclinations poses a health risk."
- Devalued the institution of marriage which appeared "less significant and less viable in the future."
- Had a reduced "desire to have children and promoted the acceptance of male dominance and female servitude."[266]

Even more concerning, other studies by the same researchers indicated that subjects exposed to prolonged pornography usage developed more tolerance for perverse sexual behavior and became desensitized to rape.[267]

Pornography Destroys Marriages

Contrary to popular belief, sexually explicit materials do not enhance marriage or a couple's intimacy—they *destroy* them. Pornography establishes false expectations for looks, intimacy and sex.

Some wives reported that their husbands became angry and disinterested in them when they refused to perform sexual acts depicted in pornography. One woman reported:

> *Although I was careful with my clothes and figure, I found that my husband was increasingly critical of the way I looked. Even when*

---

[266] Zillmann, D., & Bryant, J. (1988). Effects of prolonged consumption of pornography on family values. *Journal of Family Issues, 9*(4), 518-544.

[267] Zillmann, D., & Bryant, J. (1982). Pornography, sexual callousness, and the trivialization of rape. *Journal of Communication, 32*(4), 10-21. Zillmann, D., & Bryant, J. (1984). Effects of massive exposure to pornography. In Malamuth, N. M., & Donnerstein, E. I. (Eds.), *Pornography and sexual aggression*. Orlando: Academic Press.

friends and acquaintances told me I was an attractive woman, I wasn't attractive enough to compete with eternally young, surgically altered models. Jack also expressed irritation when I was uncomfortable with some of the sexual practices he'd seen in pornographic magazines. In the end, he lost all interest in me as a sexual partner. This had a devastating impact on my view of my worth as a woman. It created such despair in me that I began to let my appearance go. At last, I looked the way his rejection made me feel—totally unlovely.[268]

Psychiatrist Jeffrey Satinover, MS, MD, who has treated many patients for pornography addictions, explained during a Senate hearing:

The pornography addict soon forgets about everything and everyone else in favor of an ever more elusive sexual jolt. He will eventually be able to find it only among other 'junkies' like himself, and he will place at risk his career, his friends, his family, everything of value. He will indulge his habit anywhere and everywhere, at any time. No one, no matter how highly placed, is immune. And like all other addicts, the pornography addict will lie to cover it up, heedless of risk or cost to himself or to others.[269]

Clearly, pornography is an enemy to marriage and, thus, an enemy to the family!

Pornography Desensitizes the User to Deviant Sexual Behavior

When a person regularly downloads sexually explicit images or depictions of sexual acts into their brain through pictures, videos or movies, the chances that he or she will think about those images and then eventually act on some of them is high. It can be a short trip from viewing pornography to later acting it out with a consenting person or even by force.

Like drug users, addicts need harder and harder pornography in order to be aroused. Material initially perceived as revolting, shocking,

---

[268] Hall, L. (1996). *An affair of the mind.* Carol Stream: Tyndale House Publishers.
[269] Satinover, J. (2004, November 18). *The science behind pornography addiction.* Testimony given at a hearing of the United States Senate Committee on Commerce, Science and Transportation. Retrieved June 16, 2009, from http://commerce.senate.gov/public/index.cfm?FuseAction=Hearings.Testimony&Hearing_ID=e8088f9f-d8d2-4e82-b012-46337c6f9456&Witness_ID=f9da1f44-63e9-4288-966c-9cae2242977a

taboo-breaking, immoral or illegal can eventually become acceptable. In search of a new "high," the addict often turns to pornography depicting sexual aggression or violence. Once an addict has reached the "acting out" stage, individuals nearly always experience a serious erosion of personal relationships and values.

Clinical psychologist Dr. Victor Cline explains that there are four progressive levels that can develop after being exposed to pornography: addiction, escalation, desensitization, and then acting out sexually.[270]

Addiction

|

Escalation

|

Desensitization

|

Acting Out Sexually

Dr. Cline further explains that pornography addictions can escalate into many types of unwanted sexual illnesses:

"I have been treating sexual violence victims and perpetrators for 13 years. I have not treated a single case of sexual violence that did not involve pornography."

As a clinical psychologist, I have treated, over the years, approximately 350 sex addicts, sex offenders, or other individuals (96% male) with sexual illnesses. This includes many types of unwanted compulsive sexual acting-out, plus such things as child molestation, exhibitionism, voyeurism, sadomasochism, fetishism, and rape. With several exceptions, pornography has been a major or minor contributor or facilitator in the acquisition of their deviation or sexual addiction.[271]

Dr. Mary Anne Layden, director of education at the University of Pennsylvania Health System, pointed out, "I have been treating sexual

[270] Cline, V. (n.d.). *The effects of porn addiction.* Retrieved February 17, 2009, from AskMaple.com Web site: http://www.askmaple.com/porn-addiction.html.

[271] Cline, V. *Pornography's effects on adults and children.* (n.d.). Retrieved June 16, 2009, from Morality in Media Web site: http://www.obscenitycrimes.org/clineart.cfm

violence victims and perpetrators for 13 years. I have not treated a single case of sexual violence that did not involve pornography."[272]

One study showed that "males who are exposed to a great deal of erotica before the age of 14 are more sexually active and engage in more varied sexual behaviors as adults than is true for males not so exposed."[273] Another study revealed that of 932 sex addicts, 90 percent of the males and 77 percent of the females studied reported that pornography played a significant role in their addiction.[274] Yet another study found that rapists are 15 times more likely than non-offenders to have had exposure to hardcore pornography during childhood.[275]

More than two decades ago, a number of women, men and children testified before an Attorney General's Commission on Pornography. The following are disturbing excerpts from these testimonies that contain numerous accounts of sexual molestation, rape, torture and more—all fueled by pornography. I do not recommend reading the report. I became physically ill reading just parts of it. Here are a few of the milder excerpt (Skip past the next three bullet points if you prefer not to read these even milder firsthand experiences):

> *Rapists are 15 times more likely than non-offenders to have had exposure to hardcore pornography during childhood.*

- *The incest started at the age of eight. I did not understand any of it and did not feel that it was right. My dad would try to convince me that it was o.k. He would find magazines with articles and/or pictures that would show fathers and daughters and/or mothers, brothers and sisters having sexual intercourse. (Mostly fathers and daughters.) He would say that if it was published in magazines that it had to be all right because magazines could not publish lies.*

---

[272] *The effects of pornography and sexual messages.* (n.d.). Retrieved June 16, 2009, from National Coalition for the Protection of Children & Families Web site: http://www.nationalcoalition.org/effects.asp

[273] Davis, K. E., & Braucht, G. N. (1970). Exposure to pornography, character and sexual deviance. *Technical Reports of the Commission on Obscenity and Pornography, 7.*

[274] Carnes, P. (1991). *Don't call it love: Recovery from sexual addictions.* New York: Bantam.

[275] Goldstein, M. J., Kant, H. S., & Harman, J. J. (1974). *Pornography and sexual deviance.* Berkeley: University of California Press.

- *I have had my hands tied, my feet tied, my mouth taped to teach me big girls don't cry. He would tell me I was very fortunate to have a father that would teach me the facts of life. Many of the pictures he had were of women in bondage, with their hands tied, feet tied and their mouth taped.*

- *I understand pornography to be a force in creating violence in the gay community. I was battered by my ex-lover who used pornography. The pornography, straight and gay, I had been exposed to, helped convince me that I had to accept his violence and helped keep me in that destructive relationship. Then one time, he branded me. I still have a scar.*[276]

There also were reports from those who had been kidnapped or held captive during the production of pornographic materials.[277]

There is an undeniable correlation between pornography addiction and the commission of sexual crimes and violence. A number of serial killers, including the notorious Ted Bundy who confessed to 30 brutal murders, have stated that pornography fueled their crimes.

> "Research showed a 100 percent correlation between those who sought out child pornography and those who abuse children."

Moreover, Freda Briggs, a former professor at the University of South Australia, indicated that her "research showed a 100 percent correlation between those who sought out child pornography and those who abuse children."[278]

Yet, for all its demonstrated harm, pornography is sold freely and legally throughout America, poisoning minds and encouraging adultery, incest and rape.

---

[276] *Victimization.* (1986) Attorney General's Commission on Pornography, Part 4, Chapter 1. Retrieved June 16, 2009, from http://www.porn-report.com/401-victimization.htm

[277] Ibid.

[278] Secor, S. (2004, October). *A growing trend: teen pornography.* Retrieved June 16, 2009, from Morality in Media Web site: http://www.obscenitycrimes.org/espforparents/espforparents2004-10.cfm (citing Doherty, B. (2004, October). No such thing as "just looking," psychologically. *Canberra Times.* Retrieved June 16, 2009, from Stop Demand Foundation Web site: http://www.stopdemand.org/afawcs0112878/ID=25/newsdetails.html).

Pornography Can Be as Addictive as Drugs

In response to erotic stimuli, addictive chemicals called "erototoxins" are produced by the body and released in the brain. Scientific research is now confirming what therapists have recognized for many years:

> *The repeated viewing of pornographic images creates a chemical addiction in the viewer. That addiction becomes so powerful that it overrides the cognitive functions of the brain that enable a human being to make judgments, to inhibit impulsive action, or to resist engaging in conduct that will bring harm to themselves or others. Pornography addicts can become enslaved to the chemical cocktail of endogenous drugs that are produced by the body and released by the brain when it stores pornographic images.*[279]

> *The repeated viewing of pornographic images creates a chemical addiction in the viewer.*

The pornography addict seeks the flood of "feel good" chemicals similar to those created by cocaine, heroin and other drugs. So pornography addiction is not just a moral or self-control issue, but a true physiological addiction. Like other addictions, if left untreated it will escalate.

Judith Reisman, Ph.D., President of The Institute for Media Education and a specialist in the addictive properties of sexually explicit images, gave the following testimony at a Senate hearing on pornography:

> *Thanks to the latest advances in neuroscience, we now know that emotionally arousing images imprint and alter the brain, triggering an instant, involuntary, but lasting, biochemical memory trail. ... Once our neurochemical pathways are established they are difficult or impossible to delete. ... Brain scientists tell us that in 3/10 of a second a visual image passes from the eye through the brain, and*

---

[279] Harmer, J. L. (2007). *The sex industrial complex.* Salt Lake City: The Lighted Candle Society.

whether or not one wants to, the brain is structurally changed and memories are created.[280]

In the same Senate hearing, psychiatrist Dr. Jeffrey Satinover described the similarities between pornography and drugs. He noted: "The underlying nature of an addiction to pornography is chemically nearly identical to a heroin addiction: Only the delivery system is different. ..."[281]

Upon viewing pornography, the mind records the graphic images which can be replayed over and over again at will—or against your will.

Pornography is Damaging to Children

It is estimated that at least 95 percent of all teens in the United States have been exposed to pornography (intentionally or unintentionally), and 9 out of 10 children between the ages of 8 and 16 have been exposed to pornography on the Internet.[282] One survey indicated that 47 percent of school-age children receive e-mails with links to X-rated Web sites daily.[283]

It is estimated that at least 95 percent of all teens in the United States have been exposed to pornography (intentionally or unintentionally), and 9 out of 10 children between the ages of 8 and 16 have been exposed to pornography on the Internet.

Early exposure to pornography can have disastrous results for children. A 2001 report revealed that over half of all sex offenders in a particular state were adolescents, and some felony sexual assaults were being perpetrated by children as young as 8 years old.[284] Many young sex offenders say they were acting out what they had seen depicted in pornography.

---

[280] Reisman, J. (2004, November 18). *The science behind pornography addiction and the effects of addiction on families and communities.* Testimony given at a hearing of the United States Senate Committee on Commerce, Science and Transportation. Retrieved June 16, 2009, from http://commerce.senate.gov/public/index.cfm?FuseAction=Hearings.Testimony&Hearing_ID=e8088f9f-d8d2-4e82-b012-46337c6f9456&Witness_ID=29ddac76-ab1c-4fcc-8fdb-94ac0061546c

[281] Supra note 29.

[282] Ashcroft, J. (2002, June 6). Prepared statement at National Prosecutors' Symposium on Obscenity, Columbia, SC.

[283] *Symantec survey reveals more than 80 percent of children using email receive inappropriate spam daily.* (2003, June 9). Symantec News Release. Retrieved June 16, 2009, from http://www.symantec.com/press/2003/n030609a.html

[284] Child on Child. Transcript of Special Report. (2001, May 7). KSL TV. Retrieved June 16, 2009, from http://web.ksl.com/TV/series2001/child.htm

Where do children get pornography? They get it from various sources, many of which are readily available to them: the Internet/computers, magazines, iPods, cell phones, movies, videos, entertainment in hotel rooms and their TV at home.

A friend recently bought a prepaid phone for her 12 year old. She was dismayed to learn that she had supplied her son with a pornography delivery mechanism. Unbeknownst to her, the phone also had *unfiltered* Internet access and easily could send and receive inappropriate photos. She had never thought of a cell phone that way before. Unfortunately, we have to understand and guard against the negative uses of technology. "Sexting," which is a new term used to describe sending nude or suggestive pictures by cell phone, is increasingly becoming a problem among teens. Many children access pornography through their friends. Other children and teenagers are exposed to pornography after stumbling across pornographic magazines hidden in their home by another family member with a secret addiction.

Sadly, as pointed out earlier, your child is not safe from pornography even in the public schools. Some schools show graphic sexual videos under the banner of sex education, art, or under the guise of studying human sexuality.[285]

Your child is not safe from pornography even in the public schools. Some schools show graphic sexual videos under the banner of sex education, art, or under the guise of studying human sexuality.

Gateway Pornography

One of the catalysts for sexual addictions is what can be called "gateway pornography." Most young children and even teenagers are naturally repulsed by hard-core, sexually explicit images. The individuals involved in the pornography industry are clever. In order to get their customers hooked at an early age, which will maximize revenues over a person's lifetime, the pornography industry starts with "soft

---

[285] A class at Arizona State University, "Sexuality in the Media," examined issues related to explicit sexual representations in pornography, art and cinema. Topics included the representation of the male and female body and gay and lesbian sexuality. Movies shown in class depicted sexual acts, including anal sex. One of the required books was *Hard core: Power, Pleasure, and the Frenzy of the Visible.* The warning in the class description read, "This class includes sexually explicit materials and anyone offended or disturbed by viewing, reading, or discussing such materials should not enroll in the class."

core" or "gateway" pornography. These images are not legally classified as pornography, but they can serve as a catalyst to gently lead children into harder pornography.

Parents should be aware that some pornography addicts report that their addiction started as a child after viewing seemingly innocuous lingerie ads in magazines and newspapers, suggestive pictures in sports magazines (like the swimsuit edition of *Sports Illustrated*), or nude pictures in magazines like *National Geographic*.

Adults, and especially women, might not consider such things to be sexually arousing. However, a 13-year-old boy with raging hormones may have a completely different perspective. Some families remove suggestive ads from the newspaper before bringing them into the house because, to their children, those ads can have the same effect as explicit pornography.

TV sitcoms and shows with sexual themes and sexually suggestive commercials can create improper thoughts and lodge images in a child's mind that may stay with them into adulthood.

In addition, love scenes in PG, PG-13 and R-rated movies that may not be sexually stimulating to parents might have a powerful impact on a maturing adolescent. Likewise, TV sitcoms and shows with sexual themes and sexually suggestive commercials can create improper thoughts and lodge images in a child's mind that may stay with them into adulthood. Video games also should be screened, as many contain pornography as well.

Immunizing Your Children

So how do we immunize our children against ever-present pornography and help them avoid its destructive effects? Parents, talk to your children about their sexuality. Don't ignore the fact that your children are maturing. Explain the changes they are experiencing and teach them how to manage them.

Teach children that sex in and of itself is not wrong, sinful or bad—that sex in the right context, in a faithful married relationship, can be beautiful and wonderful. Teach children that youth develop sexual feelings as they mature and those feelings are normal and healthy. Teach them how to control and channel these urges appropriately so that they can be saved for marriage.

Children need to be forewarned that they will experience body changes, hormone rushes, wet dreams (boys), etc. and that this is perfectly normal. At the same time, parents can instill in their children confidence that they have the power to control these urges that someday will enable them to have children and build their own stable families. Fill your children's minds with good literature and music, and keep them busy with constructive activities.

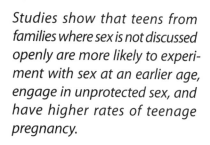

Studies show that teens from families where sex is not discussed openly are more likely to experiment with sex at an earlier age, engage in unprotected sex, and have higher rates of teenage pregnancy.

If parents do not teach their children about sex, their children may seek less worthy sources to learn from. Studies show that teens from families where sex is not discussed openly are more likely to experiment with sex at an earlier age, engage in unprotected sex, and have higher rates of teenage pregnancy.[286]

It is never too late to begin helping your children understand their sexuality and to teach them to save sex for someone they really love and respect, and thus fully commit themselves to in the sacred vows of marriage.

Family Entertainment?

"But it has great morals!" Has anyone ever used that argument to try to convince you to watch an inappropriate movie or TV show? Don't fall into that trap. And don't buy the "It will initiate a great discussion with your kids" argument. I had a school administrator try to use that one on me when I complained about some highly inappropriate literature in an English class (it had references to bestiality). Since there is plenty of

[286] Regnerus, M. D., & Luchies, L. B. (2006). The parent-child relationship and opportunities for adolescents' first sex. *Journal of Family Issues, 27*(2), 159-183; Dittus, P. J., & Jaccard, J. (2000). Adolescents' perceptions of maternal disapproval of sex: Relationship to sexual outcomes. *Journal of Adolescent Health, 26*(4), 268-278; Whitaker, D. J., & Miller, K. S. (2000). Parent-adolescent discussions about sex and condoms: Impact on peer influences of sexual risk behavior. *Journal of Adolescent Research, 15*(2), 251-273; Aspy, C. B., et al. (2007). Parental communication and youth sexual behaviour. *Journal of Adolescence, 30*(3), 449-466.

wonderful literature and wholesome entertainment available, there simply is no need to drag ourselves or our families through a filthy gutter to find moral messages.

My husband and I do not allow our children to watch a PG-13 movie unless we first review its content. Every time we have broken that rule we have regretted it. I highly recommend becoming a member of screenit.com for about 30 dollars a year. Screenit.com's reviews will tell you *everything* objectionable in a movie (without the graphic images, of course). The service's standard for objectionable material is very high.

> *Since there is plenty of wonderful literature and wholesome entertainment available, there simply is no need to drag ourselves or our families through a filthy gutter to find moral messages.*

When my daughter was 13 she begged me one evening to let her see a movie with her friends. I said, "Not until we look it up on screenit.com." She was not happy. The movie was about to start and her friends were on their way.

After reading the review, I told her I could not approve it. She became very upset and gave me the usual tirade about how "everyone else's" parents were letting them see it, and "so and so's parent's approved it." We were getting nowhere.

Suddenly I had an idea. I said, "You are 13, and this is a PG-13 movie. I am going to let you make this decision, but not until you have read the review on screenit.com." Excited that I had given her the lead, she rushed to the computer and pulled up the review.

A few minutes later, she humbly approached me and said she was not going to the movie. She was surprised at all the bad things that the review revealed, and she agreed it would be a bad idea to support the movie by buying a ticket.

We Can't Protect Children from Everything

Despite our best efforts, our children will be exposed to inappropriate things in their schools, on the beaches, in their friends' homes, and even driving along the road. As parents, we need to prepare our children for this reality and help them process the inappropriate content they will see and hear within a framework of values they understand.

When they are exposed to entertainment with themes that discuss and even glorify adultery, promiscuous sex, or other inappropriate sexual activities, point out how right is being portrayed as wrong and vice-versa. Use these opportunities as "teaching moments" to discuss the "why" behind your family's standards and values.

"For Adults Only"

One day I picked up a PG-13 movie at a video store. It looked decent, based on its cover and description, but the owner warned me that the movie was "rough." When I asked what she meant, she replied it contained sexual scenes and warned me not to watch it around children. I told her that, in our family, if it wasn't safe enough for my kids, then parents probably shouldn't be watching it either. She paused and then replied, "I never thought about it that way before."

This principle applies not only to PG-13 movies but to anything with sexually graphic content. There is a widely held view that sexually explicit materials are only harmful for children because they are not mature enough to "handle" them, and since married adults already engage in sex, supposedly there is no harm in adults watching explicit movies.

However, the harmful effects and the addictive nature of pornography do not distinguish between the young and the old, the married or the unmarried. Remember, studies show that many of the adults who have been convicted of rape, sexual assault or molestation report heavy pornography use, and many are acting out the pornography they have seen. Pornography is dangerous to everyone.

Don't Put Your Head in the Sand!

Years ago, my then 7-year-old daughter came home from school one day with a notice informing us that lice had been discovered among some students. We were asked to check our children's heads. My first thought was, "Only dirty people get lice. I'm glad we don't have to worry about that." And I promptly threw the notice away.

Several weeks later, I noticed yellow spots clinging to my hair, and sure enough, my hair was filled with lice eggs. I literally panicked. When

I checked my children, to my horror my daughter's long blonde hair was filled with lice eggs, and I found a live one in my son's hair!

How could I have been so stupid? Why had I ignored the warning, thinking our family was too good to get lice? I was humbled to say the least. How could this be happening to me and my family? After all, we showered regularly.

I didn't want to let anyone know. I knew what I would think of someone who had lice. However, I soon learned that lice is a widespread problem in the United States and, in fact, I read on a Web site that lice is one of the most common childhood ailments next to the common cold.

Because of its secrecy, lice infestations are much more pervasive than people think. And, so it is with pornography!

So why didn't I know this? Because having lice is kept a big secret. When families get infected, they don't want anyone to know for fear of being shunned. Because of its secrecy, lice infestations are much more pervasive than people think. And, so it is with pornography!

After a massive decontamination of clothes, bed sheets, and so forth, I found myself afraid to check my family's heads again because I didn't want to find that the problem had reoccurred. I wanted to think it just went away with one hair treatment. But it didn't. It came back. So it is with pornography treatment. Though it is clearly possible to be cured of such an addiction, the road to recovery can be long and difficult and almost always requires professional and/or spiritual counseling and family support.

Pornography problems, like lice, are widespread and usually kept secret. One may not discover the problem until it is very serious. Please do not ignore this warning to "check" your children and your spouse for any pornography problems! You may fear the outcome, but just like a lice infestation, the impact will be worse the longer you wait to find out.

Determine if there is a Pornography Problem in Your Home

Sometimes the only way to detect the problem is to ask probing questions of your spouse and your children. I have created a list of interview questions that can be found on our Web site (Go to family-watchinternational.org and click on "Family Policy Resource Center," then "Pornography," and then "Interview Questions.") These are sensitive questions and should be considered as guidelines only. They should be adjusted according to the maturity of the individual so that seeds are not planted prematurely.

It may take several interviews before a family member with a problem discloses anything to you. It is best to hold periodic interviews where pornography is only one of the issues discussed. Your family members may have avoided this dreaded disease for many years, but you need to make sure that remains the case.

What to Do if You Discover a Pornography Problem

If you discover that a family member has a pornography problem:

1. ***Reach out with love and support.*** They probably are living with feelings of guilt and shame, and will be devastated that you know about their problem. You may feel angry, hurt and disappointed, which is natural, but those feelings will not help your loved one overcome his or her problem.

2. ***Get help.*** If the family member has tried unsuccessfully to stop on his own, he will probably need outside intervention—professional counseling and, where possible, spiritual counseling.

3. ***Understand.*** Overcoming a pornography addiction is usually a long process that can include relapses. Realize that your loved one may have lost control and will need all the emotional support he can get to regain self-mastery, self-worth, etc.

Five Steps to Safeguard Your Family Against Pornography

1. Teach your children what pornography is and why they need to avoid it. Talk to your children regularly about pornography (including gateway pornography) and teach your family values with regard to sexuality. Remember to take into account the sexual maturity of your children. You may want to talk to them about it annually and adjust your discussion to their age level.

2. Discuss how to handle accidental viewing. Discuss with family members what to do when accidental exposure happens and help them establish a plan. For example, if pornography pops up on the computer screen despite any filtering systems you may use, teach them to immediately turn off the monitor and call a parent for help. Teach them to report to you immediately if a teacher, a friend, a neighbor or a family member asks them to view any type of pornography.

I have been surprised by the number of inappropriate things my children have encountered by chance in school and at social functions that I would have never known about had they not told me. Keep an open channel of communication on sex and sexuality. Explain that they will never be punished for telling you about an incident with exposure to pornography because you only want to help.

3. Conduct regular "head checks." Interview family members regularly to find out what is in their minds and hearts. Do not assume that just because someone is a "good" person with high moral standards that they do not have temptations or a pornography problem. Churches around the world are finding that more of their "good" members are increasingly becoming exposed, and too often addicted, to pornography.

4. Clean up your home! Realize that at least gateway pornography likely is lurking in your home somewhere. Remove it. You can enlist your children and your spouse in the process. Some of these steps may seem extreme, but the alternative may be a potential pornography addiction that your child could struggle with for years to come. The axiom "an ounce of prevention is worth a pound of cure" certainly applies here.

- Go through your videos, DVDs, music, magazines, computer games, video games, newspaper ads and so forth and throw away anything that can be sexually arousing.
- Ask your children to show you anything inappropriate on the computer and delete it. You might be surprised by what they find and consider inappropriate. Have you ever reviewed MySpace. com? Our teenage children made a decision not to use that social networking site based on the content and images some of their acquaintances posted.

- Sort through your books (including romance novels) and throw away any that portray sex outside of marriage as good or that are sexually explicit in any way.
- Block inappropriate TV channels or shows and get rid of services that offer them. MTV, for example, clearly is a gateway to pornography.

5. Safeguard your computers. If you have not done so already, install effective filters on all of your computers immediately. Do not allow computers with Internet access in the bedroom, and make sure computers are kept in a public place where the screen can be easily seen when you walk in the room. I recommend an excellent free filter which can be downloaded from www.k9webprotection.com. But please realize that kids are geniuses when it comes to getting around filters, so do not rely entirely on them.

Establish computer safety rules. (For a list of computer rules that we use in our home, go to the "Family Policy Resource Center" on our Web site, click on "Pornography," and then click on "Family Computer Rules.") You may want to establish a rule of no Internet use when a parent is not home.

Check the Internet history on your computer regularly to see where members of your family have visited, and make sure they are not erasing the history in the browser of your computer to hide intentional exposure.

Make sure that as a parent you know the passwords to your children's computers and e-mail accounts so that you can check to make sure the computer is being used properly. Establish the concept early on in your home that Internet use is a privilege, not a private activity nor a right.

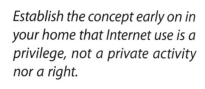

Establish the concept early on in your home that Internet use is a privilege, not a private activity nor a right.

Stand for the Family—What You Can Do

"To be silent is to approve."[287] Once we have protected our homes, we need to do what we can to protect our communities. There are many

---

[287] Hamilton, J. (2002). *To strengthen the family.* Bountiful, UT: Positive Values Publishing.

good people and organizations that have worked effectively to clean up their neighborhoods and the stores in their communities.

Sometimes all it takes is for one person to object to inappropriate material, and the store owners will remove it. Pornography expert Joan Hibbert Hamilton suggests that once you find something inappropriate in the community, do not call it pornography as there is too much controversy surrounding its definition. Instead, identify it as "inappropriate for children" and request that it be removed.[288] At a minimum, request that the materials be covered up or relocated out of the view of children. There is power in numbers, so reach out to neighbors and friends, and invite them to join you in the effort to safeguard your community.

Patronize businesses that refuse to sell pornography and let them know why you are supporting them. Inform businesses that refuse to remove pornography that you will no longer support them and tell them why. Encourage others to do the same. Finally, when traveling, choose to stay in pornography-free hotels. These are just a few things each of us can do to eliminate pornography in our homes and our communities.

To read our Family Policy Brief on pornography, which contains a summary of the important facts outlined in this chapter, go to the Family Policy Resource Center on our Web site at www.familywatchinternational. org. Remember, in the Family Policy Resource Center, you can find "Family Computer Rules," which will help you establish safe guidelines for your family's computer usage and the pornography "Interview Questions."

---

[288] Ibid.

Chapter 14

The Assault on Religion

When voters in California passed Proposition 8 to define marriage as only between a man and a woman, there was a huge backlash against the various religious denominations that were behind that victory. Church buildings were vandalized and pro-homosexual blogs were filled with hateful threats toward the various sects that supported Prop 8.

Ironically, with these threats, assaults and vandalism, homosexual rights activists displayed the very intolerance they claim to be fighting against.

A cry for "separation of church and state" was heard around the nation as homosexual activists labeled anyone who supported man/woman marriage as religious bigots and demanded that any churches supporting Prop 8 lose their tax-exempt status.

Legal scholars predict that the clash between religious freedom and those pushing for sexual rights is only going to get worse. Unfortunately, as the skirmishes worsen, it appears religion will be undermined. As such controversies have reached the courts, judges increasingly have sided with sexual rights activists at the expense of religious freedom.

If you destroy faith in God and belief in an ordered universe with moral absolutes, then sexual restraints and accountability for actions to a higher being no longer exist, and sexual chaos can ensue.

Undermining Religion

If you were bent on destroying the family, religion would have to be one of your first targets. Why? Because the teachings of almost all religions promote and protect marriage and the traditional two-parent, mother/father family.

Convince people that there is no God, and we become no more accountable for our actions than animals. Eliminate the religious motivations that channel sex into marriage, or that encourage spouses to be faithful to each other, and you are well on your way to sexual anarchy.

In other words, if you destroy faith in God and belief in an ordered universe with moral absolutes, then sexual restraints and accountability for actions to a higher being no longer exist, and sexual chaos can ensue. Research shows that people who believe in God and practice a religion regularly, tend to have stronger marriages and families. So a successful attack on religion significantly weakens both of these institutions.

Teachings on Marriage and Family From Major World Religions

For centuries, all of the world's major religions have promoted sexual morality, marriage between a man and a woman, and the traditional family. As a result, people of faith have been, and typically continue to be, the first line of defense in the assault on the traditional family. However, a concerning development is occurring as some churches have considered admitting openly gay clergy or recognizing same-sex marriage. Yet, as you likely are aware, those policy decisions have not been made without serious controversy and, so far anyway, the religions that have succumbed to this trend are the exception rather than the rule.

Protecting the traditional family effectively unites cultures and faiths across the world. I personally have worked in the family cause with Jews, Muslims and Christians of various churches including Evangelicals, Catholics, Protestants, Mormons, Pentecostals, members of the Unification Church, and members of the Bahá'í faith. Notice the consistency in support for man/woman marriage, the traditional family, and the bearing of children in the following excerpts from religious texts of the world's major religions:

Christians and Jews alike espouse that:

> ... *a man leave his father and his mother, and shall cleave unto his wife: and they shall be one flesh* (Genesis 2:24);

that couples should,

> ... *be fruitful, and multiply, and replenish the earth* (Genesis 1:28);

and that,

> ... *children are an heritage of the LORD: and the fruit of the womb is his reward. Happy is the man that hath his quiver full of them.* (Psalms 127:3, 5)

The teachings of Islam point out:

> *It is He Who created you from a single person, and made his mate of like nature, in order that he might dwell with her (in love) (Sura 7:189). He it is who created you from a single person (Adam), and then He has created from him his wife, in order that he might enjoy the pleasure of living with her ...* (Quran 7:189).

The Bahá'í teachings on marriage call it a "fortress for well-being and salvation," and they place marriage and the family as the foundation of human society. Husbands and wives are expected to be absolutely faithful to each other. The key purpose of Bahá'í marriage—beyond physical, intellectual and spiritual companionship—is to bear children. Bahá'ís view childrearing not only as a source of great joy and reward, but as a sacred obligation.[289]

The Church of Jesus Christ of Latter-day Saints (Mormon) teaches,

> *... that marriage between a man and a woman is ordained of God and that the family is central to the Creator's plan for the eternal destiny of His children, ... that the sacred powers of procreation are to be employed only between man and woman, lawfully wedded as husband and wife. ... Children are entitled to birth within the bonds of matrimony, and to be reared by a father and a mother who honor marital vows with complete fidelity.*[290]

As these passages illustrate, the world's major religions fully understand how important the family is to our wellbeing. Sadly, as noted earlier, some religions have started to stray from these age-old teachings and have begun to adopt anti-family ideologies.

Attack on God or a Creator

Teachings which undermine religious beliefs that support the traditional family are becoming more accepted. Among those teachings and philosophies are "moral relativism," which means rejecting any universal and/or fixed moral truths and "secularism," which means rejecting any

---

[289] Bahá'u'lláh, *Bahá'í Prayers*, p.105.
[290] *The Family: A Proclamation to the World*. (1995). The Church of Jesus Christ of Latter-day Saints, para. 7.

influence of religious or moral values in public affairs. Atheism, or the belief that there is no God, also works against the traditional family, as does the new concept of "tolerance," which has been redefined as accepting anything and everything as good and normal.

To one degree or another, all of these dogmas teach there are no absolute truths. Religious viewpoints or moral absolutes are dismissed as mythology, fantasy or the effects of frenzied minds and are increasingly ridiculed by the media, the entertainment industry and the "cultural elites." Therefore, those who profess these dogmas typically teach that all beliefs and lifestyles are acceptable and of equal value (even if they are contradictory), so long as they do not directly harm others.

These dogmas also demand that society accept and even promote a variety of "family forms." A new view of God under such dogmas paves the way for acceptance of things that used to be called "sin" or "morally wrong." Those who espouse such beliefs work to make "intolerance" the greatest societal sin of our day.

Here are some common distortions perpetuated worldwide:

- If there is a God, he doesn't care what we do as long as we're happy. God is love, and he will not punish us for sinning.
- All beliefs and lifestyle choices are acceptable; it is arrogant, judgmental and intolerant to assert otherwise.
- Traditional religious beliefs and values (e.g., basic morality) are outdated notions that infringe on personal liberty.
- One cannot love the sinner, as many religions require, without also tolerating and accepting his sins.
- In other words, to engage in sinful behavior is not a sin, but to call such behavior a sin is itself a sin.

Ironically, today it is increasingly common to be called "unchristian" for expressing one's Christian beliefs on family issues. Secularists twist Christian doctrines, such as the admonition to love one another, to support their secular agenda. They claim that criticizing lifestyles or another's actions is sinful, hateful, unloving and, thus, unchristian, even though the Biblical Jesus always condemned sin while at the same time advocating love for the sinner.

Attack on Religious Expression

A prevalent anti-family/anti-religion strategy is to criticize, restrict and, where possible, criminalize public religious expression. You are likely aware of the various attempts in the United States, the bastion of religious liberty, to remove God completely from government and the public square. The ACLU and other groups are working systematically to remove all religious symbols from our society.

Lawsuits have been filed across the country to remove such things as the Ten Commandments, crosses and traditional Christmas symbols from public places. Lawsuits also have been filed to remove the words "under God" from the Pledge of Allegiance, and "In God we Trust" from our currency. "Christmas vacation" has become "winter break;" and, due to concerns about offending customers, retailers now have "holiday sales" rather than "Christmas sales," even though Christmas is a holiday celebrating the birth of Christ, the founder of Christianity.

An atheist, Michael Newdow, filed a lawsuit arguing that his daughter had been forced to recite the words "under God" in the Pledge of Allegiance in her school. He claimed this violated her conscience as well as his. The words "under God" were inserted into the pledge in 1954 by an act of Congress at the height of the Cold War to contrast this country's belief in God with the Soviet Union's embrace of atheism.[291]

In a ruling that set off an uproar across the country, the United States Court of Appeals for the Ninth Circuit in 2002 agreed with Newdow and, by a narrow margin, ruled that the Pledge of Allegiance constituted government mandated prayer and thus coercion of religious observance.[292] Had this decision not been challenged, the words "under God" would have been removed from the Pledge of Allegiance recited in public schools in the Western states covered by the Ninth Circuit's jurisdiction. And, of much greater significance, such a decision would have paved the way for the removal of *all* references to God in the public sphere.

Fortunately, the school district appealed the case to the U.S. Supreme Court, and a narrow majority reversed the federal court of

---

[291] 100 Cong. Rec. 1700 (1954).

[292] *Newdow v. U.S. Congress*, 292 F. 3d 597, 612 (9th Cir. U.S. Ct. of Appeals 2002). The 9th Circuit basically ruled that both the school district's policy requiring recitation of the pledge and the statute that inserted the words "under God" in the pledge (Act of June 14, 1954, ch. 297, 68 Stat. 249) violated the clause in the First Amendment of the U.S. Constitution that prohibited Congress from making a law "respecting an establishment of religion."

appeals' decision on a technicality. They found that the father did not have a sufficient interest or injury to challenge the Pledge of Allegiance that was being recited by his daughter who had no objections to the practice herself. This means, from a strict legal perspective, that the issue is left unresolved.

The comments of some of the more conservative Supreme Court Justices during the oral arguments, however, are very encouraging and instructive. In front of the Supreme Court, Newdow proclaimed: "I am an atheist. I don't believe in God. And every school morning my child is asked to stand up, face that flag, put her hand over her heart, and say that her father is wrong." (The daughter and her mother, who is not married to Newdow, stated they had no problem with the words "under God" in the Pledge of Allegiance, and both are Christians.) Newdow also claimed that the inclusion of the words "under God" in the Pledge of Allegiance now serve to divide the nation.

Former Chief Justice William Rehnquist asked Newdow: "Do we know what the vote was in Congress apropos of divisiveness to adopt the 'under God' phrase?" Newdow correctly answered that Congress had adopted the phrase unanimously: "There was no objection." The Chief Justice then countered, "Well, that doesn't sound divisive." Newdow's response: "That's only because no atheist can get elected to public office," as if that were relevant to his lawsuit.

As Justice Rehnquist noted in a separate opinion from the majority, that there are many evidences which "strongly suggest that our national culture allows for public recognition of our Nation's religious history and character."[293] One of these evidences is the longstanding statement "In God We Trust" on our currency.

Also, many U.S. presidents have invoked the name of God in critical times, including Abraham Lincoln who used the very same words "under God" in his famous Gettysburg Address in 1863.[294] As noted by the House Report that accompanied the insertion of the phrase "under God" in the Pledge: "From the time of our earliest history our peoples and our institutions have reflected the traditional concept that our Nation was founded

---

[293] Elk Grove Unified School District and David W. Gordon, Superintendent v. Newdow, et al., 542 U.S. 1 (2004) (Rehnquist, C. J., concurring in the judgment).
[294] Commager, H. (Ed.). (1968). *Documents of American History*. New York: Appleton-Century-Crofts.

on a fundamental belief in God."[295] Justice Rehnquist saw no violation of the First Amendment in the phrase "under God," especially since any student in California could refrain from reciting the Pledge of Allegiance if he or she wanted to.

The logic underlying Newdow's argument would require that all references to deity must be removed from America's public life. In their comments on his case, the Supreme Court Justices demonstrated that, while the case was dismissed on a technicality, they also clearly understood the enormous impact accepting Newdow's assertions would have had on our nation. As one commentator put it: "After all, each session of the U.S. Supreme Court begins with the words, 'God save this honorable court.' How can the Supreme Court remove 'under God' from the Pledge of Allegiance and continue to call upon God's help as they open for business each morning?"[296]

This battle is far from over. Anti-family and anti-religion activists will not rest until America is fully secularized with a government committed to official atheism, which ironically is its own religion. Newdow himself is a "minister" in the First Atheist Church of True Science.

Indeed, these efforts to remove God from the public square and to discriminate against people of faith are intensifying. For example:

- A high school valedictorian who used the word "God" in her speech had her microphone cut off by school administrators. Another high school valedictorian was told that her diploma would be withheld until she apologized in an e-mail to students and their parents for her comments about Jesus Christ during her speech.
- Radio Disney, which claims to be the "ultimate music environment for kids and families," required that the words "chosen by God" be removed from an advertisement for the movie "The Ten Commandments." Yet, the radio station allows advertising for movies that mention mythical gods, Tiki gods, Navaho gods, and animal gods.

---

[295] H. R. Rep. No. 1693, 83d Cong., 2d Sess., 2, (1954). Our national anthem, the Star-Spangled Banner adopted as such by Congress in 1931, provides another example. 36 U.S. C. §301 and Historical and Revision Notes. The last verse ends with these words: "Then conquer we must, when our cause it is just, And this be our motto: In God is our trust. And the star-spangled banner in triumph shall wave, O'er the land of the free and the home of the brave!"

[296] Mohler, A. (2004, March 26). The pledge and the court: Will 'under God' survive? Retrieved June 16, 2009, from http://www.albertmohler.com/commentary_read.php?cdate=2004-03-26

- A British couple was denied the opportunity to adopt a child. They were told that their Christian faith might "prejudice" them against a child who may be homosexual.
- The editors of a high school yearbook changed the word "God" to "He" in an ad purchased by the parents of a student because they thought it would offend someone.

Attempts to remove God from our society are based on the false premise that the U.S. Constitution requires complete separation of "church" and "state" when, in reality, the intent was to prohibit government from endorsing one religion over another.

Attempts to remove God from our society are based on the false premise that the U.S. Constitution requires *complete* separation of "church" and "state" when, in reality, the intent was to prohibit government from endorsing one religion over another. Anti-family forces thus try to broaden the definition of "state" to include any governmental support or use of government resources so that all religious activities which touch the government however remotely will be seen as unlawful or inappropriate.

Attack on the Boy Scouts of America

Homosexual activists have targeted the Boy Scouts of America (BSA) because of their position on homosexuality. The city of Berkeley revoked the free use of a marina berth by the Sea Scouts, an organization related to the Boy Scouts, because the Sea Scouts refused to disavow the BSA's exclusion of gays and atheists. The City Attorney argued that Berkeley taxpayers should not be forced to subsidize a private organization that won't honor the city's anti-discrimination laws. The California Supreme Court agreed with the city's action.[297]

In Philadelphia, the city council passed a resolution to evict the Boy Scouts of America from its headquarters, which the Scouts had occupied rent free for 80 years, unless they agreed to back away from their policy of excluding homosexuals. The Boy Scouts didn't budge, and the city council

[297] Strack, J. (2006, March 10). Court backs city, denies free berth to scouts. *The Daily Californian.* Retrieved June 16, 2009, from http://www.dailycal.org/article/24238/court_backs_city_denies_free_berth_to_scouts (The U.S. Supreme Court declined to hear an appeal by the Sea Scouts.)

voted to renege on the 1928 ordinance that allowed the Scouts to locate their headquarters on a piece of public land in perpetuity.[298] BSA has filed a lawsuit against the city to prevent its eviction.

The Danger of Hate Crimes Legislation

A number of countries, including the United States (both at the federal and state level), have enacted hate crimes legislation that increases sentences for perpetrators who have been found guilty of crimes motivated by hatred against a minority deemed to be vulnerable. Such legislation typically covers at least race and religion as protected classes.

Of course, violence against any individual should not be tolerated. Rational people do not disagree on that point. But existing criminal laws intended to curtail violence already take into account the intent of the attacker in determining the appropriate level of punishment. Hate crimes legislation goes further and provides *special protection* for certain classes of individuals, rather than *equal protection* for everyone. Increased punishments are given to the perpetrators based on what is perceived to be their hateful thoughts and beliefs towards the victim, something very difficult to measure.

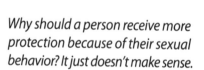

Why should a person receive more protection because of their sexual behavior? It just doesn't make sense.

In recent years there has been a push to add "sexual orientation" as a protected class under hate crimes legislation. Sexual orientation is radically different from those based on an inherent characteristic, such as race.

Why should a person receive more protection because of their sexual behavior? Why should heterosexuals receive less protection than homosexuals? Why should a person who attacks a homosexual receive a harsher punishment than a person who attacks, for example, an elderly woman? It just doesn't make sense.

Hate crimes legislation is just a small step away from criminalizing speech (without any accompanying conduct) that criticizes sexual behavior deemed by some to be "inappropriate" or "sinful." The concern

[298] Philadelphia breaks 80 year old building lease; moves to evict Scouts. (2007, June 1). Retrieved June 16, 2009, from Wikipedia: http://en.wikinews.org/wiki/Philadelphia_breaks_80_year_old_building_lease;_moves_to_evict_Scouts

is that those seeking to add "sexual orientation" as a protected class under hate crimes legislation are doing so because they intend to use this new provision against those who criticize or express a religious belief against the homosexual lifestyle.

> They intend to use this new provision against those who criticize or express a religious belief against the homosexual lifestyle.

These trends strike at the heart of freedom of speech and religion. As of the writing of this book, hate crimes legislation was pending in Congress. If we have not been successful in stopping it, we will need your help in getting it reversed.

Hate Crimes Legislation Around the World

Some countries are dealing with "hate speech" in disturbing ways:

Sweden

In Sweden "unfavorable speech" about a person's sexual orientation is itself criminalized. As a result of a 2002 amendment to Sweden's constitution, the mere public expression of beliefs about homosexuality without any accompanying criminal conduct can be criminally actionable. Swedish law offers no exclusions for religious speech, and specifically criminalizes hate speech in *"church sermons."* This is because the Swedish Federation for Gay, Lesbian, Bisexual and Transgender Rights (RFSL) had asked that religiously motivated speech not be exempt. A Pentecostal pastor in Sweden, Ake Green, was convicted of hate speech against homosexuals during a sermon in his church which focused on biblical teachings that condemn homosexual behavior. He was sentenced to 30 days in jail. The case went to Sweden's Supreme Court, with the prosecutor asking that the pastor be given a sentence of six months. Fortunately, the Swedish high court cleared Pastor Green of the hate crime charge. But the decision's reasoning is not very clear, and Sweden's law still penalizes speech against homosexuality.[299]

---

[299] *Hate speech legislation in Sweden.* (n.d.). Retrieved June 16, 2009, from Ontario Consultants on Religious Tolerance Web site: http://www.religioustolerance.org/hom_hat8.htm; *Swedish Supreme Court Acquits Pastor of 'Hate Crime'.* (2005, November 30). Retrieved June 16, 2009 from Concerned Women for America Web site: http://www.cwfa.org/articledisplay.asp?id=9549&department=CFI&categoryid=freedom

Canada

Hugh Owens was found guilty of a hate crime in Canada under Saskatchewan's Human Rights Code. Owens had placed an ad in the newspaper in response to Homosexual Pride Week that listed four Bible references opposing homosexuality. The ad included a drawing of two stick figures holding hands within a circle with a diagonal bar placed over it. The message was clear: The Bible teaches that homosexual behavior is wrong. His ad was a simple expression of belief.

Even though Owens engaged in no criminal conduct, based only on the speech in the ad, the Canadian Human Rights Board ruled that both Owens and the newspaper "discriminated against three gay men because of their sexual orientation by exposing them to hatred and ridicule and affronted their dignity."[300] Owens and the owners of the newspaper were ordered to pay damages of $1,500 to each of the three homosexual men who filed the complaint.

Although that decision was reversed on appeal, the door clearly has been opened to characterize preaching against homosexual acts as a hate crime in Canada. Indeed, other provincial human rights commissions in Canada have tried to penalize and prohibit expression opposing homosexuality and only backed down due to public opposition.[301] In Canada, being accused of a hate crime is punishment in and of itself whether you are found guilty or not. Defendants are stuck with large legal bills, while those who make the claims against them are not responsible for funding the prosecution, which is covered by the human rights tribunal. Even if defendants eventually win their case, they lose financially and sometimes suffer repercussions in terms of their reputation and employment.

United States

Although U.S. law has always provided strong protection for free speech and freedom of religion, Americans must be vigilant in protecting their right to speak out on moral issues.

---

[300] *Saskatchewan Human Rights Commission 2001-2002 Annual Report.* (2002). Saskatchewan Human Rights Commission. 22.

[301] *Canadian "Human Rights" Commissions Bear Down on Christian Clergymen.* (2008, September 25). Retrieved June 16, 2009, from the Chalcedon Foundation Web site: http://www.chalcedon.edu/articles/article.php?ArticleID=2886

In 2004, 11 Philadelphia Christians (known as the "Philadelphia 11") were arrested and jailed for peacefully passing out Christian literature at a gay pride event. Ironically, prior to their arrest, the Christians were confronted by a militant mob of homosexuals known as the "Pink Angels" who blew loud whistles, screamed obscenities at them, and carried large pink signs in front of them to block their message and access to the event. The Philadelphia police refused to take any action against the Pink Angels who continuously followed, obstructed and harassed the Christians. Instead, they took action against the Christians even though they respectfully cooperated with police.

After the Philadelphia 11 had spent 21 hours in jail, the Philadelphia District Attorney's office charged them under Pennsylvania's hate crimes law called "Ethnic Intimidation," to which "sexual orientation" was added as a victim category. A host of other felony and misdemeanor charges were filed against the Philadelphia 11 as well. Had they been convicted, each of the Philadelphia 11 could have faced up to 47 years in prison and $90,000 in fines. These charges were later dismissed by the Philadelphia County Court of Common Pleas as being without merit.

The Philadelphia 11 then filed a lawsuit against the City of Philadelphia for violations of their civil rights. However, their lawsuit was dismissed by the court which determined that the police were justified in their arrests based on their perception that the Philadelphia 11 were "disrupting the event" even though the Christians were not charged for being "disruptive," and it was the homosexuals at the event that caused the commotion. Michael Marcavage, one of the Philadelphia 11, noted that "The result in this case is another example of how hostility toward Biblical Christianity is growing in our nation. If we do not actively defend our religious liberties, homosexual extremists may succeed not only in silencing those who share their faith publicly, but also to silence the pulpit itself."[302]

Other Countries

In Holland, criticism of "fornicators" and "adulterers" is considered a hate crime; and in France, legislators have been fined for publicly criticizing homosexuality. Additional examples exist, but you get the picture.

---

[302] *Justice denied to Philadelphia 11,* (2008, July 17). Retrieved June 16, 2009, from Rempen America Web site: http://www.repentamerica.com/pressreleases/justicedenied.html; See also *Court says 'gay' rights trump Christian rights* (2008, July 18). Retrieved June 16, 2009, from World Net Daily Web site: http://www.wnd.com/index.php?fa=PAGE.view&pageId=69881

"Hate Speech" in the Work Place

Increasingly, it has become acceptable in the workplace to promote homosexuality, but not traditional family values. Government employees of the city of Oakland, California were threatened with losing their jobs for posting a flyer on the employee bulletin board in support of "marriage," "natural family," and "family values." They were warned that if they did it again they would be fired.

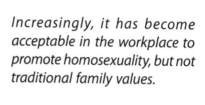

Increasingly, it has become acceptable in the workplace to promote homosexuality, but not traditional family values.

The employees challenged the warning in court and lost. On appeal, the Ninth Circuit Court concluded that the terms "marriage," "natural family," and "family values" could be censored in a municipal workplace as hate speech. The judges opined: "Public employers are permitted to curtail employee speech as long as their legitimate administrative interests outweigh the employees' interest in freedom of speech."[303] The U.S. Supreme Court declined to hear the case, so the decision stands.

Other employees of the City of Oakland posted information on a "National Coming Out Day," and a "First Annual Holiday Mixer" for the Gay-Straight Employee Alliance with no repercussions.

The Ninth Circuit Court concluded that the terms "marriage," "natural family," and "family values" could be censored in a municipal workplace as hate speech.

Other Troublesome Interferences with Religious Speech and Beliefs

It can be political suicide to oppose hate crimes legislation because those who do so are labeled "hateful." Remember the examples I gave you earlier in which businesses and even doctors have been forced to act against their religious beliefs in order to accommodate the demands of same-sex couples? Over the last several years, more and more people and businesses

---

[303] *Good News Employee Association et. al, v. Joyce M. Hicks*, 05-15467 (9th Cir. U.S. Ct. of Appeals 2007). Retrieved June, 16, 2009, from Oakland City Attorney Web site: http://www.oaklandcityattorney.org/PDFS/Opinions/GoodNewsruling2-2005.pdf

are being fined or sued for adhering to, promoting or defending their religious beliefs regarding homosexuality.

For example, Scott Brockie, a printer in Ontario, Canada, was fined $5,000 by the Ontario Human Rights Commission for refusing to print letterhead for a homosexual advocacy group. He spent $175,000 fighting the charges. The adjudicator claimed that Brockie was free to express his beliefs in his home or Christian community, but ordered him to provide printing services "to lesbians and gays and to organizations in existence for their benefit." The parties fought about who would pick up legal costs, and the Court of Appeals decided the printer was on the hook for $40,000 in legal fees.

The Assault on Religion in Children's Literature

Religion is coming under assault even in children's literature and movies. A few years ago, I purchased a set of fantasy books recommended by a friend (the second book in the trilogy had been awarded the Parent's Choice Golden Award). It wasn't until after I brought the books home that I noticed the subtitle, *His Dark Materials*, and I decided to review them before giving them to my children.

In reading the first book, I found it wasn't immediately clear which characters were the good guys and which were the bad. The plot kept twisting and turning as a good plot does. However, when I began the second book, I found the author's true agenda—the undermining of God and religion.

Pullman's *Dark Materials* subtly and subliminally gives children the message that religion is evil. Throughout book two, the witches are portrayed as the good people and, on page 44, the beautiful witch queen, Ruta Skadi, addresses her "sisters" and announces that they must fight the church because throughout history:

> *... it tries to suppress and control every natural impulse ... and every church is the same: control, destroy, obliterate every good feeling* [I've omitted the author's sexual references here] *... so if war comes and the church is on one side of it, we must be on the other, no matter what strange allies we find ourselves bound to.*

I kept waiting for the plot to twist back and portray the church as good and evil as bad, but no such luck.

In a BreakPoint commentary, Chuck Colson warned:

> *By his own admission Pullman is writing stories to "undermine the basis of Christian belief." Pullman creates a fantasy universe where God is weak and deceitful, and the Biblical Fall is the origin of human liberation. What's more, Pullman's version of the war in heaven ends with God's defeat and death.*[304]

Pullman blatantly declared in a 2003 interview with the *Sydney Morning Herald* that "my books are about killing God."[305] Peter Hitchens, a British columnist, said Pullman is "the most dangerous author in Britain," and described him as the author that "atheists would have prayed for if atheists prayed."[306]

Pullman's anti-religion, anti-God propaganda is being insidiously foisted on millions of unsuspecting children in the form of popular entertainment. A feature length film made of Pullman's first book, *The Golden Compass*, hit theaters in 2007.

Parents may be surprised to learn that one of the most popular children's series of all times, enjoyed also by millions of adults, had a hidden theme which runs counter to the religious beliefs of many of its readers. After selling 500 million copies of books and movies to families and children around the world, *Harry Potter* author J. K. Rowling announced that a beloved and trusted character, Albus Dumbledore, is a homosexual. She explained that's why he never married in the books and had a "special friendship" with another character. This announcement was made after millions of children were already hooked on the series, which was intended to endear children to Dumbledore as one of the most respected characters.

Why Religion Matters

An overwhelming case based on social science research alone can be made for the critical importance of religious practice in building and strengthening the natural family and thus society as a whole. The science

---

[304] Slater, S. (2003). Getting at our children's minds. *The Family Reporter, 7*(1).

[305] Meacham, S. (2003, December 13). The shed where God died. *The Sydney Morning Herald.* Retrieved June 16, 2009, from http://www.smh.com.au/articles/2003/12/12/1071125644900.html

[306] Hitchens, P. (2002, January 27). This is the most dangerous author in Britain. *The Mail.* p. 63. Retrieved June 16, 2009, from http://home.wlv.ac.uk/~bu1895/hitchens.htm

in this area is so overwhelming, one could easily conclude that even if all religions proved to be untrue, from a societal perspective, it would still be in government's interest to protect religion and enable it to flourish. In fact, studies show that it doesn't even matter which faith you espouse; if you attend church regularly, you and society will reap measurable benefits.

Dr. Patrick Fagan, a family scholar and a good friend of mine, wrote an excellent article called, "Why Religion Matters Even More: The Impact of Religious Practice on Social Stability." In it, Dr. Fagan stated:

> *Regular attendance at religious services is linked to healthy, stable family life, strong marriages, and well-behaved children. The practice of religion also leads to a reduction in the incidence of domestic abuse, crime, substance abuse, and addiction. In addition, religious practice leads to an increase in physical and mental health, longevity, and education attainment. Moreover, these effects are intergenerational, as grandparents and parents pass on the benefits to the next generations.*

Mr. Fagan analyzed numerous studies that show the benefits of religion to men, women, children, marriages, families and societies. Here are his findings:

> *Strong and repeated evidence indicates that the regular practice of religion has beneficial effects in nearly every aspect of social concern and policy. This evidence shows that religious practice protects against social disorder and dysfunction. Specifically, the available data clearly indicate that religious belief and practice are associated with:*

> - *Higher levels of marital happiness and stability.*
> - *Stronger parent-child relationships.*
> - *Greater educational aspirations and attainment, especially among the poor.*
> - *Higher levels of good work habits.*
> - *Greater longevity and physical health.*
> - *Higher levels of well-being and happiness.*
> - *Higher recovery rates from addictions to alcohol or drugs.*
> - *Higher levels of self-control, self-esteem, and coping skills.*
> - *Higher rates of charitable donations and volunteering.*

- *Higher levels of community cohesion and social support for those in need.*

The evidence further demonstrates that religious belief and practice are also associated with:

- *Lower divorce rates.*
- *Lower cohabitation rates.*
- *Lower rates of out-of-wedlock births.*
- *Lower levels of teen sexual activity.*
- *Less abuse of alcohol and drugs.*
- *Lower rates of suicide, depression, and suicide ideation.*
- *Lower levels of many infectious diseases.*
- *Less juvenile crime.*
- *Less violent crime.*
- *Less domestic violence.*

Dr. Fagan concludes with the following:

Although the freedom not to practice religion is intrinsic to religious freedom, that protection does not mean that this non-practice of religion is equally beneficial to society. Social science data reinforce George Washington's declaration in his farewell address: "Of all the dispositions and habits which lead to political prosperity, Religion and Morality are indispensable supports."[307]

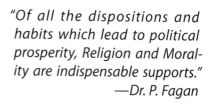

"Of all the dispositions and habits which lead to political prosperity, Religion and Morality are indispensable supports."
—Dr. P. Fagan

Stand for the Family—What You Can Do

The religious values of Americans have made our nation strong. We should not succumb to demands by minorities to remove religion from the

[307] Fagan, P. (2006, December 18). Why religion matters even more: The impact of religious practice on social stability. *The Heritage Foundation, Backgrounder #1992*. Retrieved June 16, 2009, from http://www.heritage.org/Research/Religion/bg1992.cfm

public square. Similarly, we must oppose legislation that restricts religious freedom. We should work to promote laws and policies that will protect all people equally while allowing all faiths to flourish so that our homes, families, communities, and thus our nation, will be strengthened.

On a final note, many religious people believe they cannot advocate legislation that deals with moral issues. But all laws have a moral basis. Even the U.S. Supreme Court has recognized that the law is based on "notions of morality."[308] All laws prohibit or encourage one behavior or another, and it is up to society ("We the People") to determine what to encourage or discourage according to our collective values and understanding of what is best for the welfare of our nation. It would behoove governments worldwide to encourage religious activity (although not endorsing any specific religion), rather than to succumb to demands to remove anything connected with religion from the public square.

For More Information: To read our free Family Policy Brief called "Why Religion Matters to Society," go to the Family Policy Resource Center on our Web site at www.familywatchinternational.org.

---

[308] *Bowers v. Hardwick*, 478 U.S. 186 (1986).

Chapter 15

Uncovering Common Anti-Family Strategies

The striking figure wore an exquisitely beautiful, bejeweled Indian sari. Deep turquoise, with a plunging neckline, and yards and yards of draping fabric. Absolutely stunning. The manicure was perfect. Long, pearly nails on graceful hands. The hair was shoulder length. Thick, lustrous and wavy. The makeup had been carefully and expertly applied. And the jewelry was nothing short of magnificent. The ultimate in glamour.

He was really something.

I made a valiant effort, but it was hard not to stare. There was an insurmountable disconnect between what I was seeing with my eyes and my brain's ability to process it. We were at the United Nations High Level Meeting on HIV/AIDS in New York. He was one of many transsexuals/transgenders, sex workers (i.e., prostitutes) and IV drug users in attendance, demanding the human right to engage in any high-risk behavior they wanted to with the expectation that the government would pay for the consequences.

The man in the sari was there as an official member of the Civil Society Task Force, established at the request of the UN General Assembly. (Travel and expenses for members of the Task Force were paid for by the UN.)

But here's what concerns me. On day one, I was shocked and appalled. Day two, I was amused. By day three, I just wanted to see what color sari he was wearing and hardly even glanced at him gliding down the UN hall with his pink purse.

I suspect that's exactly what he wanted.[309]

---

[309] This is adapted from an article written by FWI Communications Director Lynn Allred that first appeared in the "Have We Gone Mad" section of the *The Family Watch*, FWI's weekly e-mail newsletter. You can sign up for this free newsletter at www.familywatchinternational.org.

The above experience is an example of the Desensitization Strategy in action. A behavior that might outrage us at first can become less shocking the more we are exposed to it. Soon, we begin to tolerate it then slowly accept it, and finally, we may even embrace the behavior we previously thought to be unhealthy, abnormal or immoral. The Desensitization Strategy is very effective. Witness, for example, the increase in public "Gay Pride" events in countries across the world and in people "coming out of the closet" to announce their homosexuality. Those promoting abortion have even gone so far as to wear T-shirts proclaiming "I had an abortion." And prostitutes have organized themselves into political groups as "sex workers" to publicly promote their "work" as a legitimate profession.

The liberal media constantly use this strategy, regularly projecting sexually explicit images into our lives and gradually increasing their intensity, until many of us aren't even aware of how far our own views have been changed.

Anti-Family Strategies

If you watch the anti-family activists systematically implement their agenda at the international, national and local level, an obvious pattern emerges. Their strategies and tactics are very predictable.

Along with the Desensitization Strategy, by understanding these other strategies, you will be better able to identify and counteract them.

Bypass the People Strategy

According to the Bypass the People Strategy, if you can't get your agenda passed by a legislature or by a vote of the people, use the courts. In bypassing the legislature or the vote of the people and taking your cause straight to the courts, you can save time and money. It's much easier to convince a few judges to mandate your agenda.

Activists used this strategy to legalize abortion in the United States with the *Roe v. Wade* Supreme Court decision. They succeeded even though the Constitution nowhere mentions abortion as a fundamental right, most states at the time had laws against abortion, and polls showed that the majority of Americans were against legalizing abortion. This strategy also was used by homosexual activists to legalize same-sex marriage by judicial mandate in Massachusetts, Connecticut, California and Iowa.

Another way to apply the Bypass the People Strategy is to get policies adopted in UN documents and then use the UN to pressure countries to change their laws. For example, as noted previously, after Americans rejected the Equal Rights Amendment in the 1970s, radical feminists took their cause to the United Nations where they have infiltrated the system and are seeking to force their agenda on the United States and the rest of the world.

I'll-Make-it-Mean-What-I-Want Strategy

If you can't get what you want by popular vote, passing a law, finding a sympathetic judge, or by getting it included in a treaty or other UN document, you can always fill the entity implementing or enforcing relevant laws and regulations with *your* people. Then you can interpret a law to mean anything you want.

The State of California Superintendent of Schools used the I'll-Make-it-Mean-What-I-Want Strategy when he established an Advisory Task Force composed of 36 individuals that recommended to school districts how to implement AB 537, The California Student Safety and Violence Prevention Act of 2000. This bill was supposed to improve the educational environment for homosexual students. No conservative or pro-family individuals were included on the task force, and one of the homosexual activists who participated admitted the task force "did not feel limited by the law."

The mandate in AB 537 was simply to "prevent sexual orientation discrimination" in the schools. The resulting task force recommendations included a radical interpretation of what "prevent" means under the new law:

- Create positive, grade-appropriate visual images that include all sexual orientations and gender identities for use in common school areas (i.e., pictures of gays, transgenders etc.).
- Reduce the adverse impact of gender segregation on transgender students. In particular, best practice guidance should address issues related to locker rooms, restrooms and dress codes.
- Acknowledge lesbian, gay, bisexual and transgender historical figures, events, concepts and issues in the revisions of content standards and curriculum frameworks, when appropriate.

These recommendations seem to be aimed more at promoting homosexuality, bisexuality and transgenderism rather than preventing discrimination against those involved in such lifestyles. A couple of years later, additional legislation was introduced that made the task force's recommendations mandatory (after they had been partially implemented). By 2007, these and other curriculum requirements, which essentially indoctrinate California schoolchildren that homosexuality and transgenderism are normal and acceptable lifestyles, had all been enacted into law.

Tsunami Strategy

Using the Tsunami Strategy, introduce a plethora of bills or proposals in a variety of venues so your opponents find it difficult, if not impossible, to keep track of and stop all of them. This happens at the UN, in Congress, and in state legislatures where anti-family provisions are often tacked onto a number of unrelated bills, resolutions or documents. Anti-family forces figure that if they introduce an idea enough times in enough variations, and in enough different venues, they eventually will win. And they often do.

As I have noted, activists using this strategy successfully passed a number of pro-homosexual bills in California.

Name Calling and Discrediting Strategy

If you cannot defeat the message, attack the messenger. Call your opponents politically toxic names or otherwise discredit them. For example, label anyone who supports a moral issue an "extremist," a "right wing radical," or a "religious fundamentalist." Brand anyone who believes that homosexual behavior is unhealthy or not good for society as "hateful," "intolerant," "homophobic," "bigot" or a "Nazi." Use "anti-choice" to label those who believe that taking the life of an unborn child is wrong. Finally, characterize opposing views or positions as "hate speech" or "unchristian."

Victim Strategy

Existing laws in the United States already protect every individual (regardless of sexual orientation) from harassment and violence. Schools also have policies that protect students from being singled out and harassed. Nevertheless, claims of persecution of homosexual students in schools are used to justify mandatory "tolerance" and "diversity" programs that teach open acceptance of and respect for homosexual behavior.

The media have sensationalized accounts of people being attacked allegedly because of their sexual orientation. Yet, in some of these cases, the media later has had to reexamine their initial assertions. The most famous example of this is the Matthew Shepard case. He was cruelly beaten, tortured, and eventually died. Shepard's friends spread the word that Mathew was openly gay and that the crime likely was motivated because of his lifestyle. The media portrayed this as a bigoted attack on a homosexual.

Proposed "hate crimes" legislation in Congress has been named after Shepard and a high school play about him that promotes homosexuality is performed in schools across the nation. However, in re-examining the case years later, ABC News and others concluded that it likely was not a hate crime and that drug use and a desire for money, rather than a hatred of homosexuality, had been the motive for the attack. The lead investigator, former police detective Ben Fritzen, also believed robbery was the primary motive.[310]

In brief, we should condemn any acts of violence against anyone, but to automatically portray every attack on a homosexual as homophobic is misleading and creates unjustified support for laws, policies and programs that promote homosexuality.

Incremental Strategy

Another strategy used to promote the anti-family agenda is to subdivide it and pass it piecemeal, slowly, one step at a time, before anyone realizes it. To use a well-known metaphor, the proverbial frog (our society) is being boiled one degree at a time. Because the increase in heat is incremental and may even feel good at first, the frog fails to jump out of the pot before it's too late. The legislative history of the homosexual agenda in California is a prime example of this strategy. Pro-family policymakers take note. Monumental successes were accomplished by the following small incremental steps:

A. In 1995, California's first openly lesbian legislator was elected.

---

[310] *New details emerge in Mathew Shepard murder* [20/20 Report]. (2004, November 26). Retrieved October 11, 2008, from ABC News Web site: http://abcnews.go.com/2020/Story?id=277685&page=3

B. A second lesbian legislator was elected in California in 1996.

C. These lesbian legislators then began to propose seemingly innocuous bills to prevent "discrimination" in education.

D. The California Hate Violence Reduction Act of 1995 was enacted and required schools to "promote an appreciation of diversity and to discourage discriminatory attitudes and practices." (Notice they did not say "homosexual," but the law was used to promote homosexuality in the schools.)

E. The infamous AB 537 was enacted in 2000, which prohibited discrimination of students in the public schools on the basis of their sexual orientation or their actual or perceived gender.

F. In 2001, the California legislature enacted AB 25, which granted 13 marital rights and benefits to domestic partners. This was a deliberate attempt to circumvent the will of the people of the state of California, who had just passed Proposition 22 the year before to define marriage as being between a man and a woman.

G. Successive legislatures expanded the scope of these domestic partnerships until they now include all of the rights the state grants to married individuals.

H. The California legislature twice passed bills to try to legalize same-sex marriage, and both times they were vetoed by the governor.

I. Three very controversial bills were signed into law by the governor in 2007, further expanding mandated homosexual indoctrination in public schools.

Of course, all of this laid the foundation for the current battle over same-sex marriage in California.

Unfortunately, similar scenarios are being played out in other states and countries, most likely even in yours. But even in the worst of circumstances, reversals of anti-family policies also can happen one step at a time until there is sufficient momentum to repeal harmful laws.

Emotion Strategy

If you can't win on the merits, strike an emotional chord, start crying or tell a sad story, and compassion will take over. This Emotion Strategy was used effectively at the UN during an HIV/AIDS conference in 2006, when, for the first time, an HIV-positive person was invited to speak to the entire UN General Assembly. The woman shared a heart-wrenching story about how she had been abused and infected with AIDS by a man and the tragic consequences she had experienced. She ended her speech demanding abortion rights for women and sexual rights for homosexuals. She received a standing ovation because she got everyone emotionally involved with her story—even though her experience had nothing to do with abortion or homosexuality.

Call it a "Human Right" Strategy

At the UN, once something is labeled a human right it is considered sacred. The UN Human Rights Commission monitors human rights abuses around the world. So part of the anti-family agenda is to get the UN Committee on Human Rights to consider anything related to their agenda to be a "fundamental human right." Then the Committee can help force that "right" upon the world even if it's not specifically spelled out in a treaty. By calling such things as sodomy or abortion "human rights," anti-family advocates have made huge strides.

I witnessed UN negotiations in which delegations worked to ensure that the "sex work" of prostitutes be considered a "right."[311]

Of course, the abortion lobby is best at exploiting the "human rights" strategy at the UN and national level, claiming that women have a "right" to end the lives of their unborn babies. It's not fair, they claim, that men do not have to endure the consequences of having babies. So women must have the "right" or "choice" not to carry this burden. Most recently, some UN committees have interpreted "right to life" provisions in UN documents to mean that a woman has the right to an abortion as any pregnancy has the potential to end the mother's life. (Never mind that abortion itself can seriously impact or end a mother's life, in addition to terminating the life of the fetus.)

---

[311] In one meeting we attended, a delegate from Norway proudly announced on the UN floor that her country was among the first to decriminalize prostitution and embrace "sex work" as a legitimate occupation.

The demand for human rights can be somewhat muddled at times. An interesting dilemma some feminists have is that while they insist that abortion on demand is a human right, they condemn sex-selective abortion—aborting a child simply because it is female. In other words, they believe that women should have the right to abort a baby at any time for any reason unless the reason happens to be that the mother doesn't want to have a female baby. These feminists don't care that millions of female babies are aborted every day, they only care when the mother doesn't want a child because it is a female, then suddenly, in their view, a woman's right to abortion evaporates.

On a more general note, special interest groups such as the North American Man Boy Love Association (NAMBLA) seek to have society condone their sexually deviant acts by making "intergenerational sex" (translation: child abuse or pedophilia) a "right" for children. They believe children have a "right" to sexual experiences and to choose their own sex partners. NAMBLA seeks to lower the age of consensual sex with children so children can realize their "rights." NAMBLA has not been as public as the homosexual advocates, but if we allow our society's values to continue to degenerate, NAMBLA and other such groups will continue to become more vocal, more visible and more influential.

Useful Euphemism Strategy

If the majority would object to your agenda, re-label it with respectable nice-sounding words or phrases. For example, call abortion a "choice" and pedophilia "intergenerational sex." Pressure people into accepting your agenda in the name of "equality," "tolerance," "diversity," "freedom" or "nondiscrimination." This is one of the most common strategies, and thus it is important to understand.

Below is a list of a few of the words and phrases and their anti-family definitions used in the Useful Euphemism Strategy. Although most people certainly would not use these terms in the way defined below, they are often used in the following ways by anti-family activists.

"Sexual rights"—Complete sexual freedom for children and adults. Government is to pay for the consequences. Unlimited access for children (without parental consent) and adults to sexually explicit materials. Government funded abortion on demand.

"Unwanted pregnancy"—Baby that should be killed before it is born.

"Forced pregnancy"—When a woman is denied the right to kill her baby in the womb (abortion).

"Celebration of diversity"—Promotion of promiscuous lifestyles.

"Religion"—Radical, outdated beliefs that infringe on basic human rights and freedoms and which can cause serious harm to children.

"Human right"—The ultimate phrase used to imply that you have an overriding right to do what you want regardless of the consequences to you or to society.

"Gay, homosexual or lesbian"—People who need special rights and protections because of a condition which they perceive to be genetic.

"Hate speech"—Advancing religious views about sexual orientation or promiscuity that cause people to feel judged (e.g., publicly professing a biblical view regarding sexuality, or calling any kind of sexual activity outside of traditional marriage a sin).

"Homophobe"—Anyone who supports traditional marriage or opposes the homosexual agenda.

"Social Conservative"—A homophobe who is usually intolerant, inclined to discriminate and is working to take away the fundamental human rights of others.

"Discrimination" or "Intolerance" or "Hate"—Maintaining that marriage should be between a man and a woman, and that homosexuality should not be promoted in the schools or flaunted in the workplace.

"Tolerance"—A doctrine which calls for embracing promiscuity and sexual anarchy. "Tolerance" calls for *intolerance* of religious values or viewpoints that do not accept promiscuous behavior as normal and good.

"Lowering age of consensual sex"—Legalizing adult sex with children.

"Intergenerational sex"—Sex between an adult and a child.

"Sex worker"—A prostitute.

"Civil unions"—Legal recognition and benefits for people having sex with a partner of the same sex, i.e., legal recognition for couples who engage in sodomy.

There are many other words and phrases we could add to this list, but I'm sure you get the point.

Identifying Anti-Family Tactics

In Chapter 5 I produced a copy of an e-mail my daughter received attacking her for her position in defending man/woman marriage. You may want to go back to that chapter and reread the e-mail exchange beginning on page 61. This time as you read Jamie's e-mail, try to identify several of the anti-family strategies you just learned about in this chapter. Look for the Name Calling and Discrediting Strategy, The Emotion Strategy, The Victim Strategy, and The Call it a "Human Right" Strategy.

Stand for the Family—What You Can Do

1. Learn to recognize these strategies in articles, editorials and in discussions with others on family issues. Point them out to those who are attempting to use them.

2. Write letters to the editors of newspapers or comments in response to articles that appear on the Internet whenever you see family issues unfairly addressed using these strategies. The more readily you can identify these strategies, the more effectively you will be able to address them.

Chapter 16

Immunizing Your Family Against the Assaults

I used to think negative peer pressure ended with high school. It is amazing to watch such tactics being displayed at the United Nations among high-level representatives of various countries. Peer pressure is an effective tool that is used to advance the anti-family agenda in many situations. The following study shows that even adults can be susceptible to peer pressure.

A group of nine college students are seated in a classroom in a semicircle for an experiment in "visual judgment." The facilitator informs them that they will be comparing the lengths of lines shown on two large cards. The first card has a single vertical line, the second card has three vertical lines of various lengths. The subjects are asked to choose the line on the second card that is the same length as the line on the first card. The correct choice is quite obvious.

The experiment is set up so that each participant announces their answers in the order in which they have been seated in the room. However, all but the last subject have been secretly instructed beforehand to give the same incorrect answer. After hearing all the other subjects give the same wrong answer, the "true" test subject at the end of the row must give his answer.

The lead researcher explained, "Upon him [the test subject] we have brought to bear two opposed forces: the evidence of his senses and the unanimous opinion of a group of his peers. Also, he must declare his judgments in public, before a majority which has also stated its position publicly."

Amazingly, 75 percent of the true test subjects knowingly gave the wrong answer. Only 25 percent continued to choose the right answer despite significant peer pressure.

According to the lead researcher, those test subjects who conformed with the group did so because "[they] construed their difference from the majority as a sign of some general deficiency in themselves, which at all costs they must hide. On this basis they desperately tried to merge with the majority, not realizing the longer range consequences to themselves."

However, when just one of the subjects in collusion to give the wrong answer was told to go against the group and choose the right answer, the true subject also was emboldened to choose the correct answer instead of conforming with the group.[312]

What can we learn from this simple experiment? The bad news is that peer pressure can overrule reason. The good news is that sometimes all it takes is for one person to stand up for what is right and others will follow.

When my oldest daughter was in high school, she was invited to go to a movie by a group of popular kids that didn't usually include her in their activities. She was so excited to be invited that she didn't pay attention to the movie they were going to see as they entered the theater. As the movie began, some very graphic and inappropriate things were playing on the screen. She felt sick to her stomach but was afraid to get up and leave because she thought the other kids would think she was stupid. Finally, she couldn't take any more, and she stood up, explaining that she was going home. To her surprise, several kids followed her out of the theater. They too had felt uncomfortable but had been afraid to say anything. They thanked her for getting up and giving them the courage to do so as well.

How do we, as parents, empower the rising generation to withstand peer pressure?

We need to put a greater focus on our families. In our supercharged, multitasking, stressed out society, it is often difficult to find time for what matters most—our families. Sometimes our families get our very worst, when it is they who deserve and need our very best. Both children and adults need to feel safe, supported and loved. If we can establish a secure environment in our homes, each family member will be better prepared to resist the negative influences around them.

I am going to suggest 10 ways that you can protect and fortify your own family. My husband and I have used all of these with our family and found them very effective. Although these suggestions may seem very simple, they have proven to be extremely valuable in helping our children and other youth withstand negative peer pressure.

---

[312] Asch, S. E. (1951). Effects of group pressure upon the modification and distortion of judgments. In H. Guetzkow (Ed.) *Groups, Leadership, and Men*. Pittsburgh: Carnegie Press.

Ten Ways to Immunize Your Family Against the Assaults

1. Eat dinner together as a family on a regular basis.

Researchers have found that teens who have regular meals with their families show higher academic achievement and lower rates of smoking, drinking, marijuana use, fighting, eating disorders, and early initiation of sexual activity. Research also shows that even though teens may complain, they generally prefer eating dinner with their families.[313]

Make the family dinner a positive, interactive experience. Do not use this time to discipline or to criticize. Turn off the TV, cell phones and iPods. Put down the newspaper and focus on the family during the entire meal.

Here are sample questions you can use to initiate productive and valuable conversations at the dinner table:

- How was school/work/practice?
- What was the best/worst/funniest part of the day and why?
- Did anyone in our family help someone today that they could tell us about?
- Did anyone stand up for what was right when it was difficult?
- What did you learn that was new?

Of course, you can make up any questions or subjects you want, keeping in mind that the goal is to use dinnertime to facilitate positive family communication and build self-esteem.

Dinnertime is also a great time to discuss family standards, current events, or religious topics. I know of one family who took an article from the newspaper each day to debate during dinner. Half the family was assigned to debate one side of an issue, and the other half of the

[313] Neumark-Sztainer, D., & Doherty, W., Regular Family Dinners Offer Benefits to Modern Families. (n.d.). Retrieved June 17, 2009, from Children, Youth and Families Education and Research Network Web site: http://www1.cyfernet.org/hotnew/01-08-Dinner.html; Doherty, W. (1997). *The Intentional Family: Simple Rituals for Strengthening Family Ties.* New York: Avon. Doherty, W., & Carlson, B. Z. (2002). *Putting Family First: Reclaiming Family Time in a Hurry Up World.* New York: Henry Holt.

family the other side. All of their children became very articulate. Dinnertime also is a great time to point out positive things you have seen family members do during the day to reinforce good behavior.

In addition, family meals can be a great time to plan family activities or conduct other family business. Engaging in these activities as a family strengthens family bonds and is an important way to create a sense of belonging, identity and family unity. But keep it positive!

Listen to each family member. When a child feels they are a valued and loved family member, they will be empowered to withstand outside pressures.

2. Set aside date nights for mom and dad.

The best thing a father can do for his children is to love and honor their mother, and the best thing a mother can do is to likewise love and respect their father. Loving marriages provide the best environment for nurturing children. But, if marriages are not regularly nurtured, they can wither and die. If the parents do not take time to be with each other to nourish their relationship and then model this strong relationship, they are doing a grave disservice to their children and to each other. Children know, whether you tell them or not, what kind of marriage you have. They can feel it and it affects them.

3. Dedicate at least one night each week to your family.

Families that set aside a regular night each week to spend time together reap immense benefits. Use this time for wholesome recreation, counseling, planning, teaching, etc. Play is a child's work. Through playing games, children learn social skills, how to cooperate, how to deal with competition, and how to solve problems. Yet, more importantly, playing together strengthens family relationships and builds self-esteem.

Proactively teach your children about your religious and moral beliefs. Start when they are young, and they will look to you later as a guide in these areas when they are faced with critical choices.

During family time, you could set aside a moment for each child to share a talent, discuss the division of family chores, counsel on difficult issues that arise, or plan family vacations and activities. Encourage each family member to recommend items for a weekly "agenda." The concept is to have regular, meaningful time together as a family with no outside distractions. We often take the phone off the hook during our family time and we have asked our friends to respect this time and not interrupt us.

One of my favorite family night activities as a child was when everyone wrote down one compliment about each family member. Then we would read out loud our list of nice comments. I always walked away with a boatload of self-esteem and feeling very loved. I have repeated that tradition with my own children. A family night is also a good time to establish family rules, standards and traditions.

4. Spend one-on-one time with each child on a regular basis.

When my children were young, I took a parenting class offered in our community. It was the best investment I ever made. When we met each week and discussed our parenting challenges, it seemed that, no matter what problem a child was having, the answer was to spend some one-on-one time with him or her. And, every time it was suggested and put into practice, the parent would report back with wonderful results. If we do not give our children attention in positive ways, they will look for it in negative ways.

5. Pray together.

The family that prays together stays together. If you remember, I told you at the beginning of this book that, although I believe in God, I would not try to impose my religious views on you. Regardless of your religious faith, however, praying together with your children and for your children on a daily basis is strengthening and binding. Our family has had wonderful experiences as we have prayed together.

6. Criticize less and praise more.

Catch family members doing good, and point those things out rather than looking for the bad. If a child or a spouse receives 10 negative comments to every positive one, they are less apt to feel secure and good about themselves. Try to be less of a coach (although there are many times when our children do need coaching) and more of a cheerleader. (This works great with your spouse as well!)

7. Immunize your children against premarital sex.

With all the inappropriate material being taught to children through the media and the public schools, parents need to vigilant and do whatever they can to ensure they are the first to teach their children about their sexuality. Start by teaching your children at a young age the proper names for body parts. Talk to your children before they reach puberty about the changes that will happen to their bodies. As they reach puberty, explain the powerful nature of the sex drive and that it was intended for procreation and to bond them physically and emotionally to their future husband or wife. Let them know that this sex drive can bring them much joy and happiness when saved for marriage, but that it can wreak havoc in their lives if they do not learn to control it before marriage.

Based on research, the Heritage Foundation[314] has identified the following things parents can do to help reduce or delay teen sexual activity:

- **Mothers, stay close to your daughters, and let them know you disapprove of teen sex.** Youth who report having a good relationship with their mothers, and who know their mothers highly disapprove of them having sex, are more likely to delay sexual activity *and less likely to become pregnant.*[315]

---

[314] There is a wealth of research on family issues compiled by The Heritage Foundation available at http://www.familyfacts.org/

[315] Dittus, P. J., & Jaccard, J. (2000). Adolescents' perceptions of maternal disapproval of sex: Relationship to sexual outcomes. *Journal of Adolescent Health, 26*(4), 268-278.

- **Fathers, stay close to your daughters.** Teen girls who say they have a close relationship with their fathers are less likely to become sexually active.[316]

- **Talk to your children about sex.** In spite of the behavior of peers that would encourage sexual activity, adolescents who engage in discussions with their parents about sex are less likely to be sexually active than youth who do not have such talks with their parents.[317]

- **Discuss what is right and wrong.** Adolescents whose parents discuss what is right and wrong in terms of sexual behavior are more likely to remain abstinent than peers who do not have such talks with their parents.[318] Be very clear regarding what is acceptable and what is not.

- **Communicate with the parents of your children's friends.** Adolescent girls whose mothers communicate with the parents of their friends typically become sexually active at a later age.[319]

8. Work together.

Working together is quality time and teaches our children invaluable skills they will need for the rest of their lives. It also builds relationships. And the stronger your relationship with your children, the more able they will be to withstand peer pressure to engage in harmful activities. I am amazed at how many things I learn when I am working with my children in the kitchen, and they begin to tell me what is really going on in their lives and those of their friends. If children have trouble sticking to a task and finishing assignments, work alongside them and teach them by example.

9. Do service together as a family.

Doing service for others enhances a child's self-esteem and feelings of self-worth. Doing service together can create stronger family bonds.

[316] Regnerus, M. D., & Luchies, L. B. (2006). The parent-child relationship and opportunities for adolescents' first sex. *Journal of Family Issues, 27*(2), 159-183.

[317] Whitaker, D. J., & Miller, K. S. (2000). Parent-adolescent discussions about sex and condoms: Impact on peer influences of sexual risk behavior. *Journal of Adolescent Research, 15*(2), 251-273.

[318] Aspy, C. B., et al. (2007). Parental communication and youth sexual behaviour. *Journal of Adolescence, 30*(3), 449-466.

[319] McNeely, C., et al. (2002). Mothers' influence on the timing of first sex among 14- and 15-year olds. *Journal of Adolescent Health, 31*(3), 256-265.

Since we brought three orphans into our family from Mozambique, our family has enjoyed doing service for other orphans. You may want to participate in Family Watch's "Seven Days of Nothing" program and decide as a family what you can do without in order to help an orphan who has no family. You can go to www.familiesforoprhans. org for more information.

Of course any acts of service—such as baking something for a new neighbor, helping a widow with her yard, volunteering at a local soup kitchen, etc.—when done as a family, can strengthen your family and provide lasting positive effects for your children.

10. Never give up on a family member.

Unconditional love is the greatest gift you can give your child and your spouse. Never withhold your love or your friendship from a family member. Unconditional love can work miracles. This does not mean that you should ignore or condone negative behavior or that you should fail to discipline your children. But never punish someone by withdrawing from them or refusing to communicate. If they don't feel acceptance at home, they may look for acceptance from inappropriate sources. If you have children who stray for a time, your unconditional love may eventually reach them and help draw them back into the fold of the family.

Chapter 17

Will You Stand for the Family?

My sister and her husband volunteered to make numerous phone calls to gather support for the marriage amendment in California. They were surprised by how many people were secretly in favor of traditional marriage but were afraid to let anyone know. Conversely, those who were against the marriage amendment were quite outspoken.

Despite the many assaults on the traditional family, we know from our experience and from studying the data, that the majority of people in the world want to preserve and protect the traditional family. The problem is simple: Even though we are in the majority, too many people are remaining silent.

In Chapter 10, I related my experience of riding in a parade, holding a sign that said, "Will You Stand for the Family?"

Now, I am asking *you*. Right now. Will *you* stand for the family?

Will you stand with me and other good people across the world who are working to protect freedom, faith, family, and all that we hold dear? I hope you will, because we need you.

We Can Win the Battle to Save the Family—and We Must!

As mentioned earlier, etched in one of the remnants of the fallen Berlin Wall in Germany is this quote: *"Many small people, in many small places, doing many small things can change the face of the world."* If we all work in our spheres of influence, whether it be in our own homes, neighborhoods or communities, we can turn back the tide that is working to destroy our families. It will take our combined best efforts.

If you are not already involved, please enlist in this fight to preserve the family because we can't do it alone! Please help protect the family by taking one or more of the following actions right now.

1. Sign the "I Stand for the Family" petition at the end of this book and mail it to us or go to www.familywatchinternational.org and sign it online. Your e-mail address serves as your electronic signature. We will e-mail you *The Family Watch* newsletter, containing important updates on family issues.

Invite others to sign the petition as well. We will use this petition in our work to support the family in the United States and in our international activities to show policymakers and others the strong support for the family and family values. The more signatures we have, the stronger our voice will be.

Occasionally, we will send action alerts inviting you to act to defend marriage and the family.

2. Make a generous monetary contribution to Family Watch International or another like-minded organization. We cannot continue to do our work without the financial support of people like you. Gifts of any size are greatly appreciated, and since Family Watch is a 501(c)(3) organization, contributions are tax deductible for U.S. taxpayers. E-mail us at fwi@familywatchinternational.org for more information on how you can support our work. You can easily donate online or print out a mail-in contribution form by clicking on the "Contribute" button on our Web site at www.familywatchinternational.org. Or simply mail a check to:

Family Watch International
P.O. Box 1432
Gilbert, AZ 85299-1432

3. Help spread the word. Multiply yourself. Lend or gift a copy of this book to others who might join us. To purchase books or learn about quantity discounts, visit the site created for this book: www.standforthefamily.org. Pass along our Web address (www.familywatchinternational.org) to your friends, family, co-workers, fellow church members, and others with whom you associate, and invite them to sign the petition. Or go to the Family Watch site, print out the petition, collect signatures in your own community and mail them to us. For collecting 50 signatures, you can download a free electronic copy of the book!

4. Lead a Family Watch team in your community. Hold monthly meetings in your home or other venue and invite concerned citizens to work to identify threats to the family in your area. Work together to counteract them. Create and implement proactive plans to promote and protect the family where you live. Please contact us to learn more about how you can do this.

We Can Make This Happen

We call upon people everywhere to work together toward:

- A day when any new proposed policy, law or program would first be analyzed for its impact on the traditional family, and only those measures that strengthen the family or do no harm would be accepted.
- A day when policymakers across the globe understand the critical role that traditional marriage plays in our world, our nations, and our families and when these policymakers pledge to do everything they can to preserve, promote and protect marriage and families.
- A day when each life is valued and protected from the earliest stages until natural death.
- A day when women, the life-givers of the world, are valued and honored for their role as mothers and nurturers who create and prepare the future of our nations.
- A day when the world comes to understand the critical importance of procreation and seeks once again to channel sex in its proper and only safe place—a marriage between a man and a woman, where intimacy serves to both create and strengthen families.
- A day when laws that protect filth are replaced by laws that protect the innocence of children and the sanctity of the family.
- A day when parents make it a priority to spend quality *and quantity* time with their children.

Please join with me and many others across the world who are working to make such days become a reality.

Our Family Watch team as well as my immediate and extended family made many sacrifices to bring this book to you because it is our hope that it will help you to become involved in at least some small way to protect the family.

Neither I, nor my family, will benefit financially from this book or from any contributions made to Family Watch International. All proceeds from sales of the book will go to Family Watch International for which I am an unpaid volunteer and currently serve as president.

Please contact me at fwi@familywatchinternational.org and tell me how this book has affected you. I would love to hear from you!

"Never doubt that a small group of thoughtful, committed citizens can change the world. Indeed, it is the only thing that ever has."[320]

---

[320] Margaret Mead, cultural anthropologist, 1901-1978.

About Family Watch International

Family Watch International (FWI) is a 501(c)(3) nonprofit international organization founded in 1999. FWI is not affiliated with any religious group, political party or faction. FWI works at the United Nations (UN), in countries around the world, and in the United States to preserve and protect marriage and the family, and to promote family-based solutions to world problems.

Mission of Family Watch International

To stem the tide of family disintegration through education, family policy advocacy, and family-based humanitarian aid.

Areas of Focus

- Family Autonomy
- Motherhood
- Sex Education
- Marriage
- Pornography
- Parental Rights
- National Sovereignty
- International/Domestic Adoption
- Fatherhood
- Human Sexuality
- Abstinence
- Divorce
- Protection of Life
- Freedom of Religion
- Orphan Care Policies

Family Watch International Objectives

- Identify, analyze, and monitor the emerging cultural, social, and legal dynamics affecting family stability.
- Educate the public, policymakers, and the media about both threats and opportunities regarding the family.
- Develop and promote solutions to counteract threats to the family.
- Promote stable family life.

Family Watch Activities

Our Family Watch team works with volunteers and professionals across the world to:

- Monitor, report on, and participate in UN conferences and other international forums affecting families worldwide.
- Train pro-family advocates to identify and counteract threats to the family in their countries.
- Sponsor and report on cutting-edge research on emerging family issues.
- File AMICUS briefs in key court cases dealing with family issues.
- Educate the rising generation and prepare them for stable and successful family life. (See our "I Can Soar" Program at www.familiesfororphans.org)
- Promote policies that facilitate domestic and international adoption.
- Provide lifesaving aid to orphans and vulnerable children.

Family Watch International
www.familywatchinternational.org
480.507.2664
fwi@familywatchinternational.org

The "I Stand for the Family" Petition

Whereas, the traditional family is increasingly under attack on a variety of fronts at the international, national, state and local level; and

Whereas, weakening the family will have serious negative repercussions on families, individuals and societies; and

Whereas, it will take the best efforts of all of us working together to stem the tide of family disintegration and to preserve the family,

I pledge to support efforts to:

- Strengthen the family as the fundamental unit of society.
- Preserve and protect marriage as only between a man and a woman.
- Protect life before as well as after birth.
- Preserve the rights of all citizens to practice their religion as they choose so long as that does not infringe on the rights of others.
- Preserve the rights of parents to direct the moral, spiritual and intellectual upbringing of their children.

* * *

Join thousands of people in this worldwide movement to preserve and protect the family by signing the "I Stand for the Family" Petition!

Note: *Your e-mail address serves as your signature on this petition, so please write clearly.*

Name _____

Street Address_____

City _____ State _____ Postal Code_____

Country _____ Phone (opt.)_____

E-mail _____

Petition signers will receive free e-mail updates on important family issues and a free membership to Family Watch International.

Please Return to: Family Watch International
P.O. Box 1432
Gilbert, AZ 85299-1432
480-507-2664

Print out the petition or sign it online at www.familywatchinternational.org.

Acknowledgements

This, my first book, has been a team effort.

Foremost, I would like to thank my husband Greg for his never-ending support. He has spent hundreds of hours editing, researching, and helping document everything. Greg's legal background has been invaluable. He willingly picked up the slack at home whenever it was needed. Greg is also the best pro-family lobbyist I know!

My children—Julie, Tyler, Michael, Jessica—and our newest additions from Mozambique—Luis, Amelia and Afonso—have been gracious, supportive and patient. If they weren't such good kids I would have never finished the book.

My father Howard Ruff has been my cheerleader, support and a great source of inspiration. As a best-selling author himself, he made invaluable suggestions and critical edits.

My mother Kay Ruff taught me by her example of unselfish love the joy of motherhood. She stayed home, dedicating her life to raising her nine biological children (I was number five) and five children who were adopted. The love and stability that my mother gave each of us provided a solid foundation for our lives.

My brother Tim Ruff and my sisters Pam Patterson and Debbie Rasmussen also spent countless hours reviewing and editing. Their suggestions greatly improved the book. My brother Eric Ruff and his wife Janine contributed financially to make this possible.

I would especially like to thank Lynn Allred who wrote several sections of the book and helped me edit countless drafts. For years, Lynn has been in the trenches with me at the UN, at our state capitol, and in our schools and during many of the experiences recounted in this book. Along with my husband Greg, Lynn spent innumerable hours researching and documenting the information in the book. Lynn is the detail person I am not.

Annie Franklin also has been a comrade in arms in the trenches with Lynn and me in the cause to defend the family. Her European background (she was born and raised in Belgium and speaks fluent French) has been invaluable to our efforts on the international level. She also made valuable suggestions and edits to the book.

Sheldon Kinsel edited several drafts of the entire book. He believed in me and encouraged me to get it done.

Susan Roylance was my mentor and introduced me to the pro-family work at the UN. Anything I have done over the last decade for the pro-family cause was largely done by building on her experience, knowledge and projects.

I am also deeply indebted to Bob and Lynette Gay who provided substantial financial and moral support. Without this generous support, many of the experiences and successes recounted in this book would not have been possible.

April Parker, Diane Matthews, Al Schmeiser, Randy Van Drew, Jared Smith and Randy Jensen also made important edits and suggestions.

Finally, Cecily Markland, owner of Inglestone Publishing, walked me through the final editing process and prepared the book for publication. She spent countless hours helping to simplify and organize the book so it would flow better. She believes in this cause and put her all into making this book a success.

Help us Reach Others by Sharing
Stand for the Family

If you like this book and want to share it with others,
there are several ways to obtain more copies.
To learn how to purchase copies or receive discount prices,
or to inquire about bulk orders for your group or organization
or even how to download a free electronic copy,
please visit the Web site created especially for this book:

www.standforthefamily.org

For more information about Family Watch International
and to be updated about important issues
and ways to Stand for the Family
please visit www.familywatchinternational.org